Empathy and Counseling

Gerald A. Gladstein and Associates

Empathy and Counseling

Explorations in Theory and Research

With Contributions by John Brennan,
JoAnn Feldstein, Gerald A. Gladstein,
Mary Anna Ham, Jeanette Kreiser,
Susan MacKrell

With 17 Figures

Springer-Verlag
New York Berlin Heidelberg
London Paris Tokyo

GERALD A. GLADSTEIN AND ASSOCIATES
Center for Counseling, Family, and Worklife Studies
Graduate School of Education and Human Development
University of Rochester
Rochester, New York 14627, U.S.A.

Library of Congress Cataloging in Publication Data
Gladstein, Gerald A., 1927-
   Empathy and counseling.
   Bibliography: p.
   Includes index.
   1. Counseling. 2. Empathy. I. Title.
BF637.C6G54 1986   158'.3   86-10168

Typeset by Ampersand Publisher Services, Inc., Rutland, Vermont.
Printed and bound by R.R. Donnelley & Sons, Harrisonburg, Virginia.
Printed in the United States of America.

9 8 7 6 5 4 3 2 1

ISBN 0-387-96358-8 Springer-Verlag New York Berlin Heidelberg
ISBN 3-540-96358-8 Springer-Verlag Berlin Heidelberg New York

*This book is lovingly dedicated to my wife Barbara,
my children Richard, Deborah, Rose, and Laura,
my mother Bella,
and in memory of my father Samuel.*

Preface

Contemporary society is in constant change. Transitions and crises occur in every life, regardless of status, ethnicity, sex, race, education, or religion. Yet, the traditional societal forms for helping with these transitions and crises are changing as well. The typical nuclear family has given way to single-parent, blended, or dual-career structures. Religious, health, educational, social service, philanthropic, and other organizational support systems have also changed from their pre-1950 counterparts.

As these sometimes evolutionary, sometimes revolutionary, changes have occurred, considerable scholarship and empirical research has attempted to identify and develop methods of helping people encounter these transitions and crises. These efforts have come from various fields: psychology, sociology, anthropology, linguistics, law, social work, nursing, medicine, education, labor relations, and others. Each has brought its own theories, research methods, and practical experiences to bear on the problems.

One of the methods that these fields have universally been intrigued with is the use of empathy. Empathy, that crucial but elusive phenomenon (so the literature has reported), has been identified as important in human interactions. Labor mediators, legal arbitrators, psychiatric psychoanalysts, encounter group facilitators, classroom instructors, and kindred helpers have been told that "understanding how the other person or group is thinking and feeling" will help that person or group. The anxious parent and troubled spouse have been urged to "understand the other's point of view." Some writers have even argued that empathy is crucial to resolving international tensions and terrorist group violent actions.

Maybe they are correct. Maybe our times, especially, call out for more people understanding other people. Certainly, our hi-tech-electronic-age, our hydrogen-bomb-age, our space-travel-age has put human interactions into new perspectives. Old "man-environment" concerns have given way to new "person-person-environment" issues. Perhaps being empathic is a crucial means of helping others.

It was within this context that I first became interested in making a serious study of empathy. As a graduate student at the University of Chicago, beginning in 1950, I studied with Carl Rogers and his colleagues John Schlein and Jules Seeman. At that time they began to write about "empathic understanding" as an important part of the psychotherapeutic process. From that time to this, I have sought—through research, counseling practice, teaching, and writing—to discover what empathy is and how it may or may not be useful in the helping process. These efforts led me into diverse literature, including psychology, sociology, psycholinguistics, anthropology, aesthetics, nonverbal communication, and film. The search continues.

It continues because what I discovered is that we really know very little about empathy, and its role in counseling! Oh yes, plenty has been written, just look at the list of references at the end of this book. But, in my opinion, we lack well-founded empirical evidence. However, we know a lot more than in 1950 when empathy began to have a continuous place in the professional counseling/psychotherapy literature. Numerous theories have been developed, many empathy measures have been created, and hundreds of process and outcome studies have been carried out. I believe we are beginning to tease out empathy's multiple elements and processes as it is used in counseling people.

Therefore, the major purpose of this book is to offer to the reader what appears to be known today about empathy and its role in counseling. Three general questions guided all of the writing: (1) What is empathy? (2) How does it develop? and (3) What is its role in counseling and similar helping processes? Answers to these questions were sought by synthesizing the major theoretical writings, beginning with the late 1800s, and presenting eight recent empirical studies to illustrate efforts to test out some of these theoretical beliefs. As the title indicates, these are explorations in theory and research. Given the state of our knowledge, it would be premature to say that we have reached the "promised land."

The book begins with an analysis of the counseling/psychotherapy, social, and developmental psychology literature. Then, in Chapters 2–7, six empirical studies are presented that describe counselors' empathy and its role in counseling process and outcome. Each chapter looks at empathy as a complex, rather than as a unidimensional variable. Chapters 8–10 focus on counselor empathy training. After a theoretical presentation, two studies (Chapters 9 and 10) systematically explore multiple training procedures. The book concludes with a synthesis of the empirical studies' findings and a description of a new categorization of the various types of empathy documented in this book. Finally, suggestions for research and practice are offered.

In view of the above, I believe this book will be primarily of benefit to serious "students" of empathy. Scholars, researchers, theoreticians, graduate students, and thoughtful practitioners should find many new and challenging perspectives about empathy. For example, at the end of the book, 18 different kinds of empathy are identified and defined. Although the book is not designed to present "how to" methods of using empathy in counseling/psychotherapy and similar helping processes, the reader will find many examples of techniques that have been developed and tried out in research projects. The reader may want to try these methods in his or her own work.

Many individuals have been very helpful to me and my colleagues as we have developed and completed this volume.

First and foremost has been my wife Barbara. As a professional (family therapist) and intimate companion she has always provided the intellectual and emotional support so crucial during the lonely scholarship process. My four children, Richard, Deborah, Rose, and Laura, have also shown the type of interest and curiosity that helped me relate theoretical concepts to the real world of human relationships.

Many professional colleagues have been helpful over the years. One in particular Miron Zuckerman, has been especially important for this book. Through our co-teaching a course entitled "Empathy and Helping" he has provided valuable insights to the social psychology literature. Further, his critique of an earlier version of this book led to significant improvements. Three graduate students also need to be pointed out. Garson Herzfeld provided valuable comments on the entire manuscript. Christina Frederick tirelessly searched for references and checked their accuracy. Nancy Kizielewicz helped create the author index.

The absolutely crucial task of typing the many drafts was wonderfully achieved by Margaret Davidson, Betty Drysdale, Florence Geglia, Judy Gueli, and Margaret Zaccone. Their separate and combined efforts are greatly appreciated.

At Springer-Verlag, I am particularly pleased to thank the editorial staff, who responded so quickly and enthusiastically to the manuscript.

Finally, I am grateful to my former graduate students, some of whom are chapter authors in this book, who provided encouragement and intellectual challenge throughout the years.

GERALD A. GLADSTEIN
Rochester, New York
October, 1986

Contents

Contributors

JOHN BRENNAN, President, Interact Associates, Rochester, New York 14607, U.S.A.

JOANN FELDSTEIN, Consulting Psychologist, Harvard Community Health Plan, Cambridge, Massachusetts 02238, U.S.A.

GERALD A. GLADSTEIN, Professor of Education and Psychology, Graduate School of Education and Human Development, University of Rochester, New York 14627, U.S.A.

MARY ANNA HAM, Assistant Professor, Counseling Psychology, Institute for Learning and Teaching, University of Massachusetts-Boston, Harbor Campus, Boston, Massachusetts 02125, U.S.A.

JEANETTE KREISER, Coordinator, Student Development Programs, University of Maryland University College, College Park, Maryland 20742, U.S.A.

SUSAN MACKRELL, Assistant Professor, Graduate School of Education and Human Development, University of Rochester, Rochester, New York 14627, U.S.A.

1
The Role of Empathy in Counseling: Theoretical Considerations

GERALD A. GLADSTEIN

In the counseling and psychotherapy literature, empathy has been identified as crucial to successful outcomes. Stimulated by Rogers's (1957) discussion of empathy as one of the "necessary and sufficient conditions of therapeutic personality change," (p. 95) numerous theory, research, and application publications have appeared. At the same time, psychoanalysts, such as Stewart (1956), Greenson (1967, 1978), Kohut (1977, 1978), and Lichtenberg, Bornstein, and Silver (1984), have written about empathy, expanding on Freud's (1921/1923) brief comments concerning identification and empathy.

The importance to psychotherapy outcomes was apparently well established by Truax and Carkhuff (1967). Yet, in recent years, others have challenged their conclusion. For example, Bergin and Suinn (1975) finished their review of the literature by suggesting that empathy and other facilitative conditions are probably not sufficient "except in highly specific, client-centered type conditions" (p. 515). In other reviews, Lambert, DeJulio, and Stein (1978) and Parloff, Waskow, and Wolfe (1978) also questioned empathy's role in psychotherapy. After separating counseling from psychotherapy studies, Gladstein (1970, 1977) found that the evidence was mixed. "In effect, despite the large number of theory, discussion, case, and process articles describing the positive relationship between empathy and counseling outcome the empirical evidence still remains equivocal" (1977, p. 75). Contemporary theorists and researchers continue to investigate whether empathy is crucial to counseling and psychotherapy success. For example, Barrett-Lennard (1981) described the theoretical empathy cycle in human interactions, including psychotherapy. He supported his concepts by referring to research studies in which the clients' perceptions of empathy were positively related to

This chapter, in a slightly different form, originally was published in 1983 as "Understanding empathy: Integrating counseling, developmental, and social psychology perspectives." *Journal of Counseling Psychology, 30,* 467–482. Adapted with permission of the © American Psychological Association.

counseling outcomes. Other researchers have used empathy as a measure of successful counseling outcome.

Reflecting a more psychoanalytic perspective, Bordin (1979) recently wrote about empathy and the therapeutic working alliance. Drawing on the work of writers such as Reik (1964) and Greenson (1967), he indicated that empathy could be one of the elements involved in creating working alliances. However, he also noted that empathy would have less importance in creating this alliance in behavior therapy, compared to other therapies.

Textbooks and training manuals also document the continued interest in empathy. They typically assume its importance in counseling and psychotherapy or support its inclusion by referring to writers such as Carkhuff (1969a, 1969b, 1980). For example, Hansen, Stevic, and Warner (1982) discussed its significance in the early stage of establishing a counseling relationship. Egan (1975), in a training manual, presented eight rules for communicating more accurate empathy.

Thus, despite the recently published reviews that question empathy's importance in counseling and psychotherapy, it continues to be viewed as an important construct, probably because of the mixed findings in the research literature. Some studies show only positive relationships (e.g., Altman, 1973), whereas others do not (e.g., Irwin, 1973/1974). Hence, researchers are stimulated to continue to explore the topic; practitioners continue to use empathy.

Why have these mixed research findings occurred? One reason for this confusion seems to be the way counseling/psychotherapy theorists and researchers have defined empathy. Earlier Gladstein (1977) showed that some emphasized the cognitive aspects, whereas others concentrated on the affective. Recently, Gladstein (1984) presented an historical analysis of various writers' views of these affective and cognitive aspects. As noted there, some authors have included both. For example, Rogers (1975, p.4) defined empathy as follows:

It means entering the private perceptual world of the other and becoming thoroughly at home in it. It involves being sensitive, moment to moment, to the changing felt meanings which flow in this other person, to the fear or rage or tenderness or confusion or whatever, that he/she is experiencing. It means temporarily living in his/her life, moving about in it delicately without making judgments, sensing meanings of which he/she is scarcely aware, but not trying to uncover feelings of which the person is totally unaware, since this would be too threatening. It includes communicating your sensings of his/her world as you look with fresh and unfrightened eyes at elements of which the individual is fearful.

Hackney (1978) also discussed the confusion mentioned above. In his tracing of the changes in definitions from 1958 to 1978, he noted that recently stress has been put on empathy as a communication skill (only part of Rogers's definition). By communication skill he meant the ability to give accurate and adequate responses to a client's message. He called for more concern with the affective or emotional components. In his recent theoretical paper, Barrett-Lennard (1981) agreed with this concern. He also traced the evolution of his own thinking (stimulated originally by Rogers's ideas) and presented an empathy cycle involving three types of empathy. These are: (a) empathic resonation (in which the empathizer responds emotionally to the other), (b) expressed empathy (the communicative act), and (c) received empathy (how the other receives the empathizer's response).

This is a very helpful model because, as Barrett-Lennard (1981) demonstrated, it can provide some explanation to confusing research findings. Furthermore, it provides a connection to another perspective of empathy that did not emanate from Rogers but that has been important in the psychotherapy literature. Barrett-Lennard's term *empathic resonation* appears to be quite similar to Stewart's (1956) first stage, *identification.* Stewart used Freud's ideas (1921/1923) about identification and its relationship to empathy. This first or prestage involves raw identification; that is, unconscious emotional connections. The second is deliberate identification. "This is a conscious process involving an emotional tie between two people striving for a common goal" (Stewart, 1956, p. 40). This view appears similar to Bordin's (1979) suggestion that emotional bonding between the therapist and client is affected by empathy. The third is resistance, or distancing, which allows the empathizer to gain a better understanding of the other. The fourth is deliberate reidentification, also a conscious act. (For additional discussion of Stewart's ideas, see Gladstein [1984].) Although Stewart's ideas have not led to empirical research, Katz (1963) used them and those of Freud in writing about the uses of empathy by counselors, ministers, and social workers. He explained that empathy can be used for diagnostic as well as therapeutic purposes.

These differing perspectives on empathy—as an affective response, as raw identification, as resonation, as cognitive understanding (role taking), as a communication skill, as received by the other—exist in the counseling/psychotherapy literature. Alongside these perspectives, various empathy measures also exist. Differences in these tests and rating systems add to the confusion too. (See Chapter 3 for more detail on this point.)

As Feldstein and Gladstein (1980) indicated, most of these measures can be labeled as either objective or subjective. *Objective* refers to external, independent judgments of actual counseling sessions. These judgments are usually made from audio or video material. Truax's Accurate Empathy Scale (Truax & Carkhuff, 1967) and Carkhuff's Empathic Understanding in Interpersonal Process Scale (Carkhuff, 1969a, b) are the two most widely used examples. *Subjective* refers to the counselor's or client's perceptions of the counseling sessions. Two frequently used measures are the Barrett-Lennard Relationship Inventory (Barrett-Lennard, 1962, 1978) and the Truax Relationship Questionnaire (Truax & Carkhuff, 1967).

However, other types of empathy measures have also been created. Cartwright and Lerner (1963) used role construct concepts to develop a comparison of a therapist's rating of how the patient saw himself or herself versus how the patient rated himself or herself. "The empathy measure was the squared discrepancy between the patient's self-description and the therapist's attempt to predict the patient's self description" (p. 139). This can be called a predictive, cognitive empathy measure. Using an entirely different approach, Kagan, Krathwohl, and Associates (1967) created the Affective Sensitivity Scale. This is a standardized decoding measure based on an affect approach. Although objective in nature, this scale has counselors respond not to their own counseling sessions but to filmed scenes. Counselors select multichoice statements that they believe best represent the person's feelings.

Although all of these scales and tests were designed to measure empathy, it appears that they may be tapping different empathic aspects or that they are assessing some qualities related to but different from empathy. Several research studies suggest that they are measuring different aspects of the same construct. For example, Kurtz and Grummon (1972) correlated six commonly used empathy scales, including Kagan's Affective Sensitivity Scale, Carkhuff's Empathic Understanding Scale, and Barrett-Lennard's Relationship Inventory. They found no statistically significant relationships among these measures. Ham (1980/1981) also found no significant relationship between the Affective Sensitivity Scale and Hogan's (1969, 1975) Empathy Scale. The latter uses sets of personality scale items that represent what people believe to be true about the "empathic man." In effect, it is a trait measure of cognitive empathy.

In addition to this overall measurement concern, some writers have questioned the validity of Truax's Accurate Empathy and Carkhuff's Empathic Understanding Scales. Beginning with Chinsky and Rappaport's (1970) critique, the problem has centered on using audiotapes judged by independent raters. Gormally and Hill (1974), Hill and King (1976), Gladstein (1977), Fridman and Stone (1978), and Feldstein and Gladstein (1980), among others, have pointed out problems concerning the material rated, the training of the raters, and the inconsistencies between stated empathy definitions and actual measures. Perhaps Hackney's (1978) comment that too much attention has been put on measuring empathic communication skill and not enough on the empathic experience best summarizes the concerns with the two scales.

Thus, the confusion regarding the significance of empathy in counseling/psychotherapy can be traced to variations in definitions *and* measures used in empirical studies. As Gladstein (1977) suggested earlier, perhaps we should be looking at which type of measure to use for which type of empathy for what type of desired counseling outcome. Barrett-Lennard (1981), in viewing this same confusion, argued that each phase of the empathy cycle requires its own unique measurement.

From another perspective, this confusion could be *expected*. Psychological research concerning empathy has assumed that this complex phenomenon can be reduced to quantifiable elements. Furthermore, it has created (as noted earlier) measures that have tended to isolate the affective from the cognitive componenets. This approach is certainly consistent with reductionism but inconsistent with a holistic philosophical perspective. The latter is best represented by psychoanalytic writers such as Stewart (1956), who argued that empathy cannot be studied by using traditional scientific, psychological methods. By inserting the outsider's objective measurements, he said, we destroy what we are trying to measure (p. 120). Thus, the confusion that exists results from studying only a part or parts of a totality that do not lend themselves to traditional scientific analysis. If one were to follow this line of reasoning, empathy would be studied holistically.

Other psychoanalytic writers (e.g., Greenson, 1967, 1978; Kohut, 1977, 1978), while not directly addressing this point, have described empathy's subtle aspects, which would appear to elude the usual psychological research methods. For example, as Greenson (1967, pp. 368-369) observed:

Empathy means to share, to experience the feelings of another human being. One partakes of the *quality* [italics added] of feelings and *not* [italics added] the quantity... It is essentially a preconscious phenomonon; it can be consciously instigated or interrupted; and it can occur silently and automatically oscillating with other forms of relating to people.

Kohut (1978) argued that empathy "constitutes a powerful psychological bond between individuals that—more perhaps than love, the expression and sublimation of the sexual drive—counteracts man's destructiveness against his fellows" (p. 705). In psychoanalysis, Kohut (1978, p. 700) called empathy "vicarious introspection" and explained what the analyst does:

He uses his sensory impressions, of course, as he hears the analysand's words and observes his gestures and movements, but these sensory data would remain meaningless were it not for his ability to recognize complex psychological configurations that only empathy, the human echo to human experience, can provide.

Certainly, these views of empathy reflect a different philosophical set of assumptions from those of Truax and Carkhuff, for example, who created measures of the counselor's empathic communication skills. In view of these different philosophical and theoretical approaches to describing empathy, it should not be surprising that the results of studies of empathy and counseling/psychotherapy outcome have been interpreted differently. (Gladstein's 1984 historical tracing of the roots of these different approaches also helps explain these interpretations.)

Within this context, it would seem reasonable to go beyond the counseling/psychotherapy literature in quest of deriving some ideas that can give us greater understanding. After all, neither of the two major models, identification or role taking, is unique in psychology (Smither, 1977). Likewise, the various empathy measures exist alongside many others. Perhaps by looking at other psychological areas it would be possible to derive a broader perspective and thus obtain a better understanding of the confusing findings.

Concepts from Social and Developmental Psychology

In analyzing the literature from social and developmental pyschology, the two specialties that have contributed the most to empathy theory and research, this author hoped to find additional views and definitions, ideas for tests and measures, and new research questions and designs. (Some of the points presented below, in abbreviated form, are discussed in more detail in Gladstein [1984].)

Three observations were made. The first was that these specialties (as well as counseling and psychotherapy) have their *own* empathy literatures, and usually they do not overlap or intersect! For example, recent reviews by Deutsch and Madle (1975), Smither (1977), and M.E. Ford (1979) in developmental psychology barely refer to studies in the social area. The second observation was that each specialty has essentially two models of empathy: (a) role taking and (b) emotional contagion. *Role taking* refers to the ability to understand another's thinking or feeling— that is, perceiving the world as the other person does. This is similar to the first part of the Rogers definition quoted earlier. *Emotional contagion* refers to a person's emotional response while observing another person's actual or anticipated condition. For example, if a counselor responded to a client's sadness by feeling sad also, this would be emotional contagion. In developmental psychology, role taking is based primarily on Piaget's writings (1929/1975, 1932/1965), whereas in social psychology it is based on Mead (1934) and Cottrel (1942). Concepts regarding emotional contagion in both the developmental and social areas can be traced back to early psychologists such as Allport (1924), McDougall (1908), and Wundt (1892/1897). The third observation was that each specialty has created its own empathy measures. To illustrate, in social psychology, Dymond's (1949) Rating Test set an early pattern for measuring role taking; Hogan's (1969) test is a more recent example. In developmental psychology, Feffer (1959), Chandler (1972), and Selman (1980) created their own role- or perspective-taking measures.

Because these two models and several measures have some similarities but considerable differences with those in counseling/psychotherapy, a further discussion of the social and developmental prespectives follows.

Social Concepts and Measures

In the social psychology literature, empathy as role taking is largely based on Mead's (1934) and Cottrell's (1942) ideas. Although Mead did not refer to empathy per se, he did use the phrase "putting yourself in his place" (1934, p. 366). He argued that this ability was learned as a result of interactions with parents and others. Cottrell (1942) used Mead's ideas in developing his theory of human social interaction. He said that the trait approach to understanding interpersonal behavior was inadequate. To take its place, he developed a theoretical model that included 16 propositions that defined and explained self-other patterns. In Proposition 2, he presented a description of a process between two people that he labeled empathy. It involved responding to another by reproducing the acts of the other. This reproduction depended upon perception and an internal attitude.

Cottrell's ideas were crucial because they greatly influenced Dymond (1949), who created the first widely used (but later widely criticized) role-taking empathy measure. Here, role taking refers to being able to predict another person's thoughts. Her Rating Test had four parts, which required the person to rate himself or herself and others on six items. She then calculated the way the person rated another in comparison to the way that person rated himself or herself. This was essentially a cognitive, predictive, role-taking empathy measure. Other early attempts to develop empathy tests were also based on this approach. For example, Kerr and Speroff (1954) created the Empathy Test, which was used in industry during the 1950s. In this case, however, the subject responded to items according to the way he or she believed certain population groups would respond.

In more recent times, two other role-taking tests have been developed. Although Hogan's (1969) test does not use Dymond's approach, it does focus on the cognitive domain. Hogan was interested in moral behavior and saw empathy related to it. Subjects are required to answer 64 items that are keyed to how an empathic person would answer. The validity and reliability data for this test are much better than those for the tests of Dymond or Kerr and Speroff.

The second measure, Emotional Empathic Tendency, was developed by Mehrabian and Epstein (1972). Their interest was primarily in studying personality characteristics. Although they indicated that they were interested in measuring emotional empathy as responses to others, they actually created a trait, affective role-taking measure. In this case, affective role taking means whether a person typically *perceives* himself or herself as responding emotionally to others' emotional behaviors. The subject answers 33 items that describe how he or she respond to certain situations. So far, the reliability and validity data are encouraging.

This brief review of the role-taking model in social psychology shows that the primary focus has been on cognitive role taking. Furthermore, tests have either been situational or trait in nature. Although the early measures have proved to be questionable, recent ones have better validity and reliability. Davis (1980, 1983) used this history in creating a multielement empathy measure that taps cognitive and affective role taking. Future research will establish whether the positive, preliminary validity findings stand up.

By contrast, the second model, *affective contagion or reaction,* focuses on the observer's emotional responses to another person's actual or anticipated condition. Empathy is present if the observer acquires the same emotional state as the other (Rushton, 1980). Recent social psychologists, such as Stotland (1969), using this model typically trace their ideas back to Allport (1924), who wrote about the conditioning process involved in sympathetic responses. They also note that McDougall (1908) and Wundt (1892/1897) referred to emotional contagion as a basis for one person's response to another. Rushton (1980) discussed this type of empathy as crucial to understanding altruistic behavior. It is one of two (the other being "personal norms") motivational systems that can be hypothesized as mediating mechanisms that lead to altruism. In a recent review, Hoffman (1977) also described how empathic distress fits this general model. He was referring to an emotional reaction to another person's negative emotional condition.

It would appear that this emotional reaction model of empathy is not closely related to the role-taking model. Emotional contagion does not require cognition. Without being aware of their actions, people can respond to others' stress, fear, or delight. Beginning in the mid-1960s, a whole group of social psychologists became interested in empathy and used this emotional contagion model. (According to Latane and Darley [1970], a violent 1964 murder witnessed by 38 unaiding neighbors alerted researchers to the problems of social indifference.) In the social psychologists' studies of prosocial or helping behavior, they frequently used empathy as an important variable, or assumed it was present. In reviewing some of these studies, Rushton (1980) pointed out that although emotional contagion is related to altruism, role-taking empathy may not be. In recent research, Batson, Duncan, Ackerman, Buckley, and Birch (1981) showed that emotional, empathic responses can be created that are either egotistic or altruistic in nature.

In carrying out these studies, various measures were used. Stotland and Dunn (1963) used palmar sweating as a physiological index of empathy. Aronfreed (1970) defined empathy in terms of experimental conditions. He argued for very explicit conditions that had to be met before saying that empathy was present. There must be a differentiation between "the observer's affective response to the perception of another person's experience and the observer's more direct response to the information that is carried in the observed reward or punishment itself" (p. 107). To achieve this determination, Aronfreed set up conditioning experiments that involved social learning through modeling.

Aderman, Brehm, and Katz (1974) also used an experimental learning model to measure empathy. They combined different role-taking instructions with a videotape presentation of an electric shock victim's affective reactions. Empathy was measured by analyzing the subject's answers to the Nowlis Mood Questionnaire in describing his or her reactions in watching the victim.

In a series of studies, Stotland and his colleagues (Stotland, Mathews, Sherman, Hansson, & Richardson, 1978) combined physiological and role-taking empathy measures. At first they used palmar sweating, basal skin conductance, and vasoconstriction. When these proved to result in mixed findings in several experiments, they developed the Fantasy-Empathy Scale, a three-item questionnaire that indicated some promising validity.

All of these emotional contagion research programs drew from traditional social psychology experimental approaches. They used classical conditioning, modeling, expectancy and set, and aggression-type paradigms. They usually created empathy by giving particular instructions to the subjects. Typically, they were also interested in the relationship of empathy to helping or prosocial behavior. Although several researchers also included role-taking empathy measures, these studies were quite different from the role-taking work of Dymond and Hogan, referred to earlier.

Developmental Concepts and Measures

The development literature has been greatly influenced by Piaget's role-taking or decentering model of empathy. Although Piaget did *not* refer to empathy per se, in several of his early works he wrote of the child's problems as a result of egocentrism (inability to differentiate self from objects or others). He indicated that during the early years the infant "confuses self with the universe," and he or she is "unconscious of his self." It is not possible for him or her to separate the conceptual from the affective elements (Piaget, 1929/1975, p. 202).

From the 3rd to the 7th year, egocentric language is predominant. It is greater between 3 and 5 than from 5 to 7 years (Piaget, 1928/1959). The child is "ignorant of his own ego, takes his own point of view as absolute, and fails to establish between himself and the external world of things that reciprocity which alone would ensure objectivity" (p. 197). Furthermore, "the child experiences the greatest difficulty in entering into anyone else's point of view" (p. 216). In effect, Piaget believed that the child below age 7 is incapable of empathy (role taking).

However, after this age, egocentrism diminishes and logical thought evolves: "We have here a remarkable instance of the influence of social factors on the functioning of thought" (p. 244). After age 7-8, argument can be "what it is for the adult, namely the change from one point of view to the other, accompanied by the effort to motivate one's own and to understand that of the interlocutor" (p. 206).

From about the age of 11-12, Piaget theorized, the child begins a new era (p. 253):

Social life starts on a new phase, and this obviously has the effect of leading children to a greater mutual understanding, and consequently of giving them the habit of constantly placing themselves at points of view which they did not previously hold.

Thus, role taking is possible by this age. Egocentrism gives way to perceiving others' views. What was an unconscious, ego-centered thought process becomes an interactive awareness of others.

These concepts became the basis for numerous studies beginning about 1957. Several fine reviews (e.g., Deutsch & Madle, 1975; M.E. Ford, 1979; & Smither, 1977) have traced the evolution and controversy in the literature. Essentially, researchers have attempted to establish age-related changes in cognitive or affective role-taking abilities. Here cognitive role taking refers to the person's ability to perceive how the other is *thinking*. Affective role taking refers to the person's ability to perceive how the other is *feeling*. For example, Burns and Cavey (1957) showed pictures to groups of younger and older children. Some of the pictures showed incongruous facial expressions. The children were asked how the boy or girl in the picture felt. Similar studies were conducted by Feffer and Gourevitch (1960) and Borke (1971). Other researchers, such as Greenspan, Barenboim, and Chandler (1976), conducted more complicated experiments with more difficult empathic tasks. They tried to measure the combination of cognitive and affective role taking. Selman (1980), although originally stimulated by Piaget's ideas, drew on Mead's (1934) belief that people are uniquely perspective-taking animals. He used Mead's distinction between the self as "I" (the perspective taker) and the self as "me" (the object). "It is the integration of these two components that makes perspective taking truly social, and not simply the application of a developing reflexive or recursive thinking ability to some arbitrary social content area" (Selman, 1980, p. 34). In other words, Selman moved beyond Piaget's concepts to concentrate on social cognition.

Overall, these studies suggest that role-taking abilities do increase with age. However, M.E. Ford's (1979) review of this literature raised some pointed criticism of Piaget's concept of egocentrism. Ford's data indicate that there is very little relationship among the affective and cognitive role-taking and perspective-taking measures.

Evidence concerning children's emotional contagion type of empathy does not seem so controversial. (Emotional contagion, or affective reaction, empathy refers to one person taking on the same emotion as the other's existing emotion. This is the same way it was defined in the social literature.) This is probably due to the fact that only one measure has been frequently used. Feshbach and Roe (1968) created the Affective Situations Test, which has been used by Feshbach and Feshbach (1969) and Roe (1980) among others. This test requires children to indicate how they feel when presented with certain stimuli—usually pictures, slides, or videotapes. In a recent review of studies using this test, Feshbach (1978) discussed the relationship of empathy to social comprehension (role taking), aggression, age, and sex. She also stated a generalization that would seem to apply to not only this area but to the social and counseling/psychotherapy literature as well: "It should be clear that no one approach, no single measuring instrument, no one cognitive skill is sufficient to encompass the psychological complexity of a major social behavior such as empathy" (p. 41). This was her way of indicating that emotional contagion empathy need not be the same as role-taking empathy. This view would be consistent with the finding (Hoffman, 1977) that boys and girls seem to have the same role-taking abilities, whereas girls tend to be higher in emotional contagion empathy. In effect, age-related changes in empathy could vary, depending on whether role-taking or emotional empathy was being measured.

The developmental literature also suggests that children can learn empathic behavior. For example, Chandler (1973) showed in an experimental study that specific filmmaking and similar activities that involved cooperation and role taking resulted in higher role-taking skills when compared to a control group. These children also showed less antisocial behavior. As Rushton (1980) noted, other studies have supported these findings and have shown that role-taking abilities can be learned even by preschoolers.

Empathy and Helping

The social and developmental literature also provides some ideas concerning empathy and helping behaviors. Several of the early social psychology writers described a complex relationship. For example, McDougall (1908) said that emotional reactions to another may or may not lead to helping. If the observer becomes too close, distress can set in. Allport (1924) went even further. He argued that "the emotion sympathetically aroused leads us primarily to the removal of the unpleasant state in ourselves rather than in those whose suffering aroused it in us" (p.

237). However, he noted that when pity was added this could lead to helping.

More recent writers, such as Hoffman (1977), have also described the complex relationship between empathy and helping. After reviewing the theories and empirical evidence, he concluded that "although distress cues from another may trigger empathic distress (emotional contagion) in observers and an initial tendency to act, they may or may not help, depending on the circumstances" (p. 203). These circumstances appear to be related to expectancies, group dynamics, and egotistic motives. For example, Batson et al. (1981) found that empathy could lead to altruistic motivation to help (not egoistic). However, in their study, Stotland et al. (1978) found that high-empathy student nurses did not display more helping behavior. Perhaps they were more egoistically than altruistically motivated.

In the developmental literature, Piaget (1932/1965) differentiated role taking and emotional reactions in terms of helping. He indicated that the infant had the raw materials (sympathetic tendencies and affective reactions) that later led to moral behavior. In fact, he stated that altruism can exist within the child's first year. Yet Piaget (1928/1959) also indicated that role taking or decentering does not occur usually until ages 7–8. Thus, the very young child's helping behavior is a function of emotional reactions, not role-taking ability.

The developmental empirical literature concerning empathy and helping, according to Bryan's (1972) and Hoffman's (1977) reviews, also is quite inconclusive. Both point out that numerous methodological problems exist. At the same time, we can abstract their cautious conclusions: (a) "very young children typically respond empathically (emotionally) to another's distress but often do nothing or act inappropriately, probably because of cognitive limitations"; (b) "with children as well as adults there appears to be a drop in empathic arousal following an act of helping" (Hoffman, 1977, p. 202); (c)"observing others behave in a helpful manner will elicit helping responses from children" (Bryan, 1972, p. 100). These three conclusions seem to be quite consistent with Piaget's beliefs.

Rushton's (1980) recent analysis of the literature seems to integrate well these various ideas and findings. He emphasized the relationship of empathy and helping in terms of norms of social responsibility, equity, and reciprocity. He argued that empathy (emotional matching between people) and these types of norms are two important motivators that account for altruism, a form of helping behavior. The specific environmental events interact with empathy and norms and thus must be considered when attempting to predict altruism. In effect, when a person has internalized norms to help others in need, to be just and fair, and experiences similar emotional reactions as the person in distress, he or she will probably help if the internalized norms and situation "demand" it. For example, a father may rush into a burning building to rescue his crying child, despite the likely personal danger.

Significance for Counseling/Psychotherapy Literature

What is the significance of these ideas from the social and developmental literature? Do they suggest any leads for understanding the confusion concerning the relationship of empathy to counseling/psychotherapy outcomes? This author believes that they do. The following sections present four proposals that integrate these three different perspectives.

Empathy as Multistage Interpersonal Process

First, it is proposed that empathy be viewed as a multistage, interpersonal process that can involve emotional contagion, identification, and role taking. The counseling/psychotherapy literature points out that empathy in this type of interpersonal process involves multistages. These stages typically follow a temporal sequence. As noted earlier, Rogers (1975) stressed two stages: (a) temporarily living in the client's life, and (b) communicating the sensings of that life to the client. Stewart (1956), drawing on Freud's (1921/1923) ideas, described four stages: (a) raw identification, (b) deliberate identification, (c) resistance, and (d) deliberate reidentification. Barrett-Lennard's (1981) cycle included five stages: (a) empathic set, (b) empathic resonation, (c) expressed empathy, (d) received empathy, and (e) feedback. He indicated that Steps b, c, and d were the actual empathy phases. Thus, regardless of the specific terms used, these and other writers included an emotional stage first, which is followed by some type of cognitive (conscious) activity. For Rogers and Barrett-Lennard, the sequence then included communication by the therapist to the client. Unfortunately, at this point in time, attempting to integrate these different identified stages seems premature. However, empirical research could be carried out to determine their degree of similarity.

Regardless, at this time this author believes that the research evidence from the social and developmental literature concerning emotional contagion should be added to the above ideas. These findings should help us understand better the raw identification or resonation stage. For example, as discussed earlier, developmental theory and research indicate that even very young children have the capacity to react emotionally (the affective stage) when observing others. The social literature, however, shows that adults' emotional empathic responses may or may not lead to altruistic behavior. Thus, we can assume that counselors have the capacity for the first stage (emotional empathy) but that social norms and situational factors may interfere with effective helping. (Perhaps the therapist has internalized a norm of "keeping aloof" and not showing emotions. In this case, he or she might not even be aware of his or her emotional response.) The studies reported by Ham (Chapter 3) and Kreiser (Chapter 4) shed some light on this possibility.

The social and developmental literature also shows that empathy can be viewed as role taking. Apparently, this is the second major stage. As a conscious, deliberate, cognitive process, role taking appears to be similar to what Stewart (1956) described as "deliberate identification" and Rogers (1975) discussed as the "as if" quality of empathic understanding. This literature also demonstrates that role taking can be taught to children through social modeling as well as cognitive-behavioral methods. Hence, it appears that therapists are capable of experiencing emotional contagion and learning role taking, both theorized as crucial to empathy in the counseling/psychotherapy literature. (See Chapters 8–10 for more discussion and reports of research concerning this idea.)

The social and developmental areas also provide some ideas and methods for studying this multistage, interpersonal empathic process. Counseling/psychotherapy researchers could adapt some of the experimental designs and measures used by Aronfreed (1970) and Stotland et al. (1978) in the social literature, and of Feshbach (1978) and Roe (1980) in the developmental literature. Furthermore, Hogan's (1969) and Mehrabian and Epstein's (1972) role-taking tests—trait measures—could be used in conjection with interpersonal process state measures such as Truax's Relationship Questionnaire (Truax & Carkhuff, 1967). A new multidimensional test developed by Davis (1980, 1983) seems promising. This 28-item, four-factor measure of empathy could provide an efficient way of measuring emotional and cognitive role taking. Counseling studies involving children could use one or more of the role-taking measures developed by Borke (1971), Chandler (1972), or Feffer and Gourevitch (1960). In effect, it is necessary to broaden our perspective as to the multiple stages *and* aspects of empathy. This would lead to the use of additional tests and measures. In this way, hypotheses could be tested regarding several aspects of empathy and counseling.

If this first point is accepted, it gives a new view to the confusion in the counseling/psychotherapy outcome and empathy research findings. The fact that researchers have found very little relationship among the various empathy tests appears to make sense now. As Barrett-Lennard (1981) has pointed out, these tests are measuring different aspects and stages of a complex phenomenon. Therefore, they would not be expected to be highly correlated. Furthermore, it should not be surprising to find that some studies result in positive findings while others do not. For example, studies of client-centered counseling/psychotherapy using client-perceived, role-taking empathy typically have had positive outcomes. The measures used have been generally consistent with Rogers's (1975) theory of empathy and its relationship to therapy.

Age Differences in Empathy

Second, it is proposed that empathy in childhood is probably different from (but related to) emapthy in adolescence and adulthood. The developmental literature, both theory and research, indicates that although very young children (below age 3) can be empathic emotionally, they probably cannot be empathic cognitively. Taking another's role in complex interpersonal situations probably cannot occur until later childhood (above age 7). However, typical adolescents and adults are capable of role taking.

How does this point relate to the counseling/psychotherapy literature? It has always been assumed that counselors are capable of taking another's role. Yet, evidence from Hogan's (1969) and Mehrabian and Epstein's (1972) studies indicate the wide range of cognitive and affective role-taking abilities. Ham's (1980/1981) dissertation further documented this with 100 counselors (see Chapter 2). Thus, it seems quite reasonable to expect that some counselors' role-taking empathic abilities are more "childlike" than "adultlike." Although they may have the intellectual capacity, because of their cognitive development stage, they are still essentially egocentric. In this sense they are acting like young children. Assuming this to be true, it should not be surprising that some therapists are not easily able to learn empathic responses. Certainly, various studies (see Bath & Calhoun, 1977) document this to be true. One practical implication of this situation concerns counselor education. Some graduate students would need special help regarding their cognitive development before empathy training could be successful. (See Chapter 10 for a study that supports the point that graduate students do vary in their ability to learn empathic behaviors.)

Empathy May Not Lead to Helping

Third, it is proposed that empathy can, but does not necessarily lead to helping behaviors. It has been shown that the social literature, in theory and research, supports this point. In this instance, this author is referring primarily to emotional or affective empathy. Apparently, when emotional contagion affects an observer, an overraction or involvement can take place. As Hoffman (1977) noted, empathic distress can lead a person away from helping.

The connection to the counseling/psychotherapy literature is evident. If a therapist has too great an emotional reaction to his or her client (too much empathic distress), he or she will probably move away psychologically from the client. As noted above, Rogers (1975) referred to this by saying that there must be an appropriate amount of "as if" quality, and Stewart (1956) argued that deliberate distancing must occur after emotional involvement.

This point has great importance in terms of the counseling/psycho-therapy outcome studies. The mixed findings probably reflect the fact that we have *not* sorted out this element. We have not known when therapists have had too much empathic distress, even though they have been able to say the correct words in communicating back what the client has said. In effect, they have had empathic communication skills but lacked the proper empathic emotional contagion. (See Chapter 9 for a study that sought to increase awareness of trainees' affective states and related this awareness to the trainees' empathic communication skills.)

There is a need to develop methods for determining when emotional reactions occur and for discovering when their levels are not facilitative. As noted earlier (Gladstein, 1977), some type of physiological measure could be used. Such an approach was recently reported by Robinson, Herman, and Kaplan (1982). Finger skin temperature and skin con-ductance measures were used with counselor-client pairs during inter-views. These data were correlated with scores from the Barrett-Lennard (1981) Relationship Inventory. Although these physiological measures have been used from time to time in the counseling/psychotherapy field, by contrast they are frequently used in social psychology studies (e.g., Stotland et al., 1978, discussed earlier). A great deal more can be learned as to the strengths and limitations of these indices by studying this body of research.

Understanding what the appropriate empathic emotional reaction should be can also be viewed in terms of psychoanalytic concepts. As noted earlier, Stewart's (1956) four stages of empathy are raw identifica-tion, deliberate identification, resistance, and deliberate reidentification. These can also be thought of as one type of transference-countertrans-ference process. Assuming that there is client transference, countertrans-ference would occur—and probably not be helpful—when the counselor is unable to go beyond the raw identification stage. Theoretically, when the counselor is able to carry out the four stages, he or she is able to go beyond deliberate distancing (resistance) to reidentification, a conscious process. In effect, the counselor can regulate the initial empathic emotional reaction and use it productively.

A recent analogue study offers some support for these ideas. Although Peabody and Gelso (1982) did not draw upon Stewart's concepts, they did use Freudian and neo-Freudian definitions of countertransference. Their operational definition, withdrawal of personal involvment, suggests that they were measuring Stewart's resistance stage. Twenty clients rated their counselors on empathy (using the Barrett-Lennard Relationship In-ventory). One week after the counseling session, the counselors re-sponded to audiotapes of three types of clients (hostile, seductive, and neutral) by selecting one of two possible interpretive responses to 30 excerpts. If the counselor chose the response that interpreted the client's preceding statement without reference to the counselor, this was defined as countertransference behavior. In effect, the counselor had withdrawn from the client's statement. Another procedure was used to measure the counselor's openness to countertransference feelings. Items were rated by the counselors regarding their views of the usefulness, frequency, duration, and place of countertransference feelings in their counseling.

Their data showed that withdrawal was significantly negatively correlated with empathy for the seductive client (but not the hostile and neutral client) statements. Furthermore, empathy was significantly positively correlated with their measure of openness to countertransference feelings. Hence, empathy was present when the counselor was aware of his or her feelings but not during withdrawal. This suggests that withdrawal occurred when the emotional reactions were too strong. Or, as noted above, with too much empathic distress, he or she moved away psychologically from the client.

The psychoanalytic view of the working alliance also has relevance here. Greenson (1978) wrote that empathy is essentially feeling emotionally with the client. The therapist lets go of his rational-analytic ego and feels like the client temporarily. He or she oscillates between his or her self and that of the client. As such, it is one element of the working alliance. But there must be a "capacity for controlled and reversible regressions" (Greenson, 1967, p. 369). Without this control, it can be inferred that empathy loses its effectiveness in creating the working alliance. In effect, maintaining the proper emotional involvement facilitates the helping process. In the Peabody and Gelso (1982) study, apparently the counselors who were rated more empathic by their seductive clients were able to maintain the proper emotional involvement.

Empathy and Counseling/Psychotherapy Outcomes

Finally, it is proposed that in counseling/psychotherapy affective and cognitive empathy can be helpful in certain stages, with certain clients, and for certain goals. However, at other times they can interfere with positive outcomes. By now it should be clear there are many empathy terms and definitions used in the literature. However, most of them emphasize one of two general elements: (a) *affective* (identification, emotional reaction, emotional contagion, resonation, "I feel what you feel," etc.) or (b) *cognitive* (role taking, perspective taking, predictive, communicative, "I comprehend what you feel," etc.). The social and developmental literature documents that these types exist and that they are not the same. As noted earlier, several counseling/psychotherapy studies also indicate their differences. Furthermore, several writers have identified both and described their relationship in terms of an empathic process (e.g., Barrett-Lennard, 1981; Chandler, 1976; Hoffman, 1977; Rogers, 1975; Stewart, 1956). It has been shown that empathy may or may not lead to helping behavior. Therefore, it is necessary to determine when each may or may not be helpful in the counseling/psychotherapy process.

Past research efforts have been too global. The expected relationships to counseling outcomes should be specified for each type of empathy. In Table 1.1 some relationships regarding counseling goals and stages and client preferences have been listed. These reflect this author's best judgments, based upon an earlier review (Gladstein, 1977) and 35 years of counseling experiences. (Other researchers might hypothesize different relationships. Future empirical studies should be carried out to test these expectations.) Three common types of goals are noted. Self-exploration refers to finding out more about one's own being or identity—for its own sake, not to solve some specific problem. The second includes specific problems, whether in the career, educational, or personal/social domains. The third delineates problems that call for specific actions, such as decision making.

Table 1.1 indicates that both affective and cognitive empathy should be helpful to self-exploration goals. Certainly, client-centered therapy emphasizes this kind of goal. As noted earlier, and reviewed by Barrett-Lennard (1981), empathy usually shows positive relationships to client-centered therapy when the client judges the outcomes. Hence, this expectation seems well supported in the literature.

The prediction that affective empathy would not be helpful for problem-solving and action-oriented goals is much more speculative. Because these two goals usually call for cognitive input from the counselor, affective empathy alone (that is, identification or resonation or emotional contagion) would not be sufficient. Even cognitive empathy might not help, since this does not offer new information to the client.

The stages listed in Table 1.1 represent the synthesis from several counseling/psychotherapy theories, including trait-factor, client-centered, and behavioral. The expectations are based largely on theoretical concensus. As noted earlier (Gladstein, 1977), practically every theory states that empathy is important to initiating and building a counseling relationship. Thus, "yes" is listed for both stages for affective and cognitive empathy. However, in the problem-identification and exploration periods, affective empathy may not be helpful. These stages typically move toward more confrontation by the therapist, and, therefore, if the therapist has an emotional reaction similar to that of the client, this technique may not be effective. On the other hand, cognitive empathy (especially role taking) should be helpful here. However, when the action and termination stages evolve, even role taking may get in the way. Helping the client make plans and carry them out usually requires providing ideas and methods beyond the client's own views. Of course, having the same emotions as the client at this time could prevent moving onto the action and termination phases.

TABLE 1.1. Expected relationship of emotional and role-taking empathy to positive counseling outcomes.

Counseling aspect	Emotional empathy	Role-taking empathy
Goals		
Self-exploration	Yes[a]	Yes
Problem-solving	No[b]	Maybe[c]
Action-oriented	No	Maybe
Stages		
Initiation	Yes	Yes
Rapport establishment	Yes	Yes
Problem identification	Maybe	Yes
Exploration	Maybe	Yes
Action	No	Maybe
Termination	No	Maybe
Client preferences		
Close emotional relationship	Yes	Yes
Neutral emotional		
relationship	No	Maybe
Counselor to take client view	Yes	Yes
Counselor to present own self	No	No

[a]Yes = would help regarding positive outcome.
[b]No = would interfere regarding positive outcome.
[c]Maybe = may or may not help regarding positive outcome.

Client preferences can provide another set of expectations. Some clients want a close emotional relationship with the therapist. (Of course, this can be encouraged or discouraged.) If so, both affective and cognitive empathy would probably be helpful. As noted earlier, however, too much emotional contagion at this point can produce countertransference and lead to counselor withdrawal. Role taking would be especially valuable here. By contrast, clients preferring a neutral emotional relationship would most likely find therapist emotional contagion too threatening. Even role taking may interfere, since the therapist may be clarifying or reflecting the client's feelings as well as thoughts.

If the client prefers the counselor to take on the client's view, both affective and cognitive empathy would be appropriate. On the other hand, when the client prefers the counselor to present his or her own self, both types of empathy would be inappropriate. In this case, the client's wishes are ignored, since the therapist does not self-disclose his or her own views and feelings but presents only the client's.

Table 1.1 can also be used to suggest why some studies probably produce positive findings whereas others produce negative results. For example, Altman (1973) analyzed taped initial counseling interviews of clients who continued counseling versus those who stopped counseling after the first session. Accurate Empathy scores were significantly higher for the "stayers." This positive finding could be explained by Table 1.1 in that the Accurate Empathy Scale measures primarily cognitive empathy (Feldstein & Gladstein, 1980), and the initial session most likely incorporated the early stages only. In both instances, Table 1.1 predicts that cognitive empathy would be helpful.

By comparison, Irwin (1973/1974) found both positive and negative results. He correlated Carkhuff's Empathic Understanding scores with client-increased self-experiencing. This study also used only the initial interview. However, clients with vocational/educational concerns were separated in the analysis from the personal/adjustment clients. Although there was a significant positive correlation for the personal/adjustment clients, this did not occur for the vocational/educational clients. Thus, Altman (1973) and Irwin (1973/1974), using essentially the same type of empathy measure, found the same positive results. However, Irwin's negative result would also seem to fit one of the predictions listed in Table 1.1. Assuming that the vocational/educational clients' goals were more problem solving or action oriented than those of the personal/adjustment clients, Table 1.1 indicates cognitive empathy may or may not be helpful. This difference in goals may have been so powerful that it outweighed the fact that probably only the first three stages were reached in the initial interview.

Conclusion

It has been 29 years since Rogers (1957) stimulated the field to consider empathy as one of the crucial elements in counseling and psychotherapy. Yet, as indicated by the above review and comments, it is not clear what part empathy actually has in producing positive outcomes.

However, we have come a long way in understanding better the various aspects and stages involved in empathy. By adding the theoretical and research perspectives of developmental and social psychology to those of counseling/psychotherapy, we can move in new directions that will expand this understanding. We may not be able to resolve the existing confused picture concerning empathy and counseling/psychotherapy outcomes, but we may begin to unravel some of the enormous complexities involved. It is within this perspective that the studies that are reported in Chapters 2–10 should be viewed. Each in its own way attempted to unravel part of this very complex picture.

2
Counselor Empathy

MARY ANNA HAM

Numerous theoretical writings have argued that counselor empathy is important to successful counseling/psychotherapy. Chapter 1 discusses some of the issues concerning this point. Regardless of whether the literature documents that empathy is crucial to positive counseling outcomes, there are still these interesting empirical questions: What type and how much trait empathy do counselors have? Can their empathy be separated into components? Thus, the primary purpose of the study that is reported in this chapter was to seek answers to these questions.

Summary of Literature

The literature describing and defining empathy has not made clear whether empathy is a trait (innate or learned by a counselor/therapist) or a behavior (separate or affected by the interaction with a client). Although the question can be asked whether empathy in the therapeutic process is (a) the counselor's *ability* to be empathic, (b) the counselor's *effort* to be empathic, and/or (c) the counselor's in-session empathic *performance* (Barrett-Lennard, 1981; Bender & Hastorf, 1953; Cronbach, 1955; Kurtz & Grummon, 1972), this study examined only that aspect of empathy in the therapeutic process in which a counselor's empathic ability is a *skill*—a skill affecting the therapeutic process and preceding the therapeutic interaction between therapist and client.

There is support in the literature for conceptualizing empathy as a *skill*. From the perspective of developmental psychology, empathic skill is discussed by some as role taking, which is a skill acquired as part of an individual's cognitive development (Botkin, Flavell, Fry, Wright, & Jarvis, 1968).This role-taking skill has not only been considered a cognitive skill. From a sociological perspective, it has been suggested to have an affective component that includes a feeling of sympathy towards another and a sense of identity with another person (Sarbin & Allen, 1969). (See Chapter 1 for more discussion of this point.)

Empathic skill, as it has been discussed in the literature, involves a *covert process,* the ability to *predict* the feelings and attitudes of others (Cochrane, 1974). That is, empathic skill is considered to affect the therapeutic process *preceding* the therapeutic interaction between therapist and client.

As a predictive skill, empathy involves creating inferential strategies that can proceed even in the absence of the subject (Chandler, Greenspan, & Barenboim, 1974). The formulation of strategies has been based upon the conjecture that prediction is both a cognitive skill and an affective one.

Prediction, as an important cognitive skill (Bieri, 1961; Bronfenbrenner, Harding, & Gallway, 1968), follows Kelly's (1955) position that predictive behavior is a cognitive process involving certain behavioral variables. Kelly (1955) conceptualized a system of constructs for perceiving the social world. These constructs are used to form the basis for making predictions and are treated as personality traits. Using Kelly's conceptualization, Bieri (1961) has suggested that the greater the degree of differentiation among the constructs, the greater will be the predictive power of an individual. And he has designated the degree of differentiation of an individual's construct system as reflecting an individual's cognitive complexity or simplicity. This led to his hypothesis that there should be a significant positive relationship between an individual's degree of cognitive complexity or simplicity and the accuracy of his or her predictive behavior.

Prediction, as an affective quality, has been explored by Kagan et al. (1967). Affective sensitivity, the affective quality of empathy, is a measurable psychological trait that individuals have in varying degrees (Kagan et al., 1967). Kagan acknowledged that perhaps an individual's ability to identify accurately the feelings of another does not predict an ability to convey or communicate that sensitivity.

But is empathic skill so easily separated into either a cognitive skill or an affective skill? And, does this attempt to conceptualize predictive empathy on either a cognitive or affective level take into consideration the component of empathy that is affective in origin—affective in the sense that empathy is a projection of an individual's own feelings onto another (Chandler et al., 1974; Katz, 1963; Stewart, 1956)? Perhaps separating empathic responses into affective and cognitive components is a piecemeal approach to personality organization (Chandler et al., 1974). However, the study by Kurtz and Grummon (1972) suggested that psychotherapists' empathy, during and immediately after the therapeutic process (as measured by different instruments), had several components.

Research Question

By determining the relationship between two empathy measures, this study sought to establish whether a counselor's trait empathic skill could be separated into affective and cognitive components or would remain as a fused ability, an issue that has been highly debated in the literature (Chandler et al., 1974). Specifically, this study asked: Is a counselor's trait empathic skill the *same* or *different* as measured by two instruments: one instrument that measures a counselor's affective ability to understand another person's state of being; another instrument that measures a counselor's cognitive ability to be empathic? By measuring the correlation between two *trait* empathy instruments, Hogan's Empathy Scale (Hogan, 1969) and Kagan's Affective Sensitivity Scale (Kagan et al., 1967), the nature of counselor empathy could perhaps be determined.

Methodology

This was a descriptive, correlational study. It was the first or pretest stage of a larger research project (see Chapter 3 for its report).

Sample

One criterion for selecting subjects was used. This criterion was that the subjects had to be counselors with at least 2 years of experience in a secondary or postsecondary school setting. Other counselor characteristics were not taken into account so that the sample would be as large as possible. A list of 261 counselors who were working in secondary and postsecondary schools was compiled. Their institutions were located in a moderate-size metropolitan area in upstate New York. The counselors were requested to volunteer in the study. Of the 261 counselors who were informed of the research study, 100 counselors volunteered to participate (38% response rate). This sample of 100 counselors was composed of: 70 males, 30 females; 97 Caucasians; 3 Afro-Americans; 13 community college counselors; 2 university counselors; 85 high-school counselors (of the 85 high-school counselors, 9 were Catholic high-school counselors).

Measures[1]

The *cognitive* empathy trait measure was the Empathy Scale (Hogan, 1969). This is a 64-item self-report measure based upon the individual's capacity to adopt a broad moral perspective that reflects an empathic disposition. Hogan (1969) developed this empathy scale by comparing the responses of 57 men with high ratings and 57 with low ratings for empathy across the combined item pools of the California Psychological Inventory, the Minnesota Multiphasic Personality Inventory, and the Institute of Personality Assessment and Research. The reliability of this scale has been examined (Hogan, 1969) as well as the validity (Charles, 1973/1974; Greif & Hogan, 1973). Both appear satisfactory.

---

[1]See Chapter 3 for further details about these measures.

The *affective* empathy trait measure was the Affective Sensitivity Scale (Campbell, Kagan, & Krothwohl, 1971). It was developed as an instrument to measure an individual's ability to detect and describe the immediate affective state of another. The scale consists of multiple-choice items used with a series of short film excerpts from actual counseling sessions. The individual whose affective state is being measured views segments of the film and responds to 89 items. Each one of the 89 items consists of three statements: one statement is the correct answer and the other two statements are distractors. Two different kinds of items are included: one to reflect the client's feelings about herself or himself and the other to reflect his or her feelings about the counselor. For this scale, Campbell et al. (1971) reported test-retest reliability. Validity was also checked (Brewer, 1974; Campbell et al., 1971).

Procedures

In order to refine the procedures for administering the instruments, two subjects were asked to participate in a trial administration of both trait empathy instruments. From this preliminary testing, it was determined that it would be possible to administer the instruments in a group setting as easily as to a single counselor. The data from these two subjects were not used in the analysis of data.

A research assistant was hired and then trained to collect the data. This assistant met with the counselors at their respective institutions and at their convenience. The duties of the assistant entailed: (a) giving a brief presentation that described the research study; (b) administering the two trait empathy instruments; and (c) conducting a short discussion after the administration to allow the counselors to ventilate their feelings or to ask questions. This procedure took 1½ hours. Together the assistant and the researcher administered the instruments to groups of 10 or more counselors. The assistant, alone, handled the smaller groups and individual counselors.

Findings

The counselors' scores on the two empathy scales were the data used for this study. Three analyses of these data were conducted. The objective of these three analyses was to determine the convergent validity of the two scales; that is, to see if the two trait empathy instruments measured the same or different traits.

One analysis was made on the initial sample of 100 counselors; a second analysis was made only on the 68 males of the sample; and a third analysis was made on 46 male subjects. For the *first* analysis (the 100 subjects), descriptive statistics were computed: mean, standard deviation, and Pearson product-moment correlation. For the *second* analysis (68 male subjects), a SAS computer program was used to obtain a cross-tabulation of the data and then used to separate the data into four groups. Each group contained only those counselors who were at least one specified fraction (½, ⅓, ¼) of a standard deviation from the mean of the group of male subjects on both of the trait empathy measures. The group of 46 male subjects contained subjects as homogeneous as possible. These 46 counselors were all male, Caucasian, and were working in nonsecular high schools. For the group of 46 counselors, a *third* analysis, a correlation between their scores on the two trait empathy scales, was determined in a bivariate plot from a BMDP6D computer program.

From the first analysis made on the initial sample of 100 counselors, the correlation was −.09 (Table 2.1). Since the significance level was .38, the correlation is *not* statistically significant. In the second analysis with the group of 68 counselors, Table 2.2 presents the distribution of the four groups who were one specified fraction of a standard deviation from the mean. This demonstrates that the data diverge and form four discrete goups with a range of two, between the lowest and highest score. Since the data are divergent (can be separated into discrete groups), this is a graphic demonstration that there is no strong correlation between the two trait empathy instruments. Finally in the third analysis, with the group of 46 subjects, it is shown that the correlation of .08 (Table 2.1) is not statistically significant. As well as these three statistical analyses, two other criteria were used for determining whether the two trait empathy instruments correlated: (a) to compare the reliability coefficient of each individual instrument with the correlation coefficient between the two instruments (Guilford & Fruchter, 1978); and (b) to use inferential statistics and calculate the confidence interval using Fisher's transformation procedure (Guilford & Fruchter, 1978).

In comparing the reliability coefficient and the correlation coefficient of each instrument with one another, the calculated correlation of .08 (between the two instruments) is much smaller (lower) than either the reliability coefficient of .74 (Kagan et al., 1967) or .67−.75 (Campbell et al.,

TABLE 2.1. Descriptive statistics for empathy trait measures.

Measure	Total sample (N = 100)			Subsample (N = 46)		
	X	SD	r	X	SD	r
Affective Sensitivity Scale	68.99	14.34		69.11	13.99	
			−.09			.08
Empathy Scale	39.97	4.88		39.89	4.99	

Note. Total sample includes 70 males and 30 females. Subsample includes only homogeneous group of males.

TABLE 2.2. Distribution of subjects into groups based on distance from mean.[a]

Groups	½ SD	⅓ SD[b]	¼ SD[b]
High affective groups			
High affective, high cognitive	7	8	12
High affective, low cognitive	6	10	14
Low affective groups			
Low affective, high cognitive	5	7	10
Low affective, low cognitive	6	6	8

Note. N = 68.
[a]Based on each male subject's scores on the Affective Sensitivity Scale and the Empathy Scale. Subjects who fell within the mean are not included in this table.
[b]All calculations ⅓ and ¼ SD from the mean are cumulative.

1971) for the Kagan instrument or the reliability coefficient of .68–.86 (Greif & Hogan, 1973) for the Hogan instrument. Since the calculated correlation is lower than the previously reported reliability coefficients, there is indication that the two instruments pick up at least partially different true variance.

Using Fisher's Z-transformation procedure, the confidence interval was then calculated to be from −.225 to .245 at the .05 level of significance and is centered about the observed value of .08. Since the maximum correlation coefficient of .245 is substantially below the reported reliability coefficients, it can be stated almost certainly (at the 0.95 level of confidence) that the two trait empathy measures are divergent.

Discussion

The results indicate, from several different strategies of analysis, that there is little or almost no correlation between the two trait empathy instruments. The anlaysis of data indicates that, indeed, counselors do respond differently to these two trait empathy measures. This finding is consistent with Kurtz and Grummon's (1972) work with counselors, but it is inconsistent with Chandler et al.'s (1974) belief that empathy, at least in children, cannot be separated into components.

However, several recent studies support this research's findings and not Chandler et al.'s belief. Davis's (1980) study of college students indicated no or low positive correlations. Dolan's (1983) dissertation found no significant correlations for mothers, girls, and boys, but a moderate positive correlation for fathers. Johnson's (1983) dissertation found no significant correlations for husbands and wives.

In explanation of these results, it is necessary to point out that a trait cannot be measured independently of some method (Campbell & Fiske, 1959). Thus, it is conceivable that two separate tests might *not* correlate highly simply because *different methods* of measurement were used and *not* because *different traits* were involved. Thus, to claim without question that these results can distinguish between affective and cognitive empathy may not be possible. The importance of these results, then, is that they do begin to rend apart, expose, and perhaps clarify the underlying relationship between the trait of empathy and the measurement of empathy.

As Gladstein (1977, p. 77) has recommended, it is necessary to specify "which type of empathy is being measured by which specific type of instrument." Perhaps one key dimension that can make this separation clear is the *mode of communication* (Morocco, 1979b) that an empathy instrument requires a counselor to use in order to convey empathic understanding of client behaviors. These communication modalities have been identified by Mehrabian (1968, 1971) as verbal, nonverbal, and verbal-nonverbal communication systems (see Chapter 5 for a study based on this view).

In the two trait empathy instruments used for this research, two different modalities are required from the counselors: verbal understanding and nonverbal understanding. For the Hogan scale, a paper-and-pencil instrument, only a counselor's verbal understanding is tested. In contrast, the Kagan instrument requires that the counselors use both verbal and nonverbal understanding by requiring the counselor to respond to written responses, as well as react to the visual cues and voice tones of counselor-client exchanges portrayed on videotape. In these two instruments, the verbal-nonverbal understanding is measured by testing the counselor's verbal-nonverbal skills. The verbal skills are linguistic and the nonverbal skills are nonlinguistic. This alignment between verbal-nonverbal skill and linguistic-nonlinguistic skill is noted in the literature on nonverbal communication (Gladstein, 1974; Harrison & Knapp, 1972).

The issue can be raised of whether the mode of communication required from the counselor by the Hogan instrument is not only linguistic and verbal but also cognitive; of whether the Kagan instrument requires both nonlinguistic and linguistic, verbal and nonverbal skills, but also affective skills as well as cognitive ones. From the literature in developmental psychology, this relationship is noted in the discussion and research on how children learn to be empathic (Chandler et al., 1974; Rushton, 1980).

Distinctions between cognitive and affective empathy measures have been suggested in the measurement literature. Feldstein and Gladstein (1980) have suggested criteria for distinguishing empathy measures, including criteria for measures of affective and cognitive empathy. From their criteria, Hogan's instrument measures cognitive empathy and Kagan's instrument measures both affective and cognitive empathy. "Cognitive empathy is defined as a role taking skill ... [while] affective empathy involves an internal and unobservable motivation of the counselor's feelings and fantasies" (Feldstein & Gladstein, 1980, p. 50).

Since Hogan referred to the concept of empathy as a "major element in role-theoretical accounts of interpersonal behavior" (Greif & Hogan, 1973, p. 280), the assumption can be made that Hogan's instrument fulfills Feldstein and Gladstein's (1980) criteria for cognitive empathy. Kagan's instrument, although requiring linguistic skills of counselors, also fulfills the criteria for affective empathy instruments, because it stimulates underlying thoughts and feelings as a result of viewing videotape.

It is here in the debate that the distinction between trait and measurement can be made. The *trait of empathy,* learned as an affective and cognitive skill, is dependent upon verbal and linguistic development. Perhaps, then, the learning and the emergence of the empathic skill is integrated and holistic. However, the *measurement of empathy* can distinguish the cognitive and affective components of a counselor's learned empathic skill by the mode of communication that an empathy instrument uses to measure a counselor's empathic understanding (verbal, nonverbal, or verbal-nonverbal). This is not to say that instruments that measure empathy will be able to test all dimensions of a counselor's empathic understanding, for no instrument may be able to measure the projection of an individual's own feelings into another (Chandler et al., 1974). Instruments can, however, measure certain components of a counselor's empathic understanding and *can distinguish between those components,* namely the affective and the cognitive components. Even if the distinction of these components may be along a continuum rather than aligned as polar opposites, the critical observation made in this study was the *distinction between the components of empathy and not the degree of difference between affective and cognitive empathic dimensions.*

In addition to documenting the types of trait empathy counselors have, this study also contains data regarding their *levels* of trait empathy. This is important because most research concerning counselor empathy has focused on empathic behavior expressed during the counseling interview. This has usually been measured by having clients fill out instruments, such as the Barrett-Lennard Relationship Inventory, after the interview. The other typical procedure has been to have raters make judgments using the Carkhuff Empathic Understanding Scale (Feldstein & Gladstein, 1980).[2]

The 100 professional, experienced counselors in this study had a mean score of 68.99 (*SD* = 14.34) on Kagan's Affective Sensitivity Scales (ASS) (see Table 2.1). Of the few studies reported in the literature that include ASS scores for professionals (as opposed to trainees), Kurtz and Grummon (1972) indicated that 31 Michigan State University counselor/

---

[2]See Chapters 3–7, 9, and 10 for examples of these types of studies.

therapists (some of whom were completing their final phase of their Ph.D. training) had a mean score of 57.00 and a standard deviation of 7.23. (By comparison Kagan et al. (1967) reported a lower mean for 402 students-in-training (M = 50.00; SD = 8.19)). Thus, the counselors in this study scored considerably higher. However, with a standard deviation of 14.34 (versus 7.23 and 8.19) there was also a much greater variation. Perhaps the fact that the 100 counselors knew ahead of time that the research involved empathy may have biased the distribution. Or, since they all were experienced professionals, they may have acquired more empathic skills (or those counselors with lower skills may have left the profession). (As noted in Chapter 3, very few counselors who scored low on both the Kagan and Hogan measures volunteered for the subsequent experimental study.)

Concerning cognitive empathy, the Hogan Empathy Scale mean score of 39.97 is somewhat lower than the mean of 44.50 for two professional counselors in the study reported in Chapter 6. In a study of cognitive-behavioral therapy treatments provided for 33 elementary-school children, 13 therapists (one advanced graduate student and 12 selected upper-level undergraduates) had a mean of 43.0 and standard deviation of 4.49 on the Hogan measure (Kendall and Wilcox, 1980). Hogan's (1969) original study reported these means and standard deviations for four higher samples: (a) psychology majors (44.7; 5.2); (b) education-abroad students (43.2; 4.8); (c) medical students (42.4; 5.3); and (d) research scientists (40.3; 5.4). All of these data suggest that the counselors in this study scored lower than samples of other helpers and some non helper groups. Why they scored higher on affective empathy and lower on cognitive empathy is not clear.

Conclusion

This study documents, in at least this sample, that counselors' trait affective and cognitive empathy have little relationship to each other. In view of the similar recent findings of Dolan (1983) and Johnson (1983), briefly noted in this chapter, concerning empathy in children and adults, it appears that the empirical research is beginnning to support the theoretical notion (as presented in Chapter 1) that affective and cognitive empathy are separate domains. This conclusion is important to keep in mind when attempting to understand the research reported in this book's remaining chapters.

3
Client Behavior and Counselor Empathic Performance

MARY ANNA HAM

The framework proposed for this study was drawn from two areas of literature, role theory and communications theory. Both of these theories emphasize the importance of the interactional process occurring between two or more individuals; both theories suggest mutual involvement, influence, and alteration between participants ("actor" and "audience").

This framework can easily be related to the counseling role in which the expectation is for interaction and communication to occur between at least two individuals. If communication is to be the social matrix of the counseling process (Ruesch & Bateson, 1951), whatever occurs between counselor and client results, in part, from the way in which these two participants convey messages to each other. How these messages are conveyed is the result of the influence of individual characteristics and of role expectations for both the "actor" and "audience."

It was considered that perhaps characteristics of the counselor that existed prior to the counseling encounter would alter the interaction between the counselor and client. Therefore, two conditions, *the counselor's degree of empathic understanding* prior to the counseling encounter and *the client's interview behavior* were selected as factors highly influencing the client-counselor interaction.

Thus, the purpose of this study was to investigate whether client-counselor interaction affected, either positively or negatively, the counselor's efforts to be empathic, which, in turn, may have facilitated or prevented the counselor from enacting the counselor role in an effective and convincing way.

Summary of Literature

While there are a number of studies investigating the effects of counselor-offered empathy upon the outcome of counseling (Bergin & Suinn, 1975; Gladstein, 1970, 1977), there are few that examine those factors affecting a counselor's empathic behavior during the counseling interview (see Chapter 4 for more discussion on this point), and fewer yet that explore the effects of counselor-client interaction upon the counselor's efforts to implement empathic skills. The following studies examined those client conditions that were offered during the interview that affect the counselor's empathic skill.

A study conducted by Budman (1971) relates directly to the effect that the cognitive dimension of the client's problem has upon the counselor. In the study, he measured the relationship between a client's lexical organization (complex language organization or simple language organization) and the degree of empathy offered by a counselor. His results indicated that language organization had no significant effect upon the therapist's empathy level when rated by judges, but a significant difference existed between high- and low-empathy groups of therapists when the patient rated the therapist.

Taylor (1972), although primarily investigating the effect of the client's sex upon the counselor's level of empathic understanding, concluded that counselors achieved their lowest scores on empathic rating with clients who presented anger-hostility emotions and their highest scores on empathic ratings with clients who presented elation-excitement emotions.

Heck and Davis (1973) found, in their investigation of empathy and conceptual complexity, that the counselor's level of empathy did not maintain a constant level of expression across clients with different cognitive styles. The level at which a counselor expressed empathy was affected by whether the client was more cognitively abstract or concrete. Even though the counselor-subjects with high conceptual levels responded to both conceptually abstract and concrete clients with more empathy than counselor-subjects with low conceptual levels, counselor-subjects with high conceptual levels responded with more empathy to high conceptual clients and counselor-subjects with low conceptual levels responded with more empathy to low conceptual clients.

Melnick (1974) examined the effect of client problem upon counselor level of empathy and concluded that counselors were judged to have significantly higher levels of empathy with clients with social-personal problems than with clients with vocational-educational concerns.

More recent studies have investigated counselor variables that have affected in-session counselor-client interactions. Peabody and Gelso (1982) empirically examined the relationship between counselor empathic ability and counselor countertransference when the counselor was interacting with three different client presentations: (a) hostile, (b) seductive, and (c) neutral. It was concluded that counselors with high empathic ability are more open to conflictual feelings aroused by their clients (certain kinds of clients, e.g., seductive) and less likely to act out their countertransference reactions (withdrawal behavior).

Sladen (1982) analyzed the effects of race and socioeconomic status on the perception of process variables in counseling, including judged counselor empathy. The results of the study confirmed the hypotheses: that both black and white subjects gave highest counselor empathy ratings in those situations in which the counselor and client were similar in race and social class and lowest ratings when counselor and client were dissimilar in race and social class.

In an analogue study, Vargas and Borkowski (1982) assessed clients' ongoing impressions of a therapist's attractiveness and effectiveness after an intake session and/or after therapy was completed. Data of the study suggested that both skilled and unskilled counselors received an added boost in terms of their perceived effectiveness if they were attractive. And, when the counselor had poor counseling skills, attractiveness made little difference. However, analyses of future expectancy data collected after the third session revealed that only in the good-skills condition did attractiveness augment clients' impressions about the desirability of the counselor for treating social and behavioral problems not initially presented at the time of intake.

Research Question

The above studies provided some evidence that, indeed, the "actor" (counselor) and the "audience" (client) do affect one another and that this interaction appears to influence the counselor's ability to be empathic and, thus, his or her ability to carry out the dyadic interview, a counselor subrole.

However, the paucity of studies only pointed out the need for a more precise operational definition, and a more concise separation of empathy into meaningful components that could lead to empirical investigations of the concept, empathy. Therefore, the research question asked was: Does the relationship between the type and degree of a counselor's predictive empathic skills and a counselor's empathic behavior during a counseling session depend upon two different client behaviors, compliant and disruptive? Disruptive behaviors were selected because several studies found that client aggressive or hostile behaviors do influence the counselor's activities and perceptions (Bandura, Lipsher, & Miller, 1960; Gamsky & Farwell, 1966; Greene, 1970). Furthermore, it was assumed that compliant behaviors would have different effects.

Methodology

The analogue experimental design involved coached clients (confederates) offering either compliant or disruptive behaviors. However, this design was contingent upon the results from a pretest study. The latter was a survey of counselors' responses to two predictive empathy measures. (That study is reported as part of Chapter 2 of this book.) The goal was to identify four samples of counselors who were high and/or low in affective and cognitive empathy. However, it was not possible to find counselors who were low in both affective and cognitive empathy and were willing to volunteer for this experimental study. Therefore, the analysis was changed from a repeated measures analysis of variance to a regression coefficient analysis.

Sample

The sample consisted of two kinds of subjects: counselor-subjects and client-subjects. For the pretest sample, one criterion for selecting counselor-subjects was used. This was that the counselors would have at least 2 years of experience in a secondary or postsecondary school setting. Other counselor characteristics were not taken into account so that the pretest sample would be as large as possible. Of the approximately 260 counselors who were informed of the research, 100 counselors volunteered to participate in the pretest. This sample was composed of 70 males, 30 females; 97 Caucasians, 3 Afro-Americans; 13 junior college counselors, 2 university counselors, and 85 high-school counselors. Of the latter, 9 were Catholic high-school counselors.

For the experimental study itself a decision was made to restrict the counselor characteristics and hold constant certain factors. For several reasons the sex of the counselor-subject was selected as the most important factor to control. First, the simulated counseling session would replicate more closely the real counseling environment if the counselor-subjects were all male and the client-subjects were female. Second, because of the inconsistent findings and sparse research on the effect that the counselor's sex has on the counselor-client interaction (Feldstein, 1979), control of the sex variable was necessary in order to avoid confounding the experimental results, (see also Chapter 7 on this point). That is to say, the sex of the client rather than client behaviors would have influenced the outcome. Race and work setting were also considered important factors to be controlled. Consequently only 46 male, Caucasian, public high-school counselors were considered as possible counselor-subjects.

An analogue technique was used for this study. The client-subject sample of confederates (N = 6) consisted of female undergraduate students who had participated in drama productions at a medium-size eastern university.

Instruments

This research study utilized three instruments. For the pretest study, two were used to predict a counselor's empathic understanding. These instruments measured the independent variables (affective and cognitive empathy). They were: (a) Empathy Scale (Hogan, 1969) and (b) Affective Sensitivity Scale (Campbell et al., 1971). The other instrument measured the experimental dependent variable (a client's perception of a counselor's in-session performance behavior with her). This was the Barrett-Lennard Relationship Inventory (BLRI) (Barrett-Lennard, 1962).[1]

Empathy Scale. The Hogan Empathy Scale is a 64-item self-report measure based upon the individual's capacity to adopt a broad moral perspective that reflects an empathic disposition. Hogan (1969) developed this empathy scale by comparing the responses of 57 men with high ratings and 57 with low ratings for empathy across the combined item pools of the California Psychological Inventory (Gough, 1964), the Minnesota Multiphasic Personality Inventory (Hathaway & McKinley, 1943), and the Institute of Personality Assessment and Research (MacKinnon as cited in Hogan, 1969). The psychometric properties, including the reliability and validity of the scale, have been examined extensively (Hogan, 1969; Hogan & Dickstein, 1972; Hogan & Henley, 1970; Hogan & Mankin, 1970; Hogan, Mankin, Conway, & Fox, 1970; Kurtines & Hogan, 1972). (See Chapter 2 for further discussion.)

Affective Sensitivity Scale. This scale was developed to measure an individual's ability to detect and describe the immediate affective state of another. The scale consists of multiple-choice items used with a series of short film excerpts from actual counseling sessions. The individual views segments of the film and responds to 89 items. Each of the 89 items consists of three statements; one statement is the correct answer and the other two are distractors. Two different kinds of items are included, one to reflect the client's feelings about herself or himself and the other to reflect his or her feelings about the counselor. Campbell et al. (1971) reported satisfactory test-retest reliability. Brewer (1974), in addition, has listed validity coefficients: (a) Concurrent validity: Affective Sensitivity scores correlated 0.53 with therapist ranking of group members. Coefficients of 0.32 and 0.28 were obtained between Affective Sensitivity scores of doctoral practicum students and their supervisors' ranking of the students' sensitivity. (b) Predictive validity: Coefficients of 0.31 and 0.32 were reported between Affective Sensitivity scores and doctoral practicum students' peer rankings of counselor effectiveness.

Barrett-Lennard Relationship Inventory. This is a scale filled out by the client after the counseling interview. This scale presumes

that the client's experience of his [or her] therapist's response is the primary locus of therapeutic influence in their relationship ... that it is what the client himself [or herself] experiences that affects him [or her] directly ... [and] that the relationship as experienced by the client [rather than by the therapist] will be most crucially related to the outcome of therapy. (Barrett-Lennard, 1962, p. 2)

---

[1]In the total study reported in the dissertation, the Carkhuff Communication Index (Carkhuff, 1976) was also used.

Barrett-Lennard described the preparation of the items to involve a constant interaction between theory and operational expression. And, indeed, the instrument does assess a client's perception of a counselor's empathic understanding, congruence, regard, and unconditional regard. By using the split-half method, Barrett-Lennard (1962) assessed the internal consistency of the Relationship Inventory. As well, Lake, Miles, and Earle (1973) have reviewed studies that use the Barrett-Lennard Relationship Inventory. They stated that both test-retest and split-half reliabilities are satisfactory. Test-retest correlations for empathic understanding are reported to be 0.89 for clients. Lake et al. (1973) also give evidence of the instrument's validity by citing studies that have correlated Relationship Inventory scores with other measures (Emmerling, 1961; Snelbecker, 1961). (See Chapter 9 for more discussion.)

Procedures for Collecting Pretest Data

Several strategies for contacting and informing the counselors about the research study were considered. From among those strategies, it was decided to inform and contact counselors through their supervisors. Arrangements for administering the pretest instruments to the counselors were made, if possible, through the supervisors. In some institutions, there were as many as 14 counselors who had agreed to participate in the study, while in other school districts or institutions only one counselor wished to participate.

In order to clarify the procedures for administering the instruments to the counselors, two subjects were asked to participate in a trial administration of both predictive empathy instruments. From this preliminary testing, it was determined that it would be possible to administer the pretest instruments in a group setting as easily as to a single counselor. The data from these subjects were not used for the research study.

A research assistant was hired and then trained to collect the pretest data. This assistant met with the counselors at their institution and at their convenience. The duties of the assistant entailed: (a) giving a brief presentation to the counselor for the purpose of describing the research study, (b) administering the two predictive empathy instruments and, (c) conducting a short discussion after the administration to allow the counselors to ventilate their feelings or to ask questions. This procedure took 1½ hours. Together the assistant and the researcher administered the instruments to groups of 10 or more counselors. The assistant, alone, handled the smaller groups and individual counselors.

Procedures for Training Client-Subjects

Deciding upon a population from which to obtain client-subjects was an important initial step in the process of training client-subjects. Since the client-subjects were to be confederates, the most important criterion was the ability of the subjects to play and to maintain a role throughout a counseling session. Psychology or other social science students who were familiar with role theory and role play were possible choices as well as drama students who had actually experienced playing the role of another. A decision was made to choose drama students.

Once students had volunteered ($N = 8$) to participate in the study they were interviewed and their life histories were explored. The research study was also described to them. In order to control for conditions that would influence the counselors' responses, certain criteria were examined during the interviews: attractiveness (no one individual was to be more or less attractive than the other), age, accent, race, experience in role play or acting, voice tone, and sensitivity to their own history. From the interview, a composite description of the "experimental client" was created from the life histories of the client-subjects. From this interview process, six Caucasian female undergraduate students were selected to begin training as client-subjects.

There were three 2-hour training sessions for the client-subjects. These sessions involved their listening to a didactic presentation, observing role play on videotape, and participating and practicing role play. The last stage of the training was to make a videotape of each client-subject role playing each of the study's designated client conditions with a "live" counselor. After the training sessions for the client-subjects were completed, each videotape of the four client conditions played by the client-subjects was viewed and rated by a group of four judges, two male and two female.

The purpose for judging the videotapes was threefold: (a) To examine the performance of the client-subjects: did the client-subjects perform well in an absolute sense and perform well relative to the other roles they played? (b) To determine whether judges could agree: did the judges agree on which roles the client-subjects were playing and how well the roles were played by the client-subjects? (c) To determine whether the roles were adequately defined: could the judges identify the roles? Although these judgments were subjective, it was critical to the study to undertake this examination, for in an analogue study the researcher must have confidence that the client-subjects are as "real" as possible.

The data indicated that the judges rated the client-subjects' performances to be better than average (3.0 being average). The roles played by five of the six client-subjects were identified accurately more than 75% of the time, and 50% of the roles played by the sixth client-subject were identified correctly. The rating of the performance of the likable role was the higher, 4.29.

Experimental Procedures with Client-Subjects

Before each counseling session, the client-subject assigned for that session went to a room adjacent to the counseling room. She waited there until the research assistant came to take her to the counseling room and introduce her to the counselor. After each counseling session, the client-subject filled out the Barrett-Lennard Relationship Inventory and was assigned a client role for her next counseling session. An attempt was made to alternate the order of the client behaviors presented to the counselors: for example, if counselor I saw a compliant client first, then counselor II saw a disruptive client first. Because of the client-subjects' personal schedules, a balanced or strictly randomized order could not be carried out.

After the experimental study was completed, the client-subjects were interviewed so that they would have an opportunity to express their feelings and reactions about participating in the study. From the comments made, they all indicated having greater difficulty playing the role of a hostile client than of a compliant one.

Experimental Procedure with Counselor-Subjects

The counselors were informed that the total experiment would take 1½ hours. Within this time they would see two clients, each for 20 minutes, and then discuss their reactions to the clients with the researcher. The counselors were not informed that the clients were confederates. If they asked questions about the clients, they were given a falsified description of the client's situation. For the experiment itself, the confederate client was brought into the room by the research assistant and then introduced to the counselor. After 20 minutes, the research assistant interrupted the session. The client left the counseling room. The counselor then had the option of taking a 10-minute break. Once he was prepared to see a second client, the research assistant took the second client from the client-subject waiting room, brought her to the counseling room, and introduced her to the counselor-subject. After 20 minutes, the session was interrupted, the client-subject left, and the researcher entered the counseling room to debrief the counselor.

The researcher informed him that the experiment was a deception study. The researcher asked the counselor whether he had suspected that the client was a confederate and, if he did, what cues led him to this awareness. The responses of the counselor-subjects were varied. Two of the 20 counselors felt certain during the first session that the client was a confederate (one compliant, one disruptive) and felt this awareness interfered with their counseling. Their comments were, "She just seemed too angry." "I couldn't believe someone would be so nice." Three counselors suspected, sometime during the first session, that the clients were confederates (one compliant, two disruptive). These three counselors did not feel, however, that this awareness affected their counseling ability. Their comments were, "The client's acting seemed so believable that I did what I would have done in a 'normal' session." "I was too much into the session myself to have acted differently." The researcher also explored the counselors' feelings about participating in a deception study. Discussion continued with the counselor-subjects until they had resolved and felt comfortable with their feelings about participating in the study. The process took from 10 minutes to 1½ hours.

Analysis of Data

As noted above, due to the results of the pretest, the original plan to use a repeated measure analysis of variance procedure had to be changed to using multiple regression. This was accomplished through the computer program BMDP1R. After reviewing the results of the first computer output, the following two refinements were made: (a) The number of the sample was decreased by one (from 20 to 19 total subjects). This decrease in the sample was made because upon inspection of the plots of residuals, an outlier (outlying subject) was prominent (one of the subjects received an unusually low score on the Kagan Scale). (b) The data were weighted in order to compensate for the descriptive difference in the willingness of high-empathic and low-empathic counselors to volunteer for this research project.[2]

Results

Hypothesis Testing

The general research question stated earlier was modified to fit the regression analysis approach. It became: During a counseling session, does the difference between a counselor's empathic behavior toward a compliant client and a disruptive client depend upon the type and degree of a counselor's predicted empathic skill so that the regression slopes (coefficients) in the multiple regression equation are negative or positive but not zero? This research question was then stated as a null hypothesis: The difference scores between a counselor's empathic behavior with two different client behaviors (compliant and disruptive) do not correlate with either measure of a counselor's predicted empathic skill.

$$H_0: b_C = b_D \text{ for each predictor.}$$

Tables 3.1 and 3.2 display the regression analysis data. It can be seen that these data do not categorically support the null hypothesis. The significant values (the simple correlation r, the regression coefficient B, the multiple correlation R, and its F value) emerge in the analysis of the relationship between a compliant client's evaluation of a *counselor's*

---

[2]In the total study reported in the dissertation, other refinements were made that were not related to the data reported in this chapter.

TABLE 3.1. Summary table ($N = 19$); Relationship between counselors' predictive empathy scores and the effect of client behaviors upon counselors' in-session performance.

	Counselor interaction with compliant client					
Dependent measures	Kagan		Hogan		Kagan-Hogan	
Independent measure	r	B	r	B	R	F
BLRI	−0.618**	−0.583**	−0.284	0.137	0.632*	5.322*

	Counselor interaction with disruptive client					
Dependent measures	Kagan		Hogan		Kagan-Hogan	
Independent measure	r	B	r	B	R	F
BLRI	−0.299	−0.327	0.030	0.112	0.318	0.900

Note. Weighted regression analysis. BLRI = Barrett-Lennard Relationship Inventory; r = simple correlation; B = standard regression coefficient (slope); R = multiple correlation; F = F ratio.
*$p < .05$; **$p < .01$.

performance (behavior) during a session with her (as measured by the Barrett-Lennard Relationship Inventory) and the *counselor's predictive affective empathy score* (as measured by the Kagan Affective Sensitivity Scale). In contrast, significance is not observed in the analysis of the relationship between a compliant client's evaluation of a counselor's performance during a session with her and the *counselor's predictive cognitive empathy score* (as measured by the Hogan Empathy Scale).

The negative standard regression coefficient (slope) value of −0.583, significant at the 0.05 criterion of significance (see Table 3.1), indicates that the Barrett-Lennard score increases as the Kagan score decreases, when a compliant client is seen by the counselor. The client-type difference in relationship between the Kagan score and the Barrett-Lennard score is tested and shown in Table 3.2. (Note no significant difference in slope.) Taking the data of Tables 3.1 and 3.2, the interpretation of both of these tables together is that predictive affective empathy (Kagan score) lowers the counselor's in-session performance with compliant clients. However, there is insufficient evidence to make a specific comparison between the counselor's in-session performance with a compliant client and a disruptive client. That is, the question of whether predictive affective empathy hurts the counselor's in-session behavior as much or less for disruptive clients than for compliant clients, or even has no effect for disruptive clients, cannot be resolved.

Tables 3.1 and 3.2 show no evidence that predictive cognitive empathy (Hogan score) affects the counselor's in-session performance with either client behavior (compliant or disruptive).

TABLE 3.2. Summary table ($N = 19$); relationship between counselors' predictive empathy scores and the *difference* in the effect that client behaviors have upon counselors' in-session performance.

	Difference in the effect of the compliant and disruptive client upon the counselor					
Dependent measures	Kagan		Hogan		Kagan-Hogan	
Independent measure	*r*	*B*	*r*	*B*	*R*	*F*
BLRI	−0.217	−0.154	−0.289	−0.250	0.325	0.946

Note. BLRI = Barrett-Lennard Relationship Inventory; r = simple correlation; B = standard regression coefficient (slope); R = multiple correlation; F = F ratio.

Since only one dependent variable (compliant clients' ratings of counselors' in-session behavior as measured by the Barrett-Lennard Relationship Inventory) is shown to be significant, it is not possible to reject the null hypothesis. From the data analysis, it must be concluded that the *difference scores* between counselors' empathic in-session performance with two different client behaviors (compliant and disruptive) do not interact with counselors' predicted empathic skill.

Separate from this and in addition to answering the hypothesis, an analysis of the data was conducted to check the relevance of the hypothesis to simple effects of client behavior regardless of the counselor's predictive empathy. To check for such effects, the data were examined with a t test. The t score (for correlated observations, since each counselor had seen both types of clients) was significant at the 0.05 criterion of significance ($t = 2.640; p = .016$) for the comparison between the effects of compliant and disruptive client behavior upon counselors' in-session performances when measured by the Barrett-Lennard Relationship Inventory. The counselors performed better with compliant clients than with disruptive clients. From this finding it can be concluded that (a) a client can perceive differences in a counselor's in-session performance (behavior), and (b) differences in a client's behavior affects a client's perception of a counselor's in-session performance (behavior). In a general sense, it can be said that a counselor's in-session performance is affected by client behaviors.

Auxiliary Findings

The general findings of the research hypothesis led the researcher to ask two questions: (a) Why was a negative correlation found between compliant clients' evaluations and not disruptive clients' evaluations (perceived ratings) of counselors' empathic in-session performances and counselors' predictive affective empathy scores? (b) Why did the observed interaction effect only occur for the relationship between compliant clients' evaluation of counselors' in-session performances and counselors' predictive affective empathy scores? From the data that had

TABLE 3.3. Summary table: *Split data*—Order of client behavior. *Group I*: Compliant-disruptive (*N* = 8); *Group II*: Disruptive-Compliant (*N* = 11); Relationship between counselors' predictive empathy scores and the effect of client behavior upon counselors' in-session performance.

		Counselor interaction with compliant client					
	Dependent measure	Kagan		Hogan		Kagan-Hogan	
Order of client behavior	Independent measure	*r*	*B*	*r*	*B*	*R*	*F*
Group I	BLRI	−0.589	−0.606	−0.272	−0.306	0.664	1.966
Group II		−0.762*	−0.708*	0.393	−0.196	0.785*	6.438*

		Counselor interaction with disruptive client					
	Dependent measure	Kagan		Hogan		Kagan-Hogan	
Order of client behavior	Independent measure	*r*	*B*	*r*	*B*	*R*	*F*
Group I	BLRI	−0.224	0.226	−0.016	−0.028	0.226	0.134
Group II		−9.410	−0.492	0.159	0.296	0.499	1.323

Note. BLRI = Barrett-Lennard Relationship Inventory; *r* = simple correlation; *B* = standard regression coefficient (slope); *R* = multiple correlation; *F* = F ratio.
*$p < .05$.

already been collected, it was possible to conjecture and then test out a speculative answer for the first question.

The sequencing of client behaviors (sequence 1: compliant, disruptive; sequence 2: disruptive, compliant) was considered to be a possible reason for the differences stated in the first question. In order to test this consideration, the data were split into two groups. The first group consisted of those counselors who saw compliant clients first and disruptive clients second. The second group consisted of those counselors who saw disruptive clients first and compliant clients second. The data for these two groups were analyzed with multiple regressions.

Tables 3.3 and 3.4 give the results of these analyses. Significant values for *r*, *B*, *R*, and *F* ratio at the 0.05 criterion of significance are revealed in Table 3.3 for compliant clients' assessment (using the Barrett-Lennard Relationship Inventory) of the counselors' performances when the session with the *compliant client follows the disruptive client*. The negative slope value of −0.708, significant at the 0.05 criterion of significance, indicates that the Barrett-Lennard score increases as the Kagan score decreases when a counselor sees a compliant client immediately after a disruptive client.

Thus, there is evidence that predictive affactive empathy (Kagan score) lowers the counselor's in-session performance with a compliant client

TABLE 3.4. Summary table: *Split data*—Order of client behavior. *Group I*: Compliant-disruptive ($N = 8$); *Group II*: Disruptive-Compliant ($N = 11$); Relationship between counselors' predictive empathy scores and the *difference* in the effect that client behavior has upon counselors' in-session performance.

Difference between the effect of compliant and disruptive client upon counselor

Order of client behavior	Dependent measure Independent measure	Kagan		Hogan		Kagan-Hogan	
		r	*B*	*r*	*B*	*R*	*F*
Group I	BLRI	−0.298	−0.313	−0.246	−0.263	0.397	0.468
Group II		−0.191	−0.060	−0.487	−0.471	0.491	1.269

Note. BLRI = Barrett-Lennard Relationship Inventory; r = simple correlation; B = standard regression coefficient (slope); R = multiple correlation; F = F ratio.

when the session with the compliant client immediately follows a session with a disruptive client. There is, however, insufficient evidence to make specific comparisons between the counselor's in-session performance with a compliant and a disruptive client. To be contrasted with this significant negative standard regression coefficient (slope value) is the nonsignificance of the standard regression coefficient when counselors interact first with a compliant client and then with a disruptive client. Although the sample is small, the comparisons between Groups I and II in Tables 3.3 and 3.4 suggest strongly that counselors' in-session performances are influenced by the sequencing of client behaviors.

Discussion

The results of this experiment illuminate the counseling situation as a reciprocally contingent interaction (Heller, Myers, & Kline, 1963). That is, the experiment indicates that client behaviors do influence counselors' in-session performance, in particular, empathic behaviors. As role theory suggests, there is a reciprocal interaction between "actor and audience." The audience not only guides the actor but provides social reinforcements that shape the actor's behavior.

In this study, a counselor's in-session empathic performance (behavior) with compliant client behavior was better than with disruptive client behavior. This conclusion is supported by literature that examines the effects of disruptive and likable behavior on counselor behavior (Greene, 1970; Heller et al., 1963). These studies do not, however, distinguish counselor empathic behavior from the more generalized entity of counselor behavior.

Further refinement of counselor client interaction was anticipated. The possibility that a client with disruptive behavior would affect a counselor's in-session empathic performance more negatively than a client with likable behavior was considered. Several studies have shown positive responses from a counselor with a friendly client and negative or withdrawing behaviors with a hostile client (Greene, 1970; Heller et al., 1963). Also, Luborsky, Averbach, Chandler, Cohen, and Bachrach (1971) indicated that client likability could be a factor in positive therapeutic outcome. This study also demonstrated that counselors performed better with compliant (likable) clients.

Results from studies examining the cognitive development of empathy (e.g., Flavell et al., 1968) and theoretical discussions about the affective component of empathy (Hackney, 1978; Kagan, 1978) suggest to the researcher that, possibly, the affective component of a counselor's measured empathy would be more influenced by a client with disruptive behavior than the measured predictive cognitive component of a counselor's empathy. (See Chapters 1 and 2 for further support of this point.) If, as developmental psychologists claim, empathy is a skill related to cognitive development, then the ability to mediate (to utilize cognitive empathic skill) would assist the counselor in coping with the client who is presumed to be more difficult to treat, the disruptive client. The counselor with predictive cognitive empathy skills should be able to behave more empathically to the client with disruptive behavior. From a more psychodynamic interpretation, the measures of a counselor's predictive affective empathy would be more highly influenced by the disruptive client behavior, for deeply felt, internal, more primitive states of the counselor's state would react more strongly to behavior that appeared threatening. Interpretation of counselor-client interaction cannot be simple, for there are a myriad of factors that affect this process and the counselor's in-session empathic performance. Many of the factors that Luborsky et al. (1971) suggest as patient factors influencing the outcome of psychotherapy may also be considered as counselor or therapist traits affecting the process of therapy. Dispositional traits such as anxiety, motivation, intelligence, and personality functioning may influence highly the outcome of a therapeutic session and the interaction between counselor and client. Luborsky et al. (1971) also mention that treatment factors, such as the physical environment, the time of day, and the sequencing of clients, can influence the counseling process and, in turn, counselor's in-session empathic performance.

Determining which of these confounding factors is the most intrusive to counselor's in-session empathic performance is not easy. Although this experiment controlled counselor traits such as sex, experience, and training, other factors such as age, personality functioning, and anxiety were not controlled. Since the clients were confederates, it was hoped that many client traits were controlled. However, individual and interpersonal personality dynamics could not be monitored even though experimentally any one of these factors could be of interest. But, one factor of notable significance, sequencing, could be tested since approximately half of the counselors saw a compliant client-subject first and the remaining counselors saw a disruptive client-subject first. The effects of sequencing were tested and are discussed below as an auxiliary finding.

In the interpretation of the results, the use of the analogue method and the possible effect that confederate clients had upon the BLRI measures must be taken into consideration. It is possible that the client-subjects, even if successful in their role-play performances may have filled out the BLRI form thinking as "the actress" and not as "the client." However, the client-subjects were instructed to fill out the BLRI from the "client's" perspective. The client-subjects, themselves, said that they were able to fill out the BLRI "as if" they were the clients. Budman (1971) also reported that confederate clients were able to respond to the BLRI "as if" they were "real" clients.

In the auxiliary findings, sequencing was investigated as one possible explanation for the results from testing the hypothesis. Sequencing refers to the order in which the counselors saw the clients. Since no time elapsed between the first and second interview, the experimental conditions duplicated a "real" counseling situation, where a practitioner often may see two to four clients, one after another, with only a 5–10-minute break between each client.

The assumption behind this auxiliary testing can be explained, psychodynamically, in the following way: the male counselor participating in the study who saw a disruptive client first was able to be empathic by using both affective and cognitive empathic skills. When he saw a second client immediately following the disruptive one, he was not able to be empathic even to a compliant client. The speculative explanation for his counselor reaction is that his *affective* empathy skills when dealing with a hostile personality were so exhausted in the process of maintaining his internal self-identity that he had difficulty regaining his internal equilibrium. Thus, he could not be as empathic to the client who immediately followed. If a period of time had elapsed, for example 1 hour, perhaps the counselor would have been able to have his cognitive skills intervene once again so that this phenomenon would not occur.

The significance of this sequencing effect suggests other possible explanations for the auxiliary findings. Again, as in the discussion of the hypothesis, counselor traits may have influenced the results. Since the relationship of client behaviors and counselor performance with the predictive *affective* empathy score was significant, it would seem likely that affective dispositional traits would have the greatest effect upon the results. Thus, a trait such as anxiety would have a high probability of influencing the counselor's response to a client.

In summary, the findings of this study suggest a complex *interaction* between counselors' empathic skills (ability), underlying factors affecting counselors' empathic effort, and counselors' in-session empathic communication process (empathic performance).

Limitations

Before a discussion of the implications of this study can ensue, the limitations inherent in this research project need to be considered. In the evaluation of this study, there are four areas that limit the generalizability of the study: (a) the general methodology of the study: (b) the experimental design; (c) the instrumentation; and (d) the theoretical conceptualizations.

The limitations of the general methodology of the study include a discussion of the model for the study and of the selection of subjects. As the counseling literature has noted, the generalizability of the analogue experimental model is restricted. Controversy exists over the use of this technique, for there is no certainty that the counselor will be able to respond to the laboratory setting and the confederate clients as he would in a natural setting. In the case of an analogue study, there is always the possibility that conditions other than the experimental variables have affected the counselor's behavior.

In an analogue study, the assumption must also be made that the confederate client-subjects can be trained to role play a genuine client. The theoretical assumptions about the psychodynamics of role play can be questioned, for since the client-subject is the treatment, there is no way to test how the encounter with different genuine counselors may affect the quality of the client-subjects' performances.

The use of instrumentation was also limited by the analogue model. Crucial to this study was the assumption that a simulated client could rate the counselor's performance with the mind-set of the client she portrayed. This assumption, perhaps, places too much acceptance in role-play theory. It must be acknowledged that, although the confederate client may be able to act out a role, her judgments of the counselor might be contaminated by her own personal history, needs, and motivations.

The selection of subjects, both client-subjects and counselor-subjects, was a methodological limitation in this study. The counselor-subjects were not randomly selected. Instead, the sucess of the research depended upon the willingness of counselors to volunteer for the study. Since the group of volunteers was not large, it was impossible to select a random sample from this small body of volunteers. Although the client-subjects were carefully interviewed as a way to select individuals who had similar characteristics, only six women qualified to participate in the study. To simulate genuine counseling session conditions more accurately, it would have been preferable to have had as many client-subjects participate in the study as counselor-subjects.

In addition, if it had been possible to increase the number of client-subjects, then the matching of counselor-subjects and client-subjects could have been completely randomized or randomized under the restriction of balance required for a Latin Square design (Kerlinger, 1973; Kirk, 1968). This would have provided more favorable conditions for examining the effects of sequencing. In order for the sequencing effect to have been more thoroughly explored, experiments should have been carried out that investigated the effects of sequencing of more than two interviews (possibly three or four). With an addition of a third interview, the order in which the counselors saw the clients could have met the requirements for a Latin Square design. Although in this study the sample was small and the investigation was limited, the results gave highly convincing evidence that this experiment should be replicated as a means for clarifying how sequencing affects a counselor's interview.

The determination of sex of the subjects must be considered a limitation of the study. Controlling the sex of the counselor-subjects and the client-subjects eliminated the entire exploration of how sex differences influence the counselor-client interaction (Wiggers, 1978). (See Chapter 7 for further discussion of this point.) Because of the possible influence that sex has upon the counselor-client interaction, using only male counselor-subjects limited the generalizability of this study and raises the question of whether it could be replicated. If, for example, the confederate clients had been male rather than female, the question can be raised whether the compliant male client behavior (duplicating the compliant behavior of the female client) would have had the same effect on the counselor's in-session empathic performance. As it has been mentioned, the literature would indicte that, regardless of behavior, the sex of the client and the counselor could have produced different results in the counselor-client interaction.

The design of the study was affected by the limited number of client-subjects. Since the client-subjects had to repeat their performance many times, there was no assurance that they were not influenced by their previous performance and by events that may have occurred before or after their performance. It was also possible that the quality of their role-play performance changed over a period of time and that this change differed among the client-subjects.

The selection of instruments was subjective, for there is debate, both theoretical and methodological, over the validity of the instruments used for measuring the variables. There was no certainty that the measurement scales selected for this study would actually measure what they were set out to measure, for it was possible that the development of these instruments could have been based on inaccurate, imprecise knowledge or assumptions about the concepts. It is always questionable whether theoretical understanding of the concepts is precise enough to make them operational.

Finally, in basing an empirical study on such subjective, elusive concepts, the researcher can never truly be certain of the reasons for the experimental outcome. There is always the possibility that the theoretical definitions and framework may have been incorrect.

Implications and Recommendations

Even though the results of this study are limited in their generalizability, each conclusion drawn from the analysis of the data attempted to clarify the relationship between the operational and theoretical issues of empathy. Although other studies have examined this same relationship, new information about the elusive concept of empathy is always welcomed. In this final evaluation of the study, as in its conception, the integration of theory and method is of paramount importance to its intent.

This study offers the suggestion that empathy is both a trait and a process; it is not exclusively one or the other. The theoretical argument is as follows: counselors may not have the cognitive understanding to be aware of their empathic abilities (trait of empathy) residing within themselves. Thus, they would not know how to communicate empathy or to verbalize empathic understanding as a process of communication. Yet, their potential to be empathic could be emoted unconsciously by nonverbal means.

It is this nonverbal dimension of empathy, then, that needs to be explored. The question of whether and how empathy can be observed nonverbally should be addressed, for it is this nonverbal dimension of empathy that may clarify the distinctions and the relationship between the affective (the nonverbal) and the cognitive (verbal) components of empathy. (See Chapter 5 for one approach to this problem.)

Empathic ability (*a skill, a trait*) is only one of the many empathic conditions to be utilized in counseling. Empathic effort and empathic communication (both *processes*) are two other factors that affect counselor empathy. Corroborating Hackney's (1978) distinctions of empathy, the results of this research indicate that different conditions of empathy do exist, yet have a relationship with one another. However, as Hackney (1978) suggests, methods need to be devised that allow us to determine whether a counselor is a high sensitive/low communication skills type, a low sensitive/high communication skills type, or a high sensitive/high communication skills type. Although this research attempted to investigate the relationship between high and low predictive empathic ability with counselors' empathic performance (effort and communication), the limitations of using volunteer counselor-subjects prevented exploration of this issue. Still, future research should attempt, once again, to explore this relationship. It would be the counselor educators and practitioners who would benefit from this information. *Knowing how counselors (and potential counselors) vary in their ability to be empathic along three dimensions of empathy instead of only one dimension would help to refine and clarify the use of empathy in the counseling session.*

Counselor educators, too, may be able to use the findings of the study in their never-ending search for selection criteria for identifying future counselors. Using the predictive empathy measures, the potential empathic ability of the neophyte can be examined. The predictive empathy instrument could be a selection tool and then a diagnostic instrument for individualizing the direction of training procedures. The purpose for this type of procedure would be to utilize maximally the potential of each future counselor. While one counselor-in-training may have an internal affective sensitivity to a situation, another counselor-in-training may have developed a cognitive set of responses to that very situation. If it is the responsibility of the counselor trainer to enhance the existing abilities and develop the untapped potential of each trainee, then new and innovative training methods should be sought by the trainer.

Methods for developing a counselor's ability or sensitivity to a client could be dealt with separately from the learning of communication skills. *To enhance empathic ability in the emerging counselor, training could include psychodynamic approaches (for example, psychodrama) as well as behavioral techniques.* Perhaps those competing emotions or personality states that could block or inhibit a counselor's potential for exhibiting and demonstrating empathy to the client could best be developed by a multidisciplinary approach. By integrating the numerous theoretical definitions of empathy and broadening the methods of a counselor's expression of empathy, the potential for improving a counselor's empathic performance exists. (See Gladstein & Feldstein [1983] for one approach to this problem.)

For a practitioner, this study also has possible *practical implications.* It is evident that the *scheduling of clients* is important. Seeing one client after another may have a deleterious effect upon the counselor's empathic abilities. Although it would be impossible to know in advance a client's behavior, it would be possible to take minimal rest breaks between counseling sessions.

4
State-Trait Anxiety Level and Counselor Empathic Behaviors in the Interview

JEANETTE KREISER

The concepts of anxiety and empathy have both long been accepted as playing vital roles in the counseling process. Since Rogers (1957) first identified the construct as one of the necessary and sufficient conditions for therapeutic personality change, empathy has been considered one of the most important variables in counseling and therapy. Considerable research has focused on the role of empathy in counseling and on its relationship to successful counseling and therapy outcomes with often conflicting and confusing results (Gladstein, 1970, 1977). Gladstein (1977, 1983) proposed that the term *empathy* refers to a complex phenomenon, and that research that focuses on specific cognitive and affective aspects of empathy may lead to new insight into these contradictory findings.

In the case of anxiety, although differing explanations and definitions exist in the literature, there has been nearly universal agreement that the avoidance of this unpleasant sensation plays an important role in personality development and in the daily life of an individual, and, furthermore, is often the force motivating a client to enter a counseling relationship in the first place. For such diverse theorists as Wolpe (1958), Horney (1937), and Dollard and Miller (1950), anxiety reduction is viewed as an important goal and outcome of psychotherapy or counseling.

Within the counseling session itself, manifestations and avoidance of anxiety may provide important data for the therapist who is attempting to understand what is occurring during the counseling process. Sullivan (1954) and Kell and Mueller (1966) have pointed out the significant role played by counselor or therapist anxiety in the interactions between client and counselor. As one of the necessary conditions for therapeutic change and development, Rogers (1957) has hypothesized that in order to facilitate client change and development the therapist must be "congruent" and, as a result, not hampered by personal anxieties or conflicts in relating to a client. Followers of analytic theories also maintain that therapist conflicts and anxieties can affect the therapeutic interview; the requirement that an analyst undergo self-analysis indicates the importance placed upon the therapist's self-awareness of anxieties, on the assumption that failure to recognize and deal with them might interfere with the handling of patients.

Although there is virtually unanimous agreement on the important role that anxiety plays in personality development and in the counseling process, there is no single widely accepted empirical or theoretical definition of the term. Some of these problems of recognition and definition may lie in our usage of the term *anxiety* for a number of separate and at least partially independent phenomena. Cattell and Scheier (1961) have distinguished between *trait* anxiety, or an individual's general proneness to anxiety, and *state* anxiety, or an individual's immediate subjectively and objectively perceived emotion. Furthermore, Endler, Hunt, and Rosenstein (1962) delineated five forms of situational trait anxiety: interpersonal, physical danger, ambiguous threat, evaluation, and normal routines.

These difficulties in understanding the role of, and relationship among, empathy, anxiety, and the counseling process led to the purpose of this study: namely, to determine the relationship of a counselor's trait and state anxiety to his or her empathic behaviors during interviews.

Summary of Literature

Relatively few empirical studies have been conducted that focus on the effects of counselor anxiety on various aspects of counselor behavior during the counseling interview, and most researchers have used inexperienced counselors as subjects. Typically, the research into the relationship between anxiety and counseling effectiveness has been conducted in one of three ways.

One approach has been to investigate the relationship between counselor or therapist effectiveness and ratings of general anxiety level made by supervisors or colleagues. Utilizing this approach, both Luborsky (1952) and Bandura (1956) reported some evidence that more highly anxious therapists were considered less effective by supervisors. Other researchers examined relationships between trait anxiety as measured by a variety of self-report instruments and counselor behavior. When the Taylor Manifest Anxiety Scale was employed as the measure of anxiety, no relationship was found between anxiety and effective counselor behavior by inexperienced counselors (Brams, 1961; Dispenzieri & Balinsky, 1963; Steiberg, 1967). Using other measures, the conclusions of Jansen, Bonk, and Garvey (1973) and Wogan (1970) contradicted the findings of Brams (1961).

A third approach to the study of counselor anxiety and behavior has been to examine counselor anxiety level and/or behavior under conditions, presumably anxiety arousing, of threat or stress. Results from these studies suggest that external factors, such as recording of the interview

(Lamb & Mahl, 1956), supervision (Roulx, 1969), and evaluation (Paar & Seeman, 1973), seem to increase therapist anxiety.

There is yet another approach to the study of counselor anxiety and the counseling process. That is to monitor at least one commonly accepted physical or nonverbal indicator of anxiety as it occurs throughout the counseling interview. Some investigators (Bowman & Roberts, 1978, 1979a, 1979b; Bowman, Roberts, & Giesen, 1978; Coleman, Greenblatt, & Solomon, 1956; DiMascio, Boyd, Greenblatt, & Solomon, 1955) have measured changing physiological reactions during counseling or therapy interviews.

Despite the important role that the constructs of anxiety and empathy have independently played in counseling/therapy theory and research, only a few studies have been focused specifically on the relationship between these two variables. In these studies, measures of trait anxiety were used to determine anxiety level, and measures of primarily cognitive empathy (The Truax Accurate Empathy Scale) (Pennscott & Brown, 1972) or the Bergin-Solomon Revision of the same scale (Bergin & Jasper, 1969; Vesprani, 1969) were used to determine empathy level. Pennscott and Brown (1972) found that although counselor anxiety (as measured by the Taylor Manifest Anxiety Scale) decreased during the second semester of a training program, ratings of taped samples of interviews conducted by the same counselors did not show a statistically significant change in either direction. Bergin and Jasper (1969) found negative correlations between anxiety (as measured by the psychasthenia scale of the MMPI) and empathy, a finding supported by Vesprani (1969) for college-age companions to female mental hospital patients.

None of these researchers monitored the fluctuations of one or more physiological or nonverbal manifestations of anxiety during an actual interview while looking at concomitant changes in counselor behavior. Furthermore, since the findings of Bowman and Roberts (1978, 1979a, 1979b) and Bowman, Roberts, and Giesen (1978) suggest that the counseling practicum interview is ipso facto anxiety producing, it would seem to be important to undertake studies of counselor anxiety with more experienced counselors as subjects. Therefore, the specific purpose of this descriptive study was to investigate how experienced counselors, who differed in trait anxiety levels and in situational trait anxiety as delineated by Endler, behaved (offered empathy) in actual counseling situations during high- and low-anxiety states.

Research Questions

1. Is there a significant difference in the level of offered empathy in counselor responses when counselors differ in trait anxiety level and state anxiety level, and during the first, second, and third interviews with a client?

2. Are there significant interactions between and among the levels of state and trait anxiety and interview affecting counselor level of offered empathy?
3. Is there a significant difference in the level of offered empathy in counselor responses when counselors differ in situational trait anxiety level and state anxiety level, and during the first, second, and third interviews with a client?
4. Are there significant interactions between and among forms of situational trait anxiety, interviews, and state anxiety level upon level of offered empathy?

Methodology

Subjects

Names of potential subjects, male counselors with 1 or more years of counseling experience in their present setting, were obtained from a list of counseling personnel in the Genesee Valley region (New York State). College counseling centers in the same area were contacted for volunteers as well. The IPAT Anxiety Scale Questionnaire (IPAT) and the S-R Inventory of General Trait Anxiousness (GTA) were administered to the 53 counselors who agreed to participate. From among those who scored above and below the mean for adult males on the IPAT (Krug, Scheier, & Cattell, 1976), five high-anxious and five low-anxious individuals willing and able to audiotape counseling interviews participated in the second phase of the study. These 10 counselors ranged in age from 32 to 50 ($M = 39.9$). All had at least 5 years of counseling experience and each had obtained a master's degree. Five had completed additional graduate course work, and two held doctorates. These counselors were, then, an experienced and well-educated group. Eight of the 10 counselors were working in secondary schools; two in college settings.

Trait Anxiety Measures

The IPAT Anxiety Scale Questionnaire was used to identify high and low trait anxiety counselors. The IPAT correlates highly with other accepted measures of trait anxiety, such as the Taylor Manifest Anxiety Scale and the trait portion of the State-Trait Anxiety Inventory. Correlations with the former range from .82 to .52; Krug, Scheier, and Cattell (1976) obtained a correlation of .76 with the latter. Test-retest reliabilities ranged from .93 after 1 week to .82 after 4 weeks (Krug, Scheier, & Cattell, 1976).

The S-R Inventory of General Trait Anxiousness (GTA) is a self-report personality inventory designed to measure situational trait anxiety. The instrument produces trait anxiety measures for five situations: interpersonal, or trait anxiety involving interactions with other people;

physical danger, or trait anxiety involving actual physical harm; ambiguous, or trait anxiety associated with novel situations; daily routine, or trait anxiety associated with performing ordinary daily tasks; and evaluation, or trait anxiety associated with evaluative situations. Endler and Okada (1975) report relatively low correlations between the situational measures, with the highest correlation for a normal sample of adults being .46 between interpersonal and ambiguous. Coefficient alpha reliabilities for the different scales ranged from .71 to .83 for the interpersonal situation scale; from .69 to .86 for the ambiguous situation; and from .62 to .85 for the daily routine scale (Endler & Okada, 1975). There is no reported reliability measure of any kind for the most recently developed evaluation scale, nor any reported test-retest reliability for any of the scales.

State Anxiety Measure

The Non-Ah Speech Disturbance Ratio (SDR) developed by Mahl (1956, 1961) and by Kasl and Mahl (1965) was used as the measure of state anxiety level in this study. The instrument provides for a moment-by-moment assessment of anxiety level through measures of the number of speech disturbances (sentence corrections, repetitions, stutters, incoherent sounds, tongue slips, and omissions of words or parts of words) relative to the verbal output. The ratio has been used in a number of studies of client anxiety (Boomer & Goodrich, 1961; Mahl, 1956, 1961; Panek & Martin, 1959) and more recently with inpatients (Eisler, Hersen, Miller, & Blanchard, 1975), interviewees (Pope, Siegman, & Blass, 1970), student nurses (Pope & Siegman, 1972, Siegman & Pope, 1972), counselors (Carter & Pappas, 1975), and psychology trainees during interviews (Murphy & Lamb, 1973).

In the present study, each counselor response in every interview was rated for anxiety level using the SDR. From among the pool of counselor responses in each interview, high- and low-state responses were selected according to whether the frequency of speech disturbances was above or below the mean SDR for that particular counselor's interview. In order to get counselor statements of comparable length and content, responses selected for rating met the following minimal criteria: length of at least 20 words, preceded by a client statement at least 10 words in length. Two raters were used in the study, each scoring one-half the total number of segments. Interrater reliability, using Pearson product moment correlation based on 50 different 15 word segments, was .76.

Measures of Counselor Behavior

Empathy was measured on the 10-point Bergin-Solomon Revision of the Truax Accurate Empathy Scale (Truax & Carkhuff, 1967). The Bergin-Solomon Revision was selected because it offers additional categories in the lower regions of the scale that seemed more appropriate to the advising/counseling role of secondary school counselors. This scale, or closely related versions, has been used extensively in research on counseling and therapy (see reviews by Feldstein & Gladstein, 1980, and Gladstein, 1970, 1977). Higher scores indicate higher levels of empathy. Two graduate student volunteers served as empathy raters. Each selected segment was scored by one rater. Interrater reliability, determined by the use of a Pearson product moment correlation, was .73 based on joint ratings of counselor-client segments selected and arranged at random from 7 of the 20 interviews.

The 10 counselor-subjects audiotaped at least two consecutive interviews with any one client of their choice. Transcripts of the audiotapes were typed, and the speech disturbances were scored using the transcripts and tapes in a process described by Mahl (1956). The SDR computed for each segment was calculated by counting the number of speech disturbances and the number of words (excluding the speech disturbances) in a response, and dividing the former by the latter. This procedure differed slightly from that described by Mahl, who used the total number of words, *including* the speech disturbances, as the divisor.

On the basis of speech disturbances, at least one and no more than four segments under each anxiety condition in each interview were selected for further scoring on empathy. These high and low state segments, along with the preceding client statement, were then arranged in random order on another audiotape for independent scoring. The scoring of these segments resulted in at least one and no more than four ratings on empathy during each anxiety level in each interview. The separate ratings under each condition for each interview were averaged to obtain one mean score.

A three-way analysis of variance (ANOVA) with repeated measures on the last two factors was performed with trait anxiety, interview (first or second), and state anxiety as the independent variables and empathy behavior as the dependent variable. Similar analyses were performed using scores from the S-R Inventory of General Trait Anxiousness rather than the IPAT scores to group subjects.

Results and Discussion

Table 4.1 presents the means and standard deviations obtained for this group of subjects on each of the variables. Tables 4.2 through 4.7 summarize the results of each of the ANOVA. There were no statistically significant outcomes.

Research into the relationship between counselor anxiety and counselor behavior has been fraught with difficulties and has produced conflicting results. On the one hand, results of some research suggest that anxiety has a negative inpact on counselor ability to function effectively

TABLE 4.1. Counselor mean scores and standard deviations on IPAT, GTA, and empathy.

	IPAT	Interpersonal	Physical	Ambiguous	Daily routines	Evaluation	Empathy
All counselors tested (N = 53)							
M	18.53	26.49	55.93	37.04	24.06	37.34	
SD	12.65	8.31	11.56	9.66	6.79	12.99	
Counselors taping interviews (N = 10)							
M	21.40	26.70	54.80	38.90	23.10	35.90	3.49[a]
SD	10.87	8.03	8.20	6.26	6.49	17.86	1.14

Based on a 10-point scale.

TABLE 4.2. Summary of analysis of variance for trait anxiety, state anxiety level, and interview on level of offered empathy.

Source	SS	MS	F
Between effects			
Trait anxiety (T)	2.485	2.485	0.550
Error	36.165	4.521	
Within effects (I)			
Interview (I)	0.066	0.066	0.649
I × T	0.233	0.233	2.273
Error	0.818	0.102	
Within effects (S)			
State anxiety (S)	0.312	0.312	0.53361
S × T	0.001	0.001	0.001
Error	5.890	0.736	
Within effects (IS)			
IS	0.019	0.019	0.032
IS × T	0.113	0.113	0.193
Error	4.696	0.587	

Note. df = 1,8.

in an interview (Jansen et al., 1973; Paar & Seeman, 1973). Other researchers have failed to show any relationship at all between anxiety and counselor behavior (Brams, 1961; Dispenzieri & Balinsky, 1963; Steiberg, 1967). Still others have found a positive association between anxiety level and counseling effectiveness or a beneficial therapy outcome (Wicas & Mahan, 1966; Wogan, 1970).

TABLE 4.3. Summary of analysis of variance for interpersonal anxiety, state anxiety level, and interview on level of offered empathy.

Source	SS	MS	F
Between effects			
Interpersonal anxiety (T)	.163	0.163	0.034
Error	38.488	4.811	
Within effects (I)			
Interview (I)	.066	.066	0.509
I × T	.007	.007	0.054
Error	1.044	.131	
Within effects (S)			
State anxiety (S)	.312	.312	0.489
S × T	.792	.792	1.243
Error			
Within effects (IS)			
IS	.019	.019	0.046
IS × T	1.486	1.486	3.577
Error	3.324	.415	

Note. df = 1,8.

TABLE 4.4. Summary of analysis of variance for physical danger trait anxiety, state anxiety level, and interview on level of offered empathy.

Source	SS	MS	F
Between effects			
Physical danger (T)	9.653	9.653	2.663
Error	28.997	3.625	
Within effects (I)			
Interview (I)	.066	.066	0.510
I × T	.010	.010	0.076
Error	1.041	.130	
Within effects (S)			
State anxiety (S)	.312	.312	0.424
S × T	.007	.007	0.010
Error	5.884	.735	
Within effects (IS)			
IS	.019	.019	0.031
IS × T	.001	.001	0.002
Error	4.809	.601	

Note. df = 1,8.

Three studies have focused more specifically on the relationship between anxiety level and empathy. Two of these studies (Bergin & Jasper, 1969; Vesprani, 1969) found negative correlations between the two variables. Pennscott and Brown (1972) did not correlate anxiety scores with empathy level, but rather looked at whether each of these variables independently increased or decreased in counseling practicum students

TABLE 4.5. Summary of analysis of variance for ambiguous anxiety, state anxiety, and interview level on level of offered empathy.

Source	SS	MS	F
Between effects			
Novelty (N)	12.421	12.421	3.788
Error	26.299	3.279	
Within effects (I)			
Interview (I)	.066	.066	0.511
I × T	.012	.012	0.092
Error	1.039	.130	
Within effects (S)			
State anxiety (S)	.312	.312	0.451
S × T	.371	.371	0.537
Error	5.520	.690	
Within effects (IS)			
IS	.019	.019	0.032
IS × N	.082	.082	0.139
Error	4.728	.591	

Note. df = 1,8.

TABLE 4.6. Summary of analysis of variance for daily routine anxiety, state anxiety level, and interview on level of offered empathy.

Source	SS	MS	F
Between effects			
Daily routine anxiety (T)	.909	0.909	0.193
Error	37.741	4.718	
Within effects (I)			
Interview (I)	.066	.066	0.649
I × T	.819	.102	2.273
Error			
Within effects (S)			
State anxiety (S)	.312	.312	0.424
T × S	.016	.016	0.021
Error	5.875	.734	
Within effects (IS)			
IS	.019	.019	0.032
IS × T	.019	.019	0.032
Error	4.790	.599	

Note. df = 1,8.

during a semester. Whereas anxiety decreased, they found no change in the level of empathy offered during interviews. Thus, though the two variables were indeed included in the single study, a direct statistical relationship between the two was not established, though each seemed to

TABLE 4.7. Summary of analysis of variance for evaluation anxiety, state anxiety level, and interview on level of offered empathy.

Source	SS	MS	F
Between effects			
Evaluation anxiety (T)	.104	0.104	0.021
Error	34.532	4.933	
Within effects (I)			
Interview (I)	.183	.183	1.718
I × T	.027	.027	0.256
Error	.744	.106	
Within effects (S)			
State anxiety (S)	.000	.000	0.000
S × T	.006	.006	0.009
Error	4.646	.664	
Within effects (IS)			
IS	.714	.714	1.485
IS × T	.772	.772	1.605
Error	3.365	.481	

Note. df = 1,8.

fluctuate independently of the other. All of this research was carried out using scales measuring "cognitive" or "role-taking" empathy.

Data from the present study provide no evidence of a relationship between any trait or state anxiety variables and empathy. However, there are a number of factors to be considered when assessing the meaning of the data. First, although designed to gather data on the effects of "high" and "low" state and trait anxiety on counselor behavior, none of the subjects, whether because of a process of self-selection or as a result of chance, had very high trait anxiety scores; the highest scoring subject fell in the 77th percentile on norms for adult males (Krug et al., 1976), and all other high trait anxious counselors scored at or below the 60th percentile on the same norms. Similarly, it seems likely that state anxiety levels of the counselors, although fluctuating, never reached very high levels either. Indeed, counselors' self-reports of anxiety, completed after each interview, indicated that they experienced little or no anxiety while taping the sessions. Thus, this study of high- and low-anxiety counselors, actually, provided no data on the performance of counselors very high in trait, or at very high levels of state, anxiety.

Some attention, too, must be directed toward the manner and conditions of use of Mahl's Speech Disturbance Ratio in this study. Factors other than anxiety (such as the complexity of the communication) may have affected the SDR. Furthermore, the SDR may not be sufficiently sensitive to distinguish state anxiety reliably when used for such brief (20-30) word segments as was done in this study. It is possible, then, that the SDR may not have accurately discriminated between high and low state anxiety levels. Should further research using the SDR confirm the reliability of the measure for use with brief counselor-client communication segments, speech disturbances will prove a useful method of unobtrusively gauging changing anxiety states during a counseling interview, and thus provide researchers, counselors, and counselor-educators an additional tool for better understanding the counseling process.

Another factor concerns the counselors' empathy scores. As indicated in Table 4.1, the mean value for all interviews was 3.49 on a 10-point scale. This suggests that these counselors were not offering much empathy. Therefore, it is possible that the nonsignificant findings were partially a result of minimal counselor empathic behavior. Counselors who generally offer high empathy levels might be more affected by their own anxiety than counselors who offer low levels. The fact that the standard deviation was 1.14 suggests that less than 3% of the counselor's verbal behaviors were at the minimal facilitative level (about 6.0 on a 10-point scale). Although this finding may be surprising to some people, other studies show that typically counselors do not display more than minimal empathic behavior. (For example, see Chapters 2 and 10.)

For a number of reasons, then, the findings of this particular study cannot be regarded as conclusive. However, in looking at two aspects of anxiety, the study takes a first step toward clarifying the role of "anxiety" in all its manifestations in the counseling process. Similarly, one might investigate the relationship between state and trait anxiety levels and affective and cognitive empathy. Those who have sought to examine the relationship between these two concepts have generally looked at the relationship between trait measures of anxiety and cognitive measures of cognitive empathy. It may be that there is a differential relationship between and among these multifaceted factors. Thus, high levels of state and high levels of trait anxiety may not affect cognitive and affective empathy levels in the same way.

In conclusion, although there were no significant results, further researchers may wish to distinguish carefully between state and trait anxiety and to examine these "anxieties" at different degrees and levels and to recognize empathy, as well, as a multifaceted concept.

5
The Effect of Counselor Empathy and Communication Modality on Client Outcomes

GERALD A. GLADSTEIN

Chapter 1 of this book describes the difficulties in determining whether empathy is important to counseling and psychotherapy positive outcomes. Chapters 3 and 4 illustrate group experimental and descriptive designs and the problems inherent in each. This chapter describes a study that used $N = 1$ approach. This was used in an attempt to avoid some of the group design problems; however, this led to certain other difficulties.

Statement of Problem

Of the various dimensions related to empathy and counseling outcome, one that has not received much attention pertains to the relative importance of the communication used by counselors to convey empathy to clients. Three modalities exist: (a) verbal, (b) nonverbal, and (c) verbal-nonverbal combined.

It is important to note that most research on these systems has combined the verbal with the nonverbal modality, controlled the different levels of counselor-offered empathy, and assessed the effects of these levels on client outcomes. Further investigation into the empirical literature reveals a critical shortage of studies that isolate any one communication system, manipulate differential levels of counselor-offered empathy through it, and measure the effects of these levels on certain client behaviors. Only three studies (English & Jelevensky, 1971; Morocco, 1979b; Smith-Hanen, 1977) have been found with this particular purpose. These studies have all failed to provide conclusive results. The problem that must be resolved here is to identify the effects of

---

Adapted, with permission, from Daniel R. Morocco's doctoral dissertation, *The Psychological Impact of Varying Counselor Level of Empathic Understanding and Communication Modality on Selected In-Counseling Outcomes,* University of Rochester, 1981.

isolating each communication modality and manipulating differential levels of counselor empathy through these systems.

Another aspect of the counseling process that has been plagued by inconsistencies in research findings pertains to the effects of counselor sex on levels of offered empathy (Chapter 7). Not only is there a lack of clear findings on this dimension, but inconclusive results have been also reported overall with respect to counseling outcomes as a function of client-counselor same-sex and different-sex pairings in relation to empathy. Thus, it was the purpose of this investigation to assess the effects of manipulating different levels of counselor-offered verbal, nonverbal, and combined verbal-nonverbal empathy and various dimensions of client behaviors during the counseling process, while holding counselor-client sex pairings constant.

Review of Literature

The mode of communication used by counselors to convey empathic conditions to clients has been researched and discussed (Gladstein, 1974; Morocco, 1979a). These modalities are the verbal, nonverbal, and combined verbal-nonverbal communication systems as defined by Mehrabian (1968, 1971). Discussions on the verbal dimensions may be found in the writings of Carkhuff (1969a, 1969b) and Truax and Carkhuff (1967). Regarding the nonverbal aspect, Mehrabian (1968, 1971) pointed out that any behavior can convey some sort of communication because it is readily observable and has significance. Likewise, because the concept of nonverbal behavior is so comprehensive, a broad definition that includes conscious behaviors is considered appropriate for this study.

Preceding the literature review on this subject, one final point of importance must be brought forth. Most of the research (Graves & Robinson, 1976; Haase & Tepper, 1972; Seay & Altekruse, 1979; Shapiro, Foster, & Powell, 1968; Tepper & Haase, 1978) on these communication systems has: (a) combined the verbal and nonverbal modalities, (b) manipulated differential levels of counselor-offered empathy, and (c) assessed the effects of these levels on client outcomes. As previously mentioned, only three studies (English & Jelevensky, 1971; Morocco, 1979b; Smith-Hanen, 1977) have attempted to isolate one communication system, the nonverbal.

Given this information, and the fact that nonverbal behavior has been identified through a review of the empirical literature (Brown & Parks, 1972) as an important component of the counseling process, the pertinent literature stated above is reviewed in the following paragraphs.

The relative contribution of selected verbal and nonverbal components of the communication of empathy was studied by Haase and Tepper (1972). Twenty-six counselors rated 48 combinations of eye contact, body orientation, distance, trunk lean, and a predetermined verbal empathy message based on a modification of the Truax and Carkhuff (1967) Empathy Scale. The results of this study were that the various nonverbal behaviors as well as different combinations of these behaviors defined the nonverbal empathic behavior of the helper. Furthermore, these nonverbal behaviors accounted for twice the variability as compared to the verbal message.

Shapiro et al. (1968) investigated whether trained judges could reliably rate still photographs of helpers' level of empathy, warmth, and genuineness. It was found that trained judges were able to rate helper behavior using still photographs, and that untrained judges agreed with those having more experience. Facial cues were found to be the discriminating factor leading to agreement.

Seay and Altekruse (1979) attempted to investigate the effects of different verbal counseling styles, selected nonverbal behaviors, and client sex on the facilitative conditions of empathy, regard, and genuineness in a counseling relationship. Male and female clients were interviewed by male counselors. The results showed that the nonverbal behaviors of eye contact, smiling, leaning forward, and head nodding were all related to at least one of the facilitative conditions. It was noted that only the smiling behavior was associated with empathic communication. Finally, the point was made that the effects of the relationship characteristics were modified by the interactions with other variables such as verbal counseling style.

Tepper and Haase (1978) replicated their previous findings (Haase & Tepper, 1972) and reported that nonverbal cues accounted for significantly greater communication variance than verbal cues, and that counselors and clients differed significantly from one another in their perceptions of these cues.

The effects of inconsistencies between verbal and nonverbal behaviors of a counselor on the proxemic behavior and ratings of counselor genuineness made by clients were studied by Graves and Robinson (1976). Nonverbal behaviors included eye contact, trunk lean, body orientation, and leg positions. Verbal content reflected either high or low levels of empathic understanding. Undergraduates role played a standard concern with a confederate male counselor who communicated either contradictory or consistent verbal and nonverbal messages. The results of this study indicated that inconsistent verbal and nonverbal messages were associated with greater interpersonal distances. This was especially true when the nonverbal messages were positive. Inconsistent messages also led to lower ratings of counselor genuineness.

The final three studies all contained the same basic element; that is, studying the effects of the nonverbal empathic channel alone on some dimension of client outcome. English and Jelevensky (1971) had student counselors judge counseling videotapes of counselors in order to assess the reliability of the counselor evaluation process as a function of the audio, visual, and audiovisual modes. The results were that a significant consistency existed among judges who evaluated counselor empathy based on these three modalities. The authors stated that the claims for the audiovisual mode as being superior to others in assessing empathic behavior were not substantiated.

Smith-Hanen (1977) studied the effects of certain nonverbal counselor behaviors on client perceptions. Forty subjects rated counselor warmth and empathy after viewing video segments of a counselor's nonverbal behaviors. These behaviors included general movement, arm positions, and leg positions. The movement factor had no significant effect on the judged levels of warmth and empathy. It was reported that when the counselor's arms were crossed and when the counselor's legs were crossed (ankle to knee), the least empathic condition existed.

In the final study by Morocco (1979b), subjects were exposed to either high or low nonverbal empathy. The verbal channel was eliminated completely. Subjects were instructed to engage in a 5-minute monologue talking to a counselor who appeared on a videoscreen. This study was modeled after one conducted by Hackney (1974). Subject depth of self-exploration was hypothesized to increase as a function of high nonverbal counselor empathy, and decrease as a function of low nonverbal counselor empathy. The results may have been confounded by prolonged silence on the part of the counselor, which could have frustrated the clients. The negative findings occurred regardless of the experimental condition present. The question was raised as to whether or not the nonverbal dimension alone is sufficient to produce client outcomes.

In summary, the studies presented here serve to contribute to the literature dealing with empathy and verbal, nonverbal, and verbal-nonverbal communication. From the information obtained overall, three major points can be drawn. First, very few studies exist in the literature dealing strictly with any one communicational dimension of counselor-offered empathy and in-counseling client outcomes. Second, those that do address this topic, namely the ones isolating the nonverbal component, yield overall mixed results. In some instances, manipulating different levels of counselor-offered nonverbal empathy affected client perceptions (English & Jelevensky, 1971; Smith-Hanen, 1977), while under other conditions (Morocco, 1979b), this was not found to be so. Therefore, the conclusions drawn from the collective findings of these investigations fail to provide any clear or conclusive results because of the various inconsistencies.

Finally, the question was raised as to whether one modality alone was sufficient to effect differences related to in-counseling, client outcomes. As a result, these communication modalities must be studied in isolation of one another in order to afford a more clearly identified status of their effects on in-counseling, client outcomes. Until this is accomplished, no accurate conclusions can be drawn on exactly how these three modalities interact and affect client behaviors.

Methodology

The present study investigated the effects of manipulating high, neutral, and low levels of empathy through the verbal, nonverbal, and combined verbal-nonverbal communication modalities on client depth of self-exploration, perception of counselor-offered empathy, and interview satisfaction. A multiple-N, multiple-I single-subject experimental design (Kratchowil, 1978) was employed to test the hypotheses of this study. Multiple interventions were manipulated on different clients.

In this study, actual clients were assigned to an experienced female counselor. Because of the authenticity of the subjects as clients, the generalizability of the results is high (Gowen, 1961; Delaney, 1969; Kazdin, 1978; Munley, 1974). Also, because multiple dependent variables were employed, the concerns noted by Farnsworth (1966), Strupp and Luborsky (1962), Truax and Carkhuff (1964), and Wrenn and Parker (1960) were alleviated. Finally, clients rated their own behavior and the behavior of their counselors. This procedure addressed the issues discussed by Luborsky et al. (1971) and Rogers (1975).

Research Hypotheses

1. Client depth of self-exploration, perception of counselor empathic understanding, and satisfaction with the counseling interview will vary as a function of the level of counselor-offered empathy and the channel through which this condition is communicated.
1a. The high-empathy condition, communicated through the combined verbal-nonverbal modality, will yield greater depths of self-exploration, client satisfaction, and perceived empathic understanding than any other condition.
1b. The low-empathy condition, communicated through the combined verbal-nonverbal modality, will yield the lowest depth of self-exploration, client satisfaction, and perceived empathic understanding of any other condition.

Independent Variables

The independent variables used in this study were the level of counselor-offered empathy and the channel of counselor communication. Sex was considered as a blocking variable.

Dependent Variables

There were three dependent variables in this study. The first was the depth of self-exploration as measured by a modified version of the

Helpee Self-Exploration in Interpersonal Processes Scale (Carkhuff, 1969b). This was used to indicate the extent of client self-exploration as a function of both high and low empathic conditions as well as the three communication modalities. Truax and Carkhuff (1967) reported reliabilities ranging from .59 to .86 over 12 studies. Morocco (1979b) reported a reliability of .86.

With respect to validity, Truax and Carkhuff (1967) stated:

> ... one must depend on the face validity and the research evidence showing predictable relationships to therapeutic outcome. Beyond this, the findings that experimental manipulation of levels of conditions produces predictable changes in the measure of self-exploration, and the findings that differential reinforcement or self-exploration produced consequent differential levels of self-exploration and outcome, add to the validity and utility of the measure. (pp. 194–195)

Validity of the modified version was determined by asking five randomly selected people to match levels on the modified form with levels on the actual form. This was done until 100% agreement among raters was reached.

The second dependent variable was the level of client-perceived, counselor-offered empathic understanding. This was assessed by a modified version of the Empathic Understanding in Interpersonal Processes: A Scale for Measurement form (Carkhuff, 1969b). Carkhuff and Burstein (1970) reported reliabilities of .90 and .88, respectively, on intra- and intercorrelations among raters. The validity of this modified version was determined in the same fashion as the self-exploration scale.

The third and final dependent variable, client satisfaction, was measured by the Interview Rating Scale (Feldstein, 1979). This is a 10-item, forced-choice questionnaire where subjects respond by indicating "usually," "occasionally," or "rarely." This form was based on the work of Anderson and Anderson (1968), Linden, Stone, and Shertzer (1968), and Orlinsky and Howard (1975).

Subjects

Based on available information in the literature (see Chapter 7), only women were considered for this experiment. Four women, whose ages ranged from 27 to 40 and who were seeking vocational counseling at the University of Rochester Adult Counseling Center (URACC) participated. All subjects were experiencing moderate affect around their employment and general life circumstances. During their preliminary interview at URACC, the clients were told of this study and given a consent form to read that described the basic elements of the research. If they agreed to take part, they signed the form. Remuneration in the form of credit to their respective accounts was given. This averaged to about $5.00 per client session. The first four women who were asked during the preliminary interview whether or not they would be interested in participating agreed and were selected.

The counselor employed in this study was a female doctoral graduate student with a Master of Science degree. She was approximately 40 years old and had 2 years of supervised experience in personal/social and vocational counseling. At the end of the study she was given a small honorarium (free training in Gestalt therapy) for her participation.

Procedure

The subjects were told that this would be a four-session experiment of "Interpersonal Processes," and that the purpose of the research was to investigate certain dimensions of the relationship between a counselor and a client. The interviewer pointed out to the clients during their preliminary interview that their participation would involve meeting with a counselor and discussing their concerns with her. This would take place over three counseling sessions. At the end of the first session, they were told that they would meet with the experimenter, view five consecutive, 2-minute segments of videotape of that session, and at the end of each 2-minute segment, complete three short forms. These were the Depth of Self-Exploration Scale, the Empathic Understanding Scale, and the Interview Rating Scale. They were also instructed that at the end of the third session, the experimenter would meet with them again to make an appointment for the final meeting of the project. This last session was never more than 1 week after the third counseling session, and always before the fourth counseling session.

During this final meeting with the experimenter, the clients were told that they would view two videotapes of 10 randomly selected segments of their second and third sessions. Five were chosen from the second and five from the third. Each segment consisted of eight consecutive, 2-minute intervals. Again, at the end of each 2-minute interval, the subjects were told to complete the three forms. After they had viewed both tapes and completed all forms, the subjects were completely debriefed as to the nature of the experiment, and were told that they could continue counseling as usual if they so desired since their participation in the experiment was over.

Counselor Behavior

The counselor was trained to produce three levels of empathic behavior and to communicate these levels through the three communication systems. The three levels of empathy were high, neutral, and low. The communication modalities were verbal, nonverbal, and combined verbal-nonverbal.

In the high verbal empathic condition, the counselor employed reflection and restatement of the subject's perceived feelings and content, and also engaged in interpretation of feelings not clearly present at the surface. These procedures are considered most effective in the communication of high levels of verbal empathy (Carkhuff, 1969a, 1969b). The nonverbal behaviors of smiling, affirmative head nodding, leaning forward, and a full-body orientation to a 0-degree perspective to the client constituted the high nonverbal empathic condition (English & Jelevensky, 1971; Graves & Robinson, 1976; Haase & Tepper, 1972; Seay & Altekruse, 1979; Shapiro et al., 1968). A combination of the above verbal and nonverbal behaviors comprised the high verbal-nonverbal empathic condition.

The neutral verbal empathic condition was characterized by the counselor giving only reflection and restatement of surface level feelings and not interpretation. The neutral nonverbal condition was defined as the counselor's arms resting comfortably on the arms of the chair, with her feet crossed ankle to ankle in front of her or under the chair. Smiling and affirmative head nodding were relatively infrequent. Eye contact was frequent, and leaning forward was omitted. A combination of the above verbal and nonverbal behaviors defined the neutral verbal-nonverbal condition.

In the low empathic condition, the counselor used reflection and restatement sparingly. She often engaged in questioning and always remained on the topic as presented by the client. Her nonverbal behavior was characterized by sporadic eye contact, crossing legs knee to knee, and occasionally folding arms. Positive head nodding and smiling were also employed, but on a limited basis. Leaning forward was omitted. The combined low verbal-nonverbal condition was a union of these behaviors. At no time was the counselor blatantly nonempathic, nor did she ever show negative regard for her clients.

Counselor Training

The training of the counselor began with a detailed discussion of each condition that she was to portray. Audiotapes of counseling role plays illustrating each of the five levels of empathy defined by the Carkhuff (1969b) scale were used as models to identify high empathy (Level 5), neutral empathy (Level 3), and low empathy (Level 2). After listening to these tapes and knowing which role play corresponded to which level, the counselor was presented with seven more brief role plays, the levels being in random order. She was asked to identify the level of empathy associated with each level. She achieved 100% success on the first trial. Following this, she engaged in a variety of role plays with a research assistant practicing not only the three levels, but also switching levels on cue.

For the nonverbal behaviors, a videotape of the conditions previously described was used as a model. The counselor viewed the tape and practiced the behaviors with the research assistant.

A final videotape with the audio included was used as a model for the combined verbal-nonverbal high, neutral, and low empathic conditions. The same training procedures applied. The total training time was 4 hours.

Methodological Considerations

After the counselor developed the behavior patterns for these various empathic and communication conditions, she engaged in a series of role plays with a research assistant portraying the different levels of empathy. Audiotapes were made to accommodate the verbal mode, videotapes without sound were constructed for the nonverbal component, and videotapes with the audio were made for the combined verbal-nonverbal condition.

These tapes were subsequently shown to a group of raters who reported on the counselor's behavior. All raters were school psychologists with master's degrees and had at least 4 years of experience. Four men and three women were used. The raters were trained using the method described by Rogers and Truax (1967) to rate the levels of empathy. In this procedure, a client concern was expressed and was followed by a series of counselor responses. Each counselor response was treated individually, and was designed to illustrate a different level of empathic understanding.

The Empathic Understanding Scale (Carkhuff, 1969b) was used to rate the verbal and combined verbal-nonverbal counselor conditions. An adaptation of this form, the Gladstein Nonverbal Empathy Scale, was used to rate the nonverbal dimension (see Appendix). Reliabilities were calculated among raters for each communication modality (Winer, 1971), using the role plays described above. (Following the counseling sessions, ratings of the counselor's behavior were made by four of the seven judges to assess if deterioration in skill level had occurred.)

After approximately 4½ hours of training, acceptable levels of reliability were reached. The raters than assessed the actual counselor's level of empathy vis-á-vis the different communication modalities. A variation of the repeated measures analysis of variance described by Meyers (1969) was used to test whether the empathy levels of the counselor were significantly different from one another. The Newman-Keuls (Winer, 1971) was used to test for significant differences among levels of empathy. (See the "Results" section for a more detailed description of these analyses.)

Technological Considerations

The videotape method of assisted recall that was developed by Kagan, Kratchovil, and Miller (1963) was employed in this study. The method consists of videotaping counseling interviews, then showing these recordings to the subjects at some later date. In using this method, the subjects were able to make several responses, such as their perception of counselor level of empathy, their satisfaction with the counseling interview, and their depth of self-exploration, all on the same segment of tape.

Katz and Resnikoff (1977) reported validity data giving support for this videotape method of assisted recall. Their procedure was to have subjects make ratings of their general feeling tone during a live session, and during a video recall of that same session. The authors found a .71 correlation for client affect between the live and taped interviews.

In the present study, special videotaping effects were required because the subjects had to make ratings of both their behavior and the behavior of their counselor. Two video cameras, recording on a split screen, were employed. Both cameras were Panasonic model WV-341P. The videotape recorder was also a Panasonic, model NV-3130.

One camera recorded the behavior of the client, while the other camera was focused on the counselor. Frontal views of both individuals were recorded.

For the entire first session, the counselor was in the neutral verbal-nonverbal empathic condition. As previously reported, at the end of this interview the client viewed five consecutive, 2-minute segments of this session immediately after it ended. The starting point of the 2-minute segment was randomly chosen for each client. At the end of each 2-minute time interval, the tape was stopped and the subjects completed the three scales noted above. The purpose of this initial viewing was to desensitize the clients to seeing themselves on videotape. This reduced the confounding effects of any feelings that they may have had about seeing themselves on tape. It also gave them an opportunity to become familiar with the forms and the procedure for their completion.

The second session was the high-empathy condition of the manipulation. For the first 12 minutes of the interview, the counselor remained in the neutral verbal-nonverbal empathic condition (Baseline 1). During the next 12 minutes, the counselor's behavior changed to either a high verbal empathic condition, a high nonverbal empathic condition, or a high verbal-nonverbal empathic treatment condition. When the verbal modality was high, for example, the nonverbal modality remained neutral, and vice versa. The order of presentation of these treatment conditions was randomized across subjects for each session, and within subjects from Session 2 to Session 3. Furthermore, the order of presenting the treatment conditions to the clients for rating purposes was also randomized (see Table 5.1).

The next two 12-minute intervals were comprised of the remaining two communication modalities, with the neutral condition being present when applicable. During the final 12-minute segment, the counselor's behavior returned to a neutral verbal-nonverbal condition (Baseline 2).

TABLE 5.1. Order of communication modality presentation for all subjects.

Subject	High-empathy treatment	Low-empathy treatment	High-empathy rating	Low-empathy rating
1	B1, V-NV, V NV, B2	B1, V, NV V-NV, B2	B1, V, V-NV, B2, NV	V-NV, B1, V, NV, B2
2	B1, V, V-NV NV, B2	B1, NV, V V-NV, B2	NV, B2, V, B1, V-NV	NV, B1, B2, V, V-NV
3	B1, V-NV, NV V, B2	B1, NV, V-NV V, B2	B1, V-NV, NV, V, B2	NV, B2, V, B1, V-NV
4	B1, NV, V-NV V, B2	B1, V-NV, V, NV, B2	V-NV, B1, NV, B2, V	V, V-NV, B2 B2, B1, NV

Note. B1 = Baseline 1; B2 = Baseline 2; V = Verbal; NV = Nonverbal; V-NV = Verbal-Nonverbal.

The third session was the low-empathy condition. Once again, five 12-minute segments were used with the neutral verbal-nonverbal empathic condition being present first and last, and a randomized order of presentation of verbal, nonverbal, and verbal-nonverbal empathy occurring during the middle three intervals. At the end of this interview, the experimenter met with the client and scheduled a rating session to review the second and third interviews with the client.

The room arrangement during the counseling sessions is shown in Figure 5.1. During both the second and third sessions, the counselor was cued by a light device as to which communicational modality to portray,

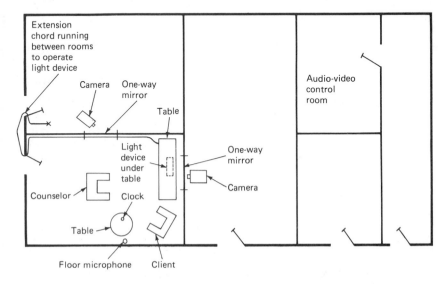

FIGURE 5.1. Floor plan and counseling room arrangement.

and when to initiate and terminate this condition. The device was the size of a shoe box. Inside were two lights, one red and one blue. When no lights were lit, the baseline condition was in effect. The red light signaled the verbal condition, the blue light indicated the nonverbal condition, and the appearance of both lights concurrently designated the combined verbal-nonverbal condition.

This device was positioned in such a manner that the client was unaware of its presence. It was operated by the experimenter from a room adjacent to the counseling room. A digital clock with a 3-inch numeric readout was strategically placed in the counseling room so that it could be seen by the experimenter and recorded on tape as well. The purpose of this was to have a systematic and direct manner to identify time intervals not only in vivo during the sessions, but also for rating purposes. (See Figure 5.1.)

Client Rating Sessions

The experimental tapes that the subjects viewed and rated consisted of selected segments of Sessions 2 and 3, with all baseline and experimental conditions being present. A total of eight of the 12 minutes per condition (i.e., Baseline 1, verbal, nonverbal, verbal-nonverbal, and Baseline 2) or 40 minutes were used in the ratings. Each 8-minute segment began at a random point. At the end of every 2-minute interval within this 8-minute segment, the tape was stopped and the subject completed the three dependent measures. Each client made 40 ratings on each of the three dependent measures, a total of 120 ratings per client. The time within these four 2-minute intervals was consecutive for each 8-minute segment. The order of presentation of the baseline and treatment conditions was random across subjects and across sessions. (See Table 5.1 for details.)

Data Analysis

In line with the multiple-*N*, multiple-*I* design, the data collected on the four subjects were represented graphically. Kratchowil (1978) stated that the use of graphs is of particular importance because information regarding experimental control and stability of change is clearly reported. Similarly, relationships between variables, trends over time, and the effects of new variables are clearly represented. In light of this, visual interpretations of mean levels of ratings within each treatment condition (i.e., communication modality) and between treatment conditions (i.e., level of counselor-offered empathy) will constitute the method of analysis of these data.

Prior to the presentation of these findings, however, the results of certain preliminary analyses, such as securing interrater reliability and achieving statistically significant differences among the different counselor empathic behaviors in the three communication modalities, are described.

Results

Reliability

In order to assess whether the three levels of empathy portrayed by the counselor were significantly different from each other, one must first establish an acceptable level of agreement among those doing the ratings. With a high interrater agreement, an experimenter can be reasonably confident that the levels of the treatment conditions are stable and not subject to variation. The analysis of these data using the analysis of variance method for calculating reliability (Winer, 1971) is reported in Table 5.2.

The reliabilities presented here indicated a very high interrater reliability over all three conditions. These data indicate that the seven judges made highly similar ratings for the counselor's empathic behavior when she was in the verbal, nonverbal, and verbal-nonverbal modalities. In view of the method used in establishing reliability, these very high results were expected. With this established, one can assume with a high degree of certainty that the judges would be as internally consistent in rating the actual counselor's behavior for the treatment check as they were under this reliability condition.

Treatment Check Data

Prior to actually conducting the study, it was important to first establish the fact that the three empathy conditions that the counselor was to portray were significantly different from one another within each communication modality. Video, audio, and audiovideotapes of the actual counselor, who was engaged in different role play conditions, were made and rated. In Table 5.3 means and standard deviation of judges' scores are presented. The marginal mean of the high-empathy condition was 4.52, with the neutral empathy condition being 3.28, while the marginal mean of the low condition was 1.90.

The data derived from the analysis of variance are reported in Table 5.4. These data clearly indicate that there was a highly significant difference in the judges' perceptions of the counselor's level of empathy. This infers that the counselor had successfully developed the necessary

TABLE 5.2. Interrater reliability for counselor level of empathy among the three communication conditions.

Empathy condition	Interrater reliability
Verbal	.98
Nonverbal	.96
Verbal-Nonverbal	.98

TABLE 5.3. Means and standard deviations of empathy conditions.

Empathy conditions	Communication modality		
	Verbal	Nonverbal	Verbal-Nonverbal
High empathy			
M	4.57	4.57	4.42
SD	.72	.72	.72
Neutral empathy			
M	3.42	3.14	3.28
SD	.49	.47	.44
Low empathy			
M	2.14	1.85	1.71
SD	.83	.63	.45

TABLE 5.4. Analysis of variance data of different levels of counselor-offered empathy as function of communication modality.

Source of variance	SS	df	MS	F
A (Communication modality)	.67	2	.34	.89
B (Level of empathy)	72.09	2	36.05	58.14**
C (Judges)	3.42	6	.57	1.50
A × B	.27	4	.10	.27
A × C	6.67	12	.56	
B × C	7.24	12	.62	
A × B × C	9.06	24	.38	

**$p < .01$.

skills required to communicate differential levels of empathy. Also, no significant differences existed in interjudge ratings. Nor were there significant differences among raters on communication modality. This further verified the fact that there was consistent agreement among the seven judges, and that the effects of communication modality were essentially the same across like empathy conditions.

Because the F value in the analysis of variance of empathy was significant, the Newman-Keuls post hoc analysis was employed to determine whether the three empathy conditions were significantly different from one another. The results of these analyses are presented in Table 5.5.

The results presented here strongly indicate that the three counselor conditions of empathy were significantly different from one another. Therefore, based on the data of these various analyses, the behavior of the counselor was consistent with the desired experimental conditions, and the subjects were ready to be recruited.

TABLE 5.5. Newman-Keuls post hoc analysis of level of counselor empathy.

	Empathy conditions		
	High vs. low	High vs. neutral	Neutral vs. low
Obtained	55.00**	26.00**	29.00**
Values	7.05	8.22	8.97

**$p < .01$.

Data on Dependent Measures

Figures 5.2–5.6 illustrate how the manipulations of the various independent variables affected the dependent variables. Tables 5.6 and 5.7 are included for additional inspection. In Table 5.6, client mean scores on the three dependent measures are reported as a function of Baselines 1 and 2 as well as the specific communication modalities. In Table 5.7 mean scores are also reported; however, collapsing occurs across communication modalities. In Figure 5.2, the perceptions of each client's level of counselor-offered empathy under high empathy with the various communication modalities within are shown, while Figure 5.3 represents the subjects' responses to the level of counselor-offered empathy in the low condition. Figures 5.4 and 5.5 pertain to subject depth of self-exploration as a function of high and low empathy, respectively. Finally, Figure 5.6 illustrates client satisfaction throughout the counseling experience.

Stable initial baselines were achieved for every subject in the high-empathy condition on the level of empathic understanding. Subjects 1, 2, and 3 began with slightly inflated ratings; however, they lowered their perceptions with the passage of time. Subject 4's mean showed a slight increase on this dimension. Subjects 2, 3, and 4 all increased in their perceptions of counselor-offered empathy in the verbal communication modality. Although Subject 1's mean level of perceived empathy was the same in this condition as in the initial baseline period, a definite increase was noted in the last two rating periods.

The counselor's switch from the high verbal condition to the high nonverbal condition yielded mixed results. Subjects 3 and 4 decreased in mean ratings, while the ratings of Subject 2 remained the same and the ratings of Subject 1 slightly increased.

The most apparent finding with regard to this dimension was that in all cases the perceived level of counselor-offered empathic understanding increased in the combined verbal-nonverbal communication condition.

Finally, the mean level of perceived empathy decreased for Subjects 2, 3, and 4 in the return to baseline. Theoretically, according to Kratchowil (1978), when the treatment conditions are withdrawn, a change in ratings in the direction of the initial baseline is expected. This change, however,

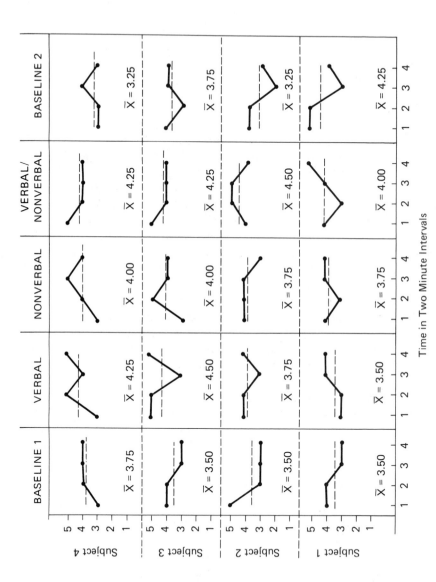

FIGURE 5.2. Level of empathic understanding in high-empathy condition.

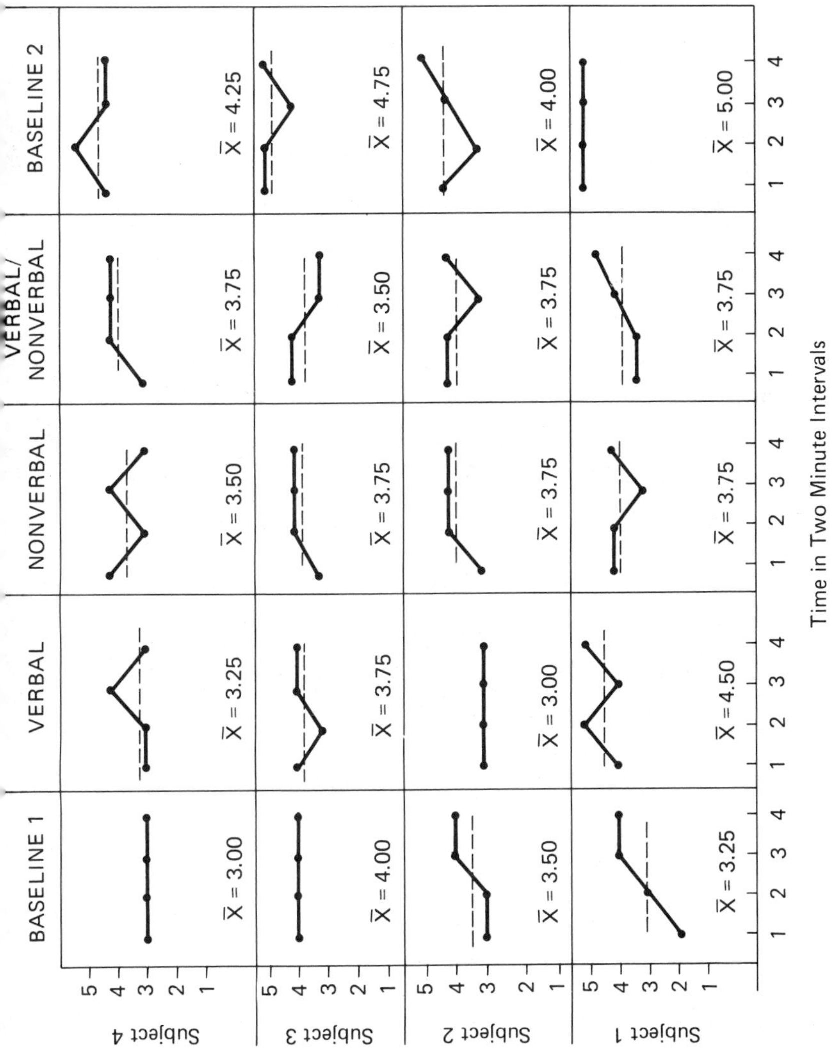

FIGURE 5.3. Level of empathic understanding in low-empathy condition.

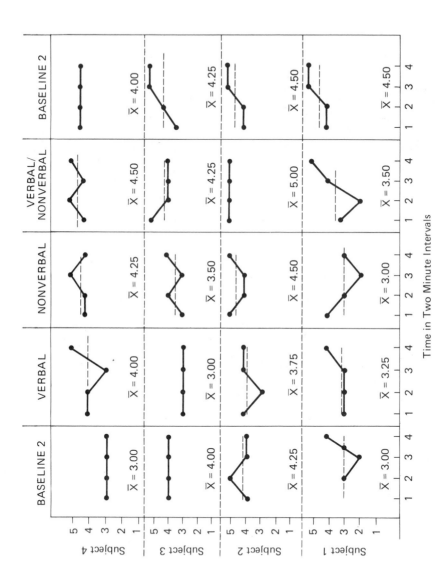

FIGURE 5.4. Depth of self-exploration in high-empathy condition.

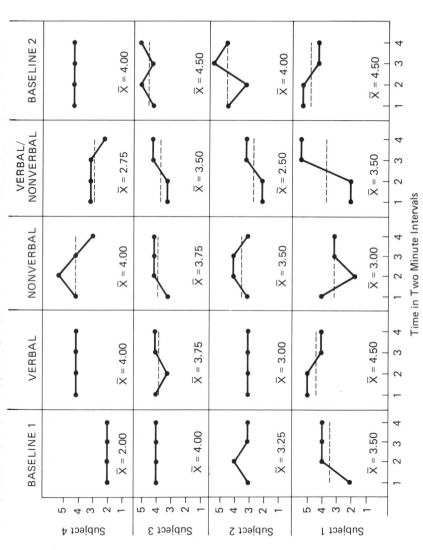

FIGURE 5.5. Depth of self-exploration in low-empathy condition.

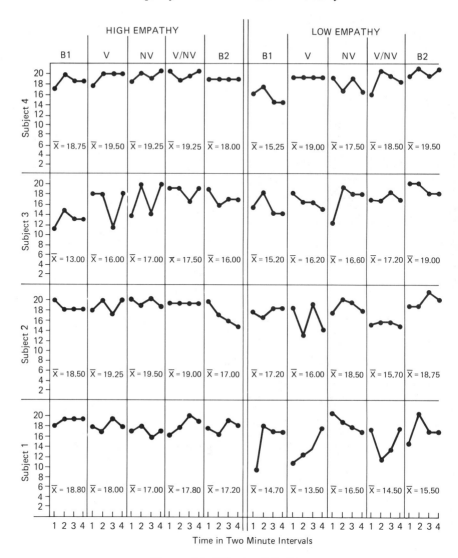

FIGURE 5.6. Client satisfaction.

will not be a complete return to the initial baseline condition in this type of single design, since the cumulative effects of subject learning prohibit this. In the case of Subject 1, a continued increase in the mean score was noted.

In the low-empathy condition, stable initial baselines were again achieved for all subjects, except Subject 1, on the level of perceived empathic understanding. Although the mean scores showed some variation, the basic pattern of responding was the same. Transition from

TABLE 5.6. Mean scores of client ratings across empathy level and communication modality on the three dependent measures.

Measures	High empathy					Low empathy				
	B1	V	NV	V-NV	B2	B1	V	NV	V-NV	B2
Empathic understanding										
Subject 1	3.50	3.50	3.75	4.00	4.25	3.25	4.50	3.75	3.75	5.00
Subject 2	3.50	3.75	3.75	4.50	3.25	3.50	3.00	3.75	3.75	4.00
Subject 3	3.50	4.50	4.00	4.25	3.75	4.00	3.75	3.75	3.50	4.75
Subject 4	3.75	4.25	4.00	4.25	3.25	3.00	3.25	3.50	3.75	4.25
Self-exploration										
Subject 1	3.00	3.25	3.00	3.50	4.50	3.50	4.50	3.00	3.50	4.50
Subject 2	4.25	3.75	4.50	5.00	4.50	3.25	3.00	3.50	2.50	4.00
Subject 3	4.00	3.00	3.50	4.25	4.25	4.00	3.75	3.75	3.50	4.50
Subject 4	3.00	4.00	4.25	4.50	4.00	2.00	4.00	4.00	2.75	4.00
Client satisfaction										
Subject 1	18.80	18.00	17.00	17.80	17.20	14.70	13.50	16.50	14.50	15.50
Subject 2	18.50	19.25	19.50	19.00	17.00	17.20	16.00	18.50	15.70	18.75
Subject 3	13.00	16.00	17.00	17.50	16.00	15.20	16.20	16.60	17.20	19.00
Subject 4	18.75	19.50	19.25	19.25	18.00	15.25	19.00	17.50	18.50	19.50

Note. B1 = Baseline 1; V = Verbal; NV = Nonverbal; V-NV = Verbal-Nonverbal; B2 = Baseline 2.

Baseline 1 to the verbal condition yielded mixed results. The means of the ratings for Subjects 1 and 4 tended to be higher, while those for Subjects 2 and 3 tended to be lower than in the original baseline.

Switching from the verbal to the nonverbal condition again offered no clear consistent pattern. Subjects 2 and 4 showed increased mean scores, Subject 3's score remained the same, and the score of Subject 1 decreased. Similar occurrences prevailed across the mean scores in the combined verbal-nonverbal empathic condition.

Baseline 2 offered a more consistent pattern. Without exception, all mean scores showed a marked increase in the level of perceived counselor-offered empathic understanding.

Initial baseline conditions for three of the four clients in the high-empathy depth of self-exploration condition are stable. The initial baseline for Subject 1 began with some stability but showed variation in Segments 3 and 4. Although this variation did exist, the trend was in the direction opposite of that which was expected. Mean ratings in the verbal condition varied; those of Subjects 1 and 4 were higher than baseline and those of Subjects 2 and 3 were lower. The mean scores in the nonverbal condition were higher than those in the verbal, with the exception of Subject 1 whose mean scores were lower, only because of one data point.

TABLE 5.7. Mean scores of client ratings across empathy level and collapsed across communication modality on the three dependent measures.

Measures	High empathy			Low empathy		
	B1	Communication modality	B2	B1	Communication modality	B2
Empathic understanding						
Subject 1	3.50	3.75	4.25	3.25	4.00	5.00
Subject 2	3.50	4.00	3.25	3.50	3.50	4.00
Subject 3	3.50	4.25	3.75	4.00	3.67	4.75
Subject 4	3.75	4.16	3.25	3.00	3.50	4.25
Self-exploration						
Subject 1	3.00	3.25	4.50	3.50	3.67	4.50
Subject 2	4.25	4.42	4.50	3.25	3.00	4.00
Subject 3	4.00	3.58	4.25	4.00	3.67	4.50
Subject 4	3.00	4.25	4.00	2.00	3.58	4.00
Client satisfaction						
Subject 1	18.80	17.60	17.20	14.70	14.83	15.50
Subject 2	18.50	19.25	17.00	17.20	16.73	18.75
Subject 3	13.00	16.83	16.00	15.20	16.67	19.00
Subject 4	18.75	19.33	18.00	15.25	18.33	19.50

Note. B1 = Baseline 1; B2 = Baseline 2.

Again the most cogent finding with regard to this aspect of the research was that in the combined verbal-nonverbal condition, subject depth of self-exploration was consistently higher than in either the initial baseline or any other treatment modality.

The Baseline 2 condition again followed the theory in that it was consistently higher than the initial baseline, but the mean scores were mixed (i.e., some were high while others were low) when compared to the combined verbal-nonverbal modality.

The initial baselines for depth of self-exploration under low empathy were the most stable overall up to this point in the presentation. Although a wide range in perception existed (from a Level 2 to a Level 4), the data points were least variable.

Changes from Baseline 1 to the verbal condition showed either a large increase in mean scores or a slight decrease. Going from the verbal modality to the nonverbal condition afforded little consistency. On the other hand, with the exception of Subject 1 whose scores showed minimal variation, the mean scores of Subjects 2, 3, and 4 were clearly lower in the verbal-nonverbal conditions than in any other treatment condition.

Furthermore, Subjects 2 and 3 had mean scores lower here than in the initial baseline.

Finally, with the return to baseline, all mean scores showed a marked increase from the combined verbal-nonverbal condition. Although this was not hypothesized, it was expected because the Baseline 2 condition, experimentally, was actually higher in empathy in both the verbal and nonverbal dimensions than the verbal-nonverbal treatment condition.

The last dependent variable to be discussed pertained to the level of client satisfaction based on the level of offered empathy and communication modality. Figure 5.6 illustrates how the treatment conditions affected this dimension, while Tables 5.6 and 5.7 provide the actual numerical data.

As with the other measures, stable initial baselines were achieved here before the onset of the treatment conditions. Little variation in mean scores occurred among Subjects 1, 3, and 4 in the high-empathy condition, and Subjects 1, 2, and 3 in the low-empathy condition. Subject 3 in the low-empathy condition tended to report a considerably lower mean rating, while Subject 2 in the low-empathy condition reported a somewhat higher mean rating. Again, although this variation existed, the pattern of the data points remained fairly consistent. Scores in the high-empathy verbal condition were higher than the initial baseline, with the exception of Subject 1 who scored lower. One of the most consistent patterns in the data with respect to this measure was the relationship between the high verbal-nonverbal empathic condition and the low verbal-nonverbal empathic condition. In all cases, clients reported higher levels of satisfaction in the former situation than in the latter.

The mean scores in the low-empathy condition across subjects and communication modalities yielded relatively inconsistent results. Aside from the consistent pattern between high and low verbal-nonverbal patterns, the other area of consistency was the increase in mean scores from the verbal-nonverbal communcation condition to the Baseline 2 condition. Again, although this was not hypothesized, it was expected because the counselor's empathy levels were higher under Baseline 2 than the verbal-nonverbal mode.

As a key element in substantiating the validity of the results of this study, the stability of the counselor's behavior through time must be assessed. Four of the seven original judges were used to rate the counselor's behavior during actual counseling sessions over different times throughout the life of the experiment. The judges rated four segments per empathy level for two clients. Therefore, 24 client-counselor interchanges were scored. The judges made ratings on one client statement followed by one counselor response, and, without exception, all four gave her consistent appropriate ratings for high empathy (Level 5), neutral empathy (Level 3), and low empathy (Levels 1 and 2).

Summary

The counselor's behavior was found to be highly illustrative of the desired experimental conditions during training as well as in the actual setting. Her behavior was also found to be stable over time, since the clients who were used for this quality check were seen about 2 months apart.

The data obtained on the Empathic Understanding Scale and on the Depth of Self-Exploration Scale clearly supported the hypotheses for the high-empathy condition. No clear findings to support the hypotheses concerning the effects of low empathy vis-à-vis the verbal-nonverbal communication modality were obtained. Consistent scores were obtained on the Interview Rating Scale indicating that clients expressed greater levels of satisfaction with the counselor when she was in the high-empathy, verbal-nonverbal mode than when she was operating from the low-empathy, verbal-nonverbal condition.

Discussion

Restatement of Purpose and Research Hypothesis

The purpose of this investigation was to assess the effects of manipulating different levels of counselor-offered verbal, nonverbal, and combined verbal-nonverbal empathy on various dimensions of client behaviors during the counseling process. One primary research hypothesis and two subcategories were identified. They were: (1) Client depth of self-exploration, perception of counselor empathic understanding, and satisfaction with the counseling interview will vary as a function of the level of counselor-offered empathy and the channel through which this condition is communicated. (1a) The high-empathy condition, communicated through the verbal-nonverbal communication modality, will yield greater depths of self-exploration, client satisfaction, and perceived empathic understanding than any other condition. (1b) The low-empathy condition, communicated through the combined verbal-nonverbal communication modality, will yield the lowest depth of self-exploration, client satisfaction, and perceived empathic understanding of any other condition.

Hypothesis 1

Looking first at the level of empathy component of this hypothesis, one can readily note that a variety in mean ratings exist. [1] In a single-subject

---

[1] It is important for the reader to keep in mind that the order of presentation of the communication modalities was randomized across clients during counseling and further randomized during rating. Therefore, when effects due to treatment are discussed, the implication is not of sequencing of communication modality presentation, but more importantly of consistent pattern development.

research design, it is crucial to be able to identify consistent data patterns and/or trends in order to infer treatment effects (Glass, Willson, & Gottman, 1975; Krachowil, 1978; Thoresen & Anton, 1974). *The levels of self-exploration overall showed no consistent pattern as a function of the level of empathy offered.* Should the level of empathy have been a substantial influence on client behavior, more consistent patterns in the direction of low empathy, low self-exploration and vice versa would have emerged. This finding supports the results of the Kratchovil, Aspy, and Carkhuff (1967) study as well as the research done by Morocco (1979b). Effects contrary to these findings are found in the works of Hountras and Anderson (1969) and Banks (1972). In the former study, cultural differences were manipulated concurrently, while in the latter, other facilitative conditions, such as genuineness and respect, were manipulated. These additional factors may have been the source or at least may have contributed substantially to the findings. *As a result of the data obtained from the clients, this portion of the hypothesis was not supported.*

Continuing with the level of self-exploration, the second element of the hypothesis was that the level of self-exploration would vary with the communication modality. One can readily observe that the data presented in Figure 5.4 and Table 5.6 identified *three of the four subjects as showing greater mean depths of self-exploration with the progression across treatment communication systems.* Subject 1's nonverbal level was somewhat less than her verbal level; however, she recovered to an even higher rating in the combined situation than in the verbal alone.

Because communication mode presentation during counseling and rating was completely randomized, these effects can be attributed to treatment rather than order or time of exposure during the session.

Aside from the treatment effects, it is also interesting to note the variations in mean ratings across subjects in the high-empathy condition when the transition is made from Baseline 1 to the treatment condition to Baseline 2. Subjects 1 and 4 rated their levels of self-exploration in Baseline 1 lower than in any other condition, while Subjects 2 and 3 were higher initially here than, at least, in the verbal mode. Baseline 2 scores tended to drop for Subjects 2 and 4, remained the same for Subject 3, and actually increased for Subject 1.

The patterns of Subjects 2 and 4 give empirical support to the theoretical basis of this type of experimental design in that the scores are expected to reverse during the withdrawal of a treatment phase albeit to a level slightly higher (in this case) than the original baseline. The lack of complete reversal to the original levels is theorized to be primarily due to the cumulative effects of learning (Kratchowil, 1978). In the case of Subjects 1 and 3 where this reversal in scores was not present, one might suggest that learning has played an even greater role for these individuals, and that the cumulative effects of exposure to the high-empathy condition combined with the element of learning produced more idiosyncratic results.

In Figure 5.5 and Table 5.6, however, different results are portrayed. Only two Subjects, 3 and 4, established a similar pattern. Depth of self-exploration under verbal and nonverbal levels remained stable for these individuals, with the combined modality showing a decrease. Considerable variation existed in the mean scores for Subjects 1 and 2. *As a result, only marginal support could be given to this portion of the hypothesis pertaining to the effects of communication modality on level of self-exploration in the low-empathy condition.*

Variation in mean scores from Baseline 1 to the treatment conditions existed here as they did in the high-empathy condition. Effects in the expected direction were indicated for Subjects 2 and 3, and in the opposite direction for Subjects 1 and 4 for the baseline, verbal transition. Effects in the opposite direction continued through the nonverbal condition for Subjects 3 and 4, and in the expected direction for Subject 1. The combined verbal-nonverbal condition showed greater stability and is discussed in detail under Hypothesis 1b.

Transitions to Baseline 2 were unanimously consistent in that the level of self-exploration for each subject was greater here than in any other communication modality. The return to the neutral verbal-nonverbal empathic condition had pronounced effects on the level of self-exploration. For the majority of this session, clients were deprived of some form of empathy, either verbal, nonverbal, or both. What appears to have happened was that the client level of self-exploration showed greater sensitivity to the return to the neutral verbal-nonverbal empathy than to Baseline 1, since the combined verbal-nonverbal Baseline 2 communication was more congruent than any other system in the treatment function in terms of the message being communicated, and also because the levels of empathy presented were perceived by the subjects as higher in this mode than in any other modes (see Figure 5.3 and Tables 5.6 and 5.7, Baseline 2).

The combined effects of the level of counselor-offered empathy and the channel through which it was communicated on client perceptions of this counselor-offered empathy was another major element of Hypothesis 1. *This element was clearly supported in the high-empathy condition as illustrated in Figure 5.2 and reported in Table 5.6.* Only minor variations in the data contradicted this position. This finding would be in support of the research conducted by English and Jelevensky (1971), who found that a significant consistency existed among individuals who evaluated counselor empathy based on audio, visual, and audiovisual systems. Similarly, these results are in agreement with those of Smith-Hanen (1977), who in fact identified the nonverbal behaviors associated with differential levels of empathy.

Through closer inspection of the data under this circumstance in the present study, it is clear that the mean level in Subject 1's ratings showed no change from Baseline 1 to the verbal mode; however, it thereafter increased in the expected direction. The mean level of scores for Subjects

2 and 4 showed a lower than expected level during Baseline 2. The possible explanation here is that these two women were highly sensitive to the withdrawal of empathy and so reflected this sensitivity in their ratings.

In the low-empathy condition, client perceptions of counselor behavior failed to support the hypothesis. Highly stable patterns across communication modes and between high and low counselor-offered empathy conditions prevailed. Hence, the findings of Kratchovil et al. (1967) and Morocco (1979b) are again supported. The possible explanations for this are presented individually and discussed in detail.

First, client expectation of counselor behavior may have affected to a large degree the data obtained. Sullivan's (1956) theory of selective attention and inattention, the findings of Cash, Kehr, and Salzbach (1978), and the results of a study conducted by Young (1979) affirm this idea. When a counselor actively engages in behavior that is contrary to a preconceived expectation that a client has, the behavior may be unnoticed, rationalized, or misinterpreted by the client. Along these lines, although the client may perceive the counselor behaving in a low empathic fashion, she may be reluctant to rate her as such because people sometimes have difficulty giving low ratings to others.

The sequence in the presentation of the level of empathy may have been a factor for the lack of clear findings. Due to ethical reasons, the high-empathy condition was presented during the second counseling session for all subjects. Because the first session was neutral empathy and the second session was basically high empathy, the halo effect may have been in operation. Previous learning had set the stage for future expectations. As a result, the client may not have been accurately perceiving the behavior of the counselor.

A fairly consistent pattern emerged in the transition from Baseline 1 to the verbal modality in the high-empathy condition. Subjects 2, 3, and 4 showed higher levels in their mean scores for perceived counselor-offered empathy. The mean score for Subject 1 remained the same as in Baseline 1. Considerable variation existed in the transition from the verbal to the nonverbal mode. The ratings from Subjects 3 and 4 decreased, Subject 2's score remained the same, and the rating made by Subject 1 increased. The inference here is that the verbal behavior of the counselor tended to have more of a consistent impact across clients than the nonverbal behavior of the counselor. This data is in contradiction to the findings reported by Mehrabian (1968, 1971), who spoke generally of people's communication systems. More tentative agreement may be found with Davitz (1964) and Ruesch (1965), who contended that verbal and nonverbal communication are interrelated.

The effects of the combined verbal-nonverbal communication modality were quite consistent and are discussed with regard to Hypothesis 1a.

Finally, a fairly stable pattern existed in the transition from the combined modality condition to Baseline 2. Again, empirical support for this type of single-subject experimental design was found in that when the reversal occurred, scores tended also to reverse. Subject 1 was the exception with a continual increase in her mean rating. The speculation here is that this difference was idiosyncratic and due to the fact that the overriding effects of the combined modality sufficiently affected her perceptions of the counselor's behavior in the direction indicated.

In examining the communication modality systems in the low-empathy condition, considerable fluctuation was apparent. Only two Subjects, 1 and 3, showed somewhat of a downward pattern. Subjects 2 and 4 showed either a continual increase in mean scores across communication modalities or an initial increase followed by plateauing. The most consistent pattern in ratings that held true for all subjects was in the transition from the combined verbal-nonverbal communication system to the Baseline 2 modality. Without exception, all subjects had mean ratings higher in this baseline than anywhere else in the low-empathy condition. Once again it appeared as though the effects of empathy deprivation had come into focus. Because the counselor in Baseline 2 was more congruent in terms of verbal and nonverbal behavior as well as in terms of the level of empathy being communicated, her behavior may have been easier to interpret. Furthermore, the empathy level of the counselor increased under this condition from the previously low levels that were offered in the other three communication modality conditions. As a result, the perceptions of the clients may have been inflated as a function of the deprivation experience.

The final consideration under Hypothesis 1 pertains to the level of client satisfaction with regard to the independent variables. Inspections of the level of empathy revealed that client satisfaction was greater in the high-empathy condition than in the low, as evidenced in Table 5.7. *Therefore, the portion of Hypothesis 1 that stated client satisfaction will vary as a function of the level of counselor-offered empathy was supported.* On the other hand, no trends or patterns were either clearly established or given minimal support for the expectation that client satisfaction would vary as a function of the counselor's communication system.

Hypothesis 1a

Hypothesis 1a basically states that in the high-empathy condition with the verbal-nonverbal modality in operation, the greatest depths of self-exploration, perceived empathic understanding, and client satisfaction will be realized. *One can readily observe from Figure 5.4 and Table 5.6 that this in fact did occur across subjects, within the three levels of communication modality, for depth of self-exploration in the high empathy condition.* It is therefore clear that it was the combination of the two communication systems that had the greatest effect on this client variable.

Similarly, with the exception of Subject 3, the findings supported this hypothesis for level of empathic understanding in the high-empathy condition. In turn, these results affirmed the point that Brown and Parks (1972) made concerning the importance of the interaction between the verbal and nonverbal dimensions in communication.

When comparing the effects of the verbal-nonverbal modality in the high-empathy condition with all other communication conditions in low empathy for depth of self-exploration, the hypothesis continued to be supported for Subjects 2, 3, and 4. Mention should be made of the fact that the Baseline 2 condition in low empathy was inflated across subjects, most likely due to the explanations given previously.

Hypothesis 1a is further supported when tested against the data derived from the empathy ratings. The only element that tended to disrupt the predicted pattern was the mean score for Subject 1, low empathy, verbal modality. *Other than this, no other mean rating surpassed any of those found in the high-empathy, combined verbal-nonverbal modality. The combined effects of the communication systems prevailed.* Again, Baseline 2 conditions tended to be high as previously discussed.

The scores reported on the client satisfaction index were highly variable and gave no clear support for this hypothesis.

Hypothesis 1b

The hypothesis states that low empathy communicated through the verbal-nonverbal channel will yield the lowest depth of self-exploration, perceived empathic understanding, and client satisfaction than any other condition. *The patterns existing on the Depth of Self-Exploration Scale were highly variable when compared to the other modes of communication within the low-empathy system.* A comparison of findings between the combined communication modality in low empathy and all scores in high empathy afforded minimal understanding. *The exception lay in a comparison of the verbal-nonverbal modality between high and low empathy. Without exception client satisfaction was depressed in the low empathic condition.*

The same basic pattern held true for the perceived level of empathic understanding variable. The only exception here was, again, that the combined verbal-nonverbal communication system in low empathy yielded scores consistently lower than the combined verbal-nonverbal communication system in the high-empathy condition.

Keeping the two exceptions noted above in mind, the client satisfaction dimension afforded little opportunity for inference.

Summary

In summary, the following points can be made with respect to the relationship between the three hypotheses and the data on the dependent variables: (a) The combined effects of the verbal and nonverbal communication systems produced consistently high levels of perceived empathic understanding when the counselor was in fact operating from high verbal-nonverbal empathic levels. Hence, the stance posited by Delaney (1968) quoted earlier is clearly supported. (b) Similarly, the combined effects of the verbal-nonverbal communication modalities produced consistently high levels of client self-exploration when the counselor was operating from a high empathic condition. *Therefore, some empirical confirmation has been demonstrated for the importance of counselor-offered empathic behavior during counseling.* The fact that this finding did not occur for client satisfaction tends to weaken this finding somewhat. (c) The combined effects of the verbal-nonverbal modality coupled with low counselor-offered empathy produced relatively stable scores, comparatively speaking, to the combined verbal-nonverbal high-empathy condition. These scores were consistently lower on all three dependent variables than their counterparts.

Related Findings

Aside from the results obtained from the hypothesis testing, certain ancillary findings are important to discuss. *In reviewing the mean scores on the levels of self-exploration and empathic understanding for both high- and low-empathy conditions, little variation in numerical value existed.* One would expect the client to rate the counselor lower (i.e., Level 1 or 2) at least on the empathic understanding scale when she was operating from the low-empathy condition. On the contrary, minimal differences were reported, albeit in the expected directions.

Coupled with this finding is the fact that *there was a large discrepancy in how the judges rated the counselor's low level of empathic understanding during the two treatment checks and how the four clients rated her behavior.* This finding is in direct opposition to the data reported by Bozarth and Grace (1970) and Carkhuff and Burstein (1970), all of whom report either positive correlations or no significant differences between ratings of clients and judges on counselor facilitative behavior. On the other hand, these findings are consistent with Truax (1966) and Travers (1959), who found that not only are measures less meaningful when assessed subjectively, but they are also unable to control for the effects of immediate and unstable circumstances that confound the clients' responses. Possible explanations for this phenomena would include the unwillingness of the client to give low scores to her counselor and the fact that clients often come to counseling with a certain set of expectations, as previously noted, about counselor behavior and attitude. Similarly, the raters who were employed in the treatment check were a highly specialized group of individuals, well versed in counseling at the practitioner level. They underwent a rigorous training program, achieved high reliability, and then made their ratings. Three of the four clients had no counseling background (Subject 4 was a social worker) and no training in how to rate empathy, and were coming to counseling preoccupied with affect-oriented issues. Hence, lack of experience coupled with psychological interferences may have served as a confounding factor in their inability to identify these low levels of empathy.

Of equal importance is the fact that during the training, judges listened to only one client statement followed by one counselor response, whereas the clients listened to 2 consecutive minutes of dialogue. The nature of the difference in this procedure could have been sufficient enough to produce such wide variations. The question therefore arises as to whether valid comparisons can be made between heterogeneous groups on this dimension.

The final point of importance rests in the experimental design used in this study. Typically, the research discussed in Gladstein's reviews (1970, 1977) employed traditional group designs and analyzed data accordingly (Banks, 1972; Hountras & Anderson, 1969; Irwin, 1973/1974; Kratchowil et al., 1967). Similarly, the recent study by Morocco (1979b) followed these methods. Results were based primarily on statistically significant differences, allowing little discussion related to trends. With single-subject experimental research, one has a more clearly defined perspective on the effects of the independent variable manipulations (Glass et al., 1975; Kratchowil, 1978). Subtle changes often missed through the use of inferential statistics readily appear within this context. It seems as though the responsibility lies not with the design or data analysis procedures, but more with the instrumentation (i.e., the scales, in particular, used in this study). With only a 5-point variation allowance, the nuances inherent within subjects are unnoticed, hence results become obscure. To ameliorate this, scales providing more latitude for variation might be employed. Furthermore, as Feldstein and Gladstein (1980) pointed out, the use of several forms of instrumentation, both subjective (client report) and objective (judge report) are also recommended.

Conclusions and Limitations

These results lead to the following three conclusions:

1. High counselor-offered verbal-nonverbal empathic behavior influenced client responses on self-perceived levels of empathic understanding, depth of self-exploration, and satisfaction with the interview. These influences were most apparent and consistent when compared to counselor-offered low verbal-nonverbal empathy. This finding must be considered when reviews examining the importance of empathy in relation to in-counseling, client outcomes are quoted.
2. The single-subject experimental design afforded greater opportunity to study subtle trends in client behavior that might otherwise be unnoticed in using the more traditional group designs.

3. Judges rated counselor empathic behavior substantially different from clients when the counselor was operating in a low empathic condition.

Yet, certain design limitations must be considered. One is that the intervention effects could occur as a function of historical coincidence (Kratchowil, 1978). This problem could have been addressed by staggering the interventions. In addition, with such a limited sample, only trend data become available. As a result, the experimenter does not enjoy the same confidence of decreasing the effects due to chance as she or he would in using inferential statistics.

Another problem that directly affected the clients was fatigue. During the fourth session when the ratings were done, each client spent about 2½ hours scoring, with only a 10-minute break. The results may have been influenced by this time factor.

Finally, because there was no random selection of either counselor or clients, the differences found may have been due to individual behavior rather than treatment effect, thus decreasing the external validity of the results.

Given the limitations, the data at this point clearly indicate that the communication of high levels of empathy communicated through the verbal-nonverbal modality is perceived as such by clients, increases client self-exploration, and improves client satisfaction when compared with low empathy communicated through the same modalities. As a result, the importance of empathy in counseling has become better defined, giving support to its continued usage in counselor training programs.

Also, the use of the single-subject experimental design has proven fruitful. However, its use needs further refinement (i.e., effects due to history). The question of trend rather than statistical significance may be a more appropriate direction to pursue, given the status of the instrumentation at this point.

The combined effects of the verbal-nonverbal systems remain without question. Concerted effort must be taken in the training of counselors to ensure that their background is comprehensive and complete in verbal as well as in nonverbal communication. As a result, those who seek the services of helping professionals in this area stand to achieve potentially greater outcomes.

6
Counselor Empathy and Client Outcomes

GERALD A. GLADSTEIN

Chapter 5 describes a study in which verbal and nonverbal components were experimentally manipulated while also varying high and low counselor empathic behaviors. This chapter describes a study that was based on the same literature background and concerns, but that differed somewhat in design and methods. Whereas the former focused primarily on the communication modality, the latter emphasized an entirely natural counseling sequence, except for varying the empathy levels during each counseling session. In addition, this research sought to utilize five clients and five counselors compared to four clients and one counselor. Thus, the purpose was to determine whether manipulating different levels of counselor-offered empathy would be manifested in client behaviors during segments of sessions throughout the natural counseling process. The goal was to determine whether in vivo studies could be made of empathy while maintaining tight experimental controls.

Background and Hypotheses

As pointed out in Chapter 1, in the counseling literature, we still lack clear-cut evidence that empathy leads to positive counseling outcomes. Chapter 5 reports an experimental study that used a multiple-N and multiple-I single-subject design, combining verbal-nonverbal high empathic behaviors, which resulted in higher client self-exploration and satisfaction; the study also showed that low empathy did *not* result in lower self-exploration and satisfaction. However, as also pointed out in Chapter 5, one of that study's weaknesses is that only two counseling sessions were studied and that high and low empathic behaviors were not manipulated during each session.

Thus, while that study was a significant improvement over previous studies, its design fell short of being totally in vivo.

But why try to carry out a study in the real counseling world? The obvious answer is the more a study uses real counselors, clients, and the counseling process, the more the findings can be extrapolated beyond that one study. Clearly, if an experimental design can be used in such a setting, most experts agree that this would maximize internal and external validity.

However, in studying empathy, Stewart (1956) argued that approaching it with traditional scientific methods would destroy that which is being studied. That is, empathy involves a unique emotional relationship that entails goodwill and caring by both concerned parties. The presence of empathy is known only by the subjective reporting by the persons involved. Manipulation by the experimenter, Stewart stated, prevents the relationship from evolving. Hence, if counseling is studied in vivo, theoretically the type of study reported in Chapter 5 cannot be used.

Despite Stewart's position (but consistent with the point of view presented in Chapters 2–4), this study sought to use a completely real counseling setting and process, with the only exception of experimentally manipulating the counselor's empathic behaviors. The general hypothesis was that client behaviors would be a direct function of these counselors' differential empathic behaviors. The specific hypotheses were: (a) Client self-exploration will be higher during high-empathy segments than during low-empathy segments; (b) clients' perceptions of counselor effectiveness will be higher during high-empathy segments than during low-empathy segments; and (c) client-perceived satisfaction will be higher during high-empathy segments than during low-empathy segments.

Methodology

As noted above, this study used the same basic $N = 1$ approach as the one reported in Chapter 5. However, due to the differences in purpose, several important distinctions existed. First, five counselors each counseled one client. These were to be staggered in a time sequence so that experimental control could be demonstrated. Figure 6.1 illustrates the design. If this had been carried out, the segment patterns of beginning and ending high and low empathy and the resulting high and low client-dependent behaviors (self-exploration, perceived counselor effectiveness and satisfaction) would document the cause-and-effect connections.

A second difference concerned the counseling process itself. Although the same agency was used (University of Rochester Adult Counseling Center [URACC]), this time each client continued his or her natural sequence. It was assumed that this would range from 3 to 10 sessions, which was typical for URACC at that time. The goal was to have the counselors carry out their normal activities.

The third difference concerned the experimental treatment. Chapter 5's study involved three counseling sessions. The first session had the counselor in the neutral-empathy condition and was used as an

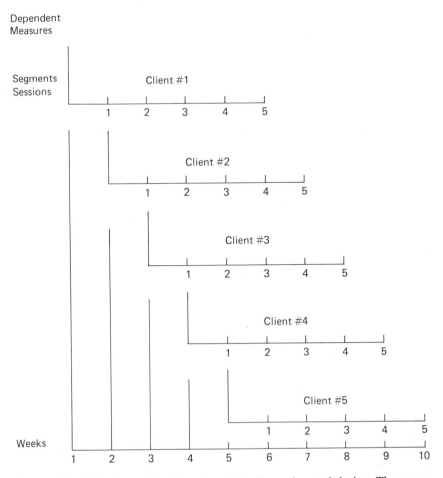

FIGURE 6.1. Original multiple-*N* and multiple-*I* experimental design. There were six segments each session: A, B, A, B, A, B (A = low empathy; B = high empathy). The number of sessions per client was expected to vary.

opportunity for the client to be desensitized to the scoring procedures. The second session had the counselor in the high-empathy condition but varied the verbal and nonverbal modalities from high to neutral empathy. The third session had the counselor in the low-empathy condition, but also varied the verbal and nonverbal modalities from low to neutral empathy. The fourth session did not involve experimental manipulation; it was used for data gathering.

By contrast, this study, as illustrated in Figure 6.1, divided each counseling session into 10-minute segments. The first was high, the second low, the third high, etc. This sequence began with the first session and continued to the end of the counseling sequence. Beyond this manipulation, each counselor carried out her or his usual activities.

The fourth difference concerned the counselors and clients. In order to maintain the in vivo conditions, males and females were included. By contrast, Chapter 5's study used only females for both. This decision, of course, added considerable variance, which in $N = 1$ small sample design can significantly affect the hypothesis testing.

The fifth difference concerned the counselors' training. As pointed out in Chapter 5, the one female counselor was given intensive training in offering high, neutral, low verbal, nonverbal, and verbal-nonverbal empathy. This was deemed crucial since the modalities were being manipulated. This training proved to be very successful, as evidenced by the very high interrater reliabilities and by the conditions check. By contrast, this study did not use such a prolonged and intensive training period. Because each counselor had already received general training in counseling (including skills in offering empathy), it was assumed that a brief, special training time was all that was needed. Furthermore, because there was no desire to have the counselor systematically vary the verbal and nonverbal modalities (rather, to combine them) while offering high or low empathy, it was assumed that a brief training period was all that was needed.

Sample

As noted above, five counselors each counseled one client. Two doctoral level (one male, one female) and three master's level (one male, two female) counselors volunteered for the study. All had been at URACC at least one semester.

The two male and three female clients were volunteers from the regular self-referred clientele. The first five clients who consented to participate were given monetary credit toward their regular fees. During the study, one client had three counseling sessions, three clients had four sessions, and one client had five sessions. In this sense, the study achieved its in vivo goal.

Independent Variable and Measures

The one independent variable was level of counselor-offered empathy. Two conditions were established: high or low. Two methods were used to determine the actual empathy levels achieved by the counselor. One utilized the client's perceptions of the counselor's general nonverbal behaviors, while the other used the client's perceptions of many different specific counselor behaviors.[1]

---

[1]In this chapter only these two client-based measures are described. However, in the larger study—from which this one evolved—judges' ratings of counselor offered empathy were also determined. These data will be reported in a subsequent publication.

Gladstein Nonverbal Empathy Scale. This scale was developed for this research project. Based on Carkhuff's (1969a, b) approach, and utilizing the findings from studies of counselor nonverbal behaviors (see Chapter 9 for a review of the literature), a 5-point Likert scale was created. (See Appendix for a copy of this scale.) As noted in Chapter 5, interrater reliability was .96 in one study. Its validity was partially established in that same study too. Table 5.3 documented its similarity to the Carkhuff Empathic Understanding measure, since the scores for the high-, neutral-, and low-empathy conditions between the two measures were extremely similar (high = 4.57 versus 4.57; neutral = 3.14 versus 3.42; low = 1.85 versus 2.14).

In this study, clients used the Gladstein Nonverbal Empathy Scale (GNES) after each counseling session. They viewed a 10-minute segment and then made a rating (1–5). For each session, there were six ratings. Because Segments 2, 4, and 6 were designed as the high-empathy conditions, it was expected that high GNES scores would occur for those segments. Similarly, Segments 1, 3, and 5 would receive low GNES scores.

Truax Relationship Questionnaire: Empathy Scale. This 45-item questionnaire was derived from the complete Relationship Questionnaire developed by Truax and reported in Truax and Carkhuff (1967). The 45 empathy items were selected and made up this scale. Truax, Altmann, and Millis (1974) used these items and referred to this as *accurate empathy.* However, because this title was also attached by Truax to his 9-point scale used to score audiotapes, in this chapter it is referred to as the TRQ:Empathy Scale.

Reliability and validity for the complete TRQ were discussed by Feldstein and Gladstein (1980). Although the TRQ has not been used extensively, the available evidence indicates that it has reasonable construct validity. It appears to measure cognitive empathy, but not affective empathy. Truax et al. showed that mental health professionals, lawyers, clergy, and general practitioners score somewhat higher than high-school and college/university faculty and much higher than nurses and manufacturing plant supervisors. Face validity seems fairly obvious in view of the item content. For example, Item 5 says: "S/he often misunderstands what I am trying to say." Item 10 is more subtle: "Sometimes s/he is so much 'with me', in my feelings, that I am not at all distracted by his/her presence." All items are answered by a true-false format. In this study, the client filled it out for each 10-minute segment after each counseling session.

By using both the GNES and the TRQ:Empathy Scale, it was assumed that the client's perceptions of the counselor's empathic global behaviors and his or her more specific behaviors would be tapped. This was a deliberate decision, based on the research findings that it is the client's perception that is most related to positive counseling outcomes (Barrett-Lennard, 1981; Gladstein, 1977).

Dependent Variables and Measures

The three dependent variables were counselor effectiveness, client satisfaction, and client self-exploration. As noted above, the evidence suggests that positive counseling outcomes occur when it is the *client's* perceptions of *both* the offered empathy and the outcomes themselves that are used as data (Barrett-Lennard, 1981). Therefore, client perceptions of counselor effectiveness and their own satisfaction were used as data. However, as noted by Feldstein and Gladstein (1980), externally judged data should be used too. In this study, this was obtained by having judges rate the client's degree of self-exploration as evidenced in the counseling session audiotapes. It was assumed that these three measures combined would give an accurate picture of the client's in-counseling outcomes. (See Chapter 8 for a discussion of the nature of in-counseling outcomes.)

Counselor Effectiveness Scale. This 25-item, semantic differential measure was created by Haase, Miller, Ivey, Morrill, and Normington, and reported by Ivey and Authier (1978). Their available research findings suggest that its reliability is low (.37 for seven undergraduates who rated a videotape). The authors caution about its use for other than immediate posttraining purposes, because of its sensitivity to changes in a client's environment. The validity data suggest that the Counselor Effectiveness Scale (CES) does easily discriminate between "good" and "bad" video-taped counselor models (means of 131 versus 66 for scale for #1) as rated by 18 undergraduates.

URACC Single-Session Reaction Form. The University of Rochester Adult Counseling Center Single-Session Reaction Form (URACC:SSRF) was created for this research project. This is a slight modification of the URACC Reaction Form developed in 1981. The latter uses a 5-point Likert scale system to measure the client's opinions of the service he or she received. The 10 items were created from the life span developmental model of counseling used in URACC. The items concern the counselor's behavior, the client's perceptions of his or her own changes, and the counseling process. While the entire URACC:RF is used to gather data after the completion of the entire counseling sequence, the URACC: SSRF was used in this study after each session. As with the other independent and dependent variable measures, the client filled it out after viewing each 10-minute segment of videotape. No reliability or validity data existed prior to this study. It was assumed that the client's scores represented his or her satisfaction with the counseling.

Helpee Self-Exploration in Interpersonal Processes: A Scale for Measurement. This Self-Exploration Scale (SE) was developed by Carkhuff (1969b) and was used in this study by external judges who reviewed audiotapes of the counseling sessions. After each 10-minute segment, the judge assigned a 1, 2, 3, 4, or 5 score by following the explicit definitions. (Reliability and validity for the SE Scale are discussed in Chapter 5.)

Procedures

Following the procedures described in Chapter 5, each client came for his or her counseling session. In this study, after each session he or she reviewed the videotape and filled out the measures for each 10-minute segment. During each session, the counselor varied the high- and low-empathy treatments as noted in Figure 6.1. Following the end of each client's last counseling session, debriefing was carried out.

Contrary to the study reported in Chapter 5, no in-process checks were made of the counselor's treatment procedures. It was assumed that, after training, the counselors were able to carry out the high- and low-empathy conditions. Data analysis was then performed.

Findings and Discussion

Treatment Check

As part of the data analysis, checks were made to see if the counselors had been able to establish the high- and low-empathy conditions. Unfortunately, the counselors were not able to do this. Using Truax's Relationship Questionnaire (TRQ:ES) as the main criterion, there were very few differences. Figure 6.2 illustrates this with Client 2. The fact that Segments 1, 3, and 5 were almost identical to Segments 2, 4, and 6, and that the low-empathy condition was perceived as slightly higher (Segment 5) at one point documents the problem.

Using the Gladstein Nonverbal Empathy Scale (GNES), a slightly more positive picture emerged. While the clients did perceive the high-empathy condition higher than the low-empathy condition, the differences were very slight. Figure 6.3 illustrates this with Client 2. Although the high-empathy scores are higher, all of the low segments (1, 3, and 5) are still above 3.0. This indicates that the client perceived the counselor as empathic (using Carkhuff's view that 3.0 or above is facilitative). Thus, the experimental manipulation was not successful.

Hypotheses Testing

In view of this finding, it was not possible to test the hypotheses. Instead, a case study approach was used in an effort to explore possible

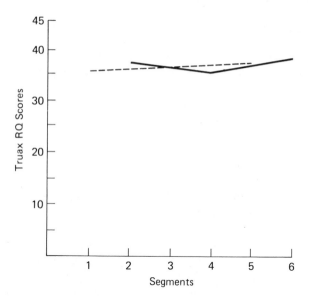

FIGURE 6.2. Mean Truax Relationship Questionnaire scores by segments for all sessions (Client 2). Segments 5 and 6 were in four sessions only. (— — — = low empathy; ——— = high empathy)

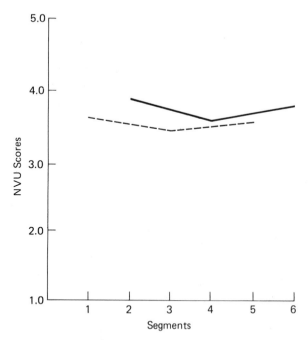

FIGURE 6.3. Mean Client 2 view of nonverbal understanding by segments for all sessions. Segment 4 was in four sessions only; Segment 5, two sessions only; Segment 6, three sessions only. (— — — = low empathy; ——— = high empathy)

relationships. Client 2 was selected, since she seemed to be typical of URACC clients. Her counselor was a master's level male with 2 years of counseling experience.

Case Study of Client 2

Figures 6.2 and 6.3 indicate that the counselor was unable to manipulate his high and low empathic behaviors. Figures 6.4 and 6.5 show that, overall, his level of empathy increased steadily from the first through fifth session. Anecdotal data from the counselor indicate that his concern for the client made it very difficult for him to deliberately carry out the low-empathy condition, even though he tried to do this. In effect, although in training he was able to display low empathy, in the real counseling situation he could not. Perhaps this illustrates what Stewart (1956) meant when he said that it is not possible to study empathy in the typical experimental way, since it will destroy the empathy. In this instance, the counselor chose (or unconsciously behaved) not to fulfill the research expectation with the result that the client perceived him as quite empathic.

Likewise, Figures 6.6 and 6.7 show that the client rated the counselor as very effective during all segments and all sessions. By the fourth session, she gave him a maximum score of 7 and none of the segments or sessions was lower than 5.6.

The URACC:SSRF data also show that the client was generally satisfied with her counseling experience. Figures 6.8 and 6.9 document an

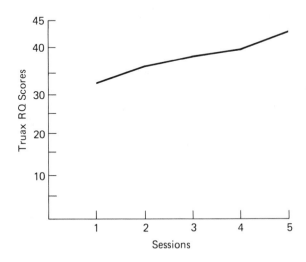

FIGURE 6.4. Mean Truax Relationship Questionnaire scores by sessions for all segments (Client 2). Session 4 had only four segments.

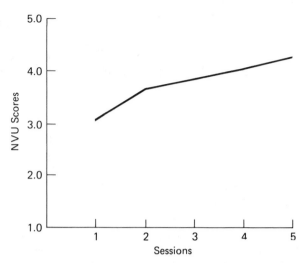

FIGURE 6.5. Mean Client 2 view of nonverbal understanding by sessions for all segments. Session 2 had only five segments; Session 4, four segments; Session 5, three segments.

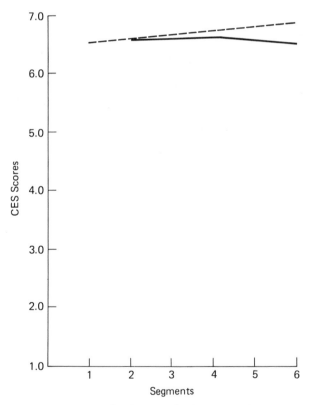

FIGURE 6.6 Mean Counselor Effectiveness Scale scores by segments for all sessions (Client 2). (— — — = low empathy; ——— = high empathy)

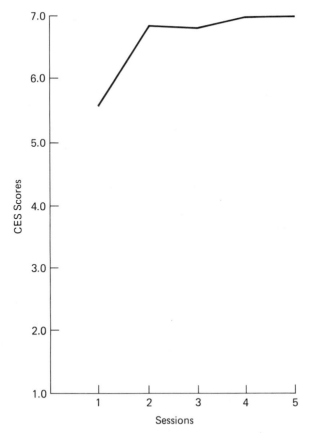

FIGURE 6.7. Mean Counselor Effectiveness Scale scores by sessions for all segments (Client 2).

average score of 3.5 (on a 1.0–5.0 scale) regardless of the high- or low-empathy segment and regardless of the specific session.

The client self-exploration data show the same consistency, but slightly lower scores. Figures 6.10 and 6.11 indicate essentially no differences in the high- and low-empathy segments (average 2.5 on a 1.0–5.0 scale) and across sessions.

Thus, although the client perceived the counselor as quite effective and empathic and was generally satisfied with the counseling, she was only moderately self-exploratory. This finding is somewhat surprising in view of theoretical expectations. Hence, although Barrett-Lennard (1981) has argued that client self-exploration should result when the client perceives the counselor as empathic, this did not occur to a great extent for this client.

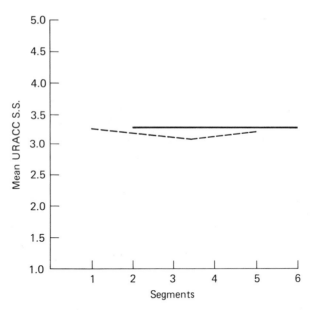

FIGURE 6.8. Mean URACC Single-Session Satisfaction score by segments for all sessions (Client 2). (— — — = low empathy; ——— = high empathy)

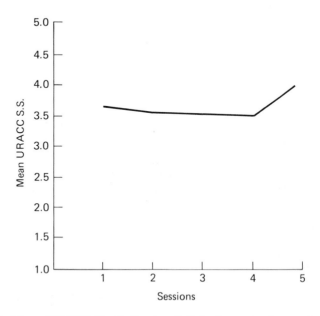

FIGURE 6.9. Mean URACC Single-Session Satisfaction score by sessions for all segments (Client 2).

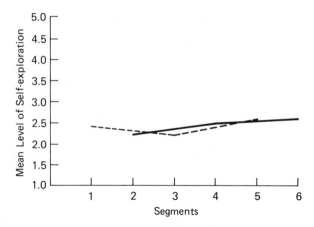

FIGURE 6.10. Mean level of self-exploration score by segments for all sessions (Client 2). (— — — — = low empathy; ———— = high empathy)

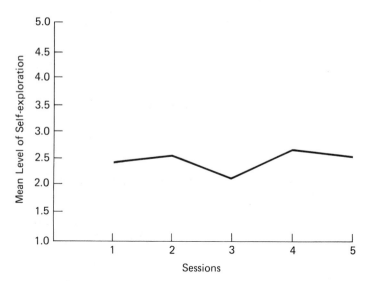

FIGURE 6.11. Mean level of self-exploration score by sessions for all segments (Client 2).

Conclusion and Implications

On one level this study was a failure: the counselors were unable to carry out the experimental treatment. They could not display low empathy during the predetermined counseling segments. This made it impossible to test the hypotheses. Yet, on another level this study achieved its goal.

As stated earlier, this goal was to find out whether in vivo studies could be made of empathy while maintaining tight experimental controls. At least for this project, the answer is no. The counselors became too involved with the clients and were unable to deliberately display low empathy.

This finding can be contrasted to the results in Chapter 5. In that study, one counselor was able to maintain the experimental conditions of high, neutral, and low empathy. However, this did not occur for the entire natural counseling process. The counselor knew that after Session 3 she would be able to carry on her usual activities. This expectation may have made it possible for her to maintain her "experimental self" until the study was completed.

Thus, some way must be found to make it possible for the counselor to maintain the experimental conditions during an otherwise entirely natural counseling process. Conceivably, as Stewart (1956) has argued, this is not possible. If so, researchers will have to be content with using either descriptive designs or experimental designs within an analogue model. In either case, this means that less than ideal methods will have to be accepted in studying empathy and counseling/psychotherapy outcomes.

7
Relationship of Counselor and Client Sex and Sex Role to Counselor Empathy and Client Self-Disclosure

JoAnn Feldstein

One of the significant controversies in current counseling theory and practice concerns the relationship of empathy to counseling outcome. Both theory (Rogers, 1975) and empirical research (Carkhuff, 1969a, b; Truax, 1966; Truax & Carkhuff, 1967) agree on the crucial role of empathy for therapeutic effectiveness. Advocates of this position view empathy as one of "the necessary and sufficient conditions for therapeutic personality change" (Rogers, 1957). Recent empirical and conceptual reviews of empathy and counseling outcome (Gladstein, 1970, 1977), however, have challenged this conclusion. According to Gladstein (1977), the empirical evidence regarding the positive relationship between empathy and counseling treatment remains equivocal.

Contemporary theorists, researchers, and practitioners, however, continue to emphasize the role of empathy in counseling. Specifically, the effect of counselor and client sex on empathy in a therapeutic relationship has received considerable attention. There have been many observations and suggestions that same-sex pairing, particularly with females, is desirable in counseling in order to provide the necessary conditions for personal growth (Carter, 1971; Chesler, 1972). Proponents of this position believe that men empathize better with men than they do with women and that a similar correspondence holds for women, because biological gender defines similarity in personality and experiences. The argument for shared experiences increasing empathy has intuitive appeal. For instance, gender-linked biological events can, of course, only be directly experienced by members of the same sex. Because only a woman experiences menstruation, pregnancy, rape, or mastectomy, only a woman can truly understand the feelings associated with these events.

Parts of this chapter are adapted from Feldstein, (1979). Effects of counselor sex and sex role and client sex on clients' perceptions and self-disclosure in a counseling analogue study. *Journal of Counseling Psychology, 26,* 439–443, Adapted with the permission of the American Psychological Association.

Recent results of research investigating the same-sex pairing in the counseling relationship, however, are inconsistent. Whereas several studies have indicated that same-sex pairing increases levels of empathy offered by counselors to clients (Daane & Schmidt, 1957; Hill, 1975), a study by Cartwright and Lerner (1963) found that experienced therapists with opposite-sex patients responded with the highest levels of empathic understanding. Further evidence has indicated that neither same-sex nor opposite-sex pairing is a predictor of levels of empathy offered by counselors (Breisinger, 1976; Feldstein, 1982; Petro & Hansen, 1977; Taylor, 1972).

Prevailing cultural stereotypes, in addition to advocating same-sex pairing to increase empathic understanding, also suggest that "being a counselor is more natural for a woman" (Carter, 1971, p. 297). Because role expectations for boys and girls differ in our society, girls are taught the expressive role—to be responsive to the needs and feelings of others (Hoffman, 1977)—and are expected to experience and express a wide range of feelings, while in contrast, boys are taught to perform an instrumental role in which they are rewarded for acquiring traits of mastery, problem solving, and emotional control. In other words, helping others at an emotional level is more often thought of as a feminine rather than masculine activity (Foushee, Davis, Archer, 1979), and females have traditionally been socialized to acquire expressive traits such as empathy. Whereas a substantial number of studies and literature reviews of developmental sex differences indicate that females are more empathic than males (Eisenberg-Berg & Mussen, 1978; Feshbach, 1978; Feshbach & Roe, 1968; Hoffman, 1977; Hoffman & Levine, 1976; Hogan, 1969; Jensen, Perry, Adams, & Gaynard, 1981), research findings also indicate that maternal child-rearing practices are related to empathy for males. (See Dolan [1983] for a discussion of this point and some evidence contrary to this general finding.) Warm, sympathetic mothers produce highly empathic sons (Eisenberg-Berg & Mussen, 1978).

The results of research examining counselor sex differences in levels of offered empathy do not support the conclusion that female counselors are more empathic than male counselors. Although female counselors were found to be more empathic than male counselors in several studies (Abramowitz, Abramowitz, & Weitz, 1976; Hill, Tanney, Leonard, & Reiss, 1977; Rappaport, 1975), a greater number of studies indicate no differences in levels of empathy offered by male and female counselors (Breisinger, 1976; Feldstein, 1982; Hill, 1975; Petro & Hansen, 1977; Taylor, 1972). This raises two interesting questions. First, do differences exist between males who select counseling as a profession and males in general? Second, is counselor training successful in eliminating the early developmental differences in empathy generally found between males and females?

Perhaps a possible explanation for the inconsistent research findings regarding developmental sex differences in empathy and the lack of evidence for counselor sex differences in empathy concerns the omission of counselor and/or client sex-role identity. This may be a serious omission because, although most individuals learn behavior characteristics of their sex by means of social reinforcement and learning-modeled behaviors (Williams, 1977), individuals may also learn behaviors that deviate from the sex-role stereotypes of society (Bem, 1974; Eisenberg-Berg & Mussen, 1978). As previously discussed, maternal child-rearing practices are related to the development of empathy in males (Eisenberg-Berg & Mussen, 1978). More specifically, in addition to feminine women and masculine men, there are masculine women and feminine men. Consequently, it seems germane to question whether it is biological gender or sex-role identity that is critical to empathic understanding in the counseling relationship.

Purpose and Hypothesis

Therefore, the overall purpose of this study was to determine the effects of counselor sex and sex role and client sex on the counseling relationship. There were three specific objectives that followed from this overall purpose. First, the effect of client sex on client perception of counselor empathy was examined. The second objective was to investigate the effects of counselor sex and sex-role identity on client perception of counselor empathy. The third objective was to investigate the effects of counselor sex and sex-role identity on the frequency of client affective and nonaffective self-references.

The general hypothesis of the study was that there would be no significant main effects, but there would be significant interactions of subject sex and counselor sex and sex role on clients' perceptions of the counselor's empathy and on client self-disclosure during the interview.

Methodology

The laboratory analogue methodology was employed in conducting this study. This has been defined by Cowen (1961, p. 9) as "controlled laboratory situation involving two or more people, in which the behavior of the one person is designed along some relevant dimension to simulate that of a psychotherapist."

It was believed that the effect of counselor and client sex on empathy could best be studied by this methodology for the following reasons. The analogue format provided greater control over situational variables that might have obscured the treatment effects. In addition, it allowed for the manipulation of subject sex, counselor sex, and counselor sex-role identity. The necessity for control over the interview situation and the manipulation of the independent variables in order to study more clearly client perceptions of counselor empathy supported the use of the analogue design. The inconsistency of the research in this area, as pointed out in the review of the literature, may be related to idiosyncratic behavior of either counselors or clients rather than actual differences due to sex.

Subjects

The subjects were 35 male and 39 female undergraduate students enrolled in an introductory psychology course at a moderate-size private eastern university. The students received course credit for participating in research.

The four experienced counselors, two male and two female, were in their mid-twenties. They all had recently completed a master's program in counseling at a public institution that included supervised practicum experience with college students.

Experimental Treatment

The experimental treatment in this study was manipulation of counselor sex and sex role. Therefore, each male and female counselor was trained to role play both a masculine and a feminine counseling role. The counselor roles varied in three ways: (a) Counseling interventions of the masculine sex-typed counselor were more action oriented (e.g., use of confrontation), whereas the feminine sex-typed counselor employed more responsive interventions (e.g., reflection of feeling). (b) The affect of the feminine sex-typed counselor was warm, supportive, and emotional, and the affect of the masculine sex-typed counselor was cognitive, assertive, and controlled (Bem, 1974). (c) The nonverbal behavior of the feminine sex-typed counselor included a softer voice, more smiling, more body lean, and more head nods than the masculine sex-typed counselor, whereas the nonverbal behavior of the masculine sex-typed counselor included a louder voice, more postural relaxation, and more shifts in leg movements (Wiggers, 1978).

The 10 hours of counselor training, based on written descriptions of counselor roles, included videotaped demonstrations of desired counselor behavior and critiques of the audiotaped role plays of the counselors with a simulated client. The investigator attempted to anticipate the kinds of client behaviors and problems the counselors might meet and prepared them for as many contingencies as were possible in the role-play situation.

Each counselor was videotaped interviewing simulated clients of each sex in both experimental roles. The videotapes were shown to a group of 10 judges (graduate students in a research seminar and blind to the purpose of the study) to check for counselor effect. The judges rated each counselor in both roles on 5-point Likert-type scales for physical attractiveness, genuineness, empathy, and clarity of expression. In addition to verifying the quality and accuracy of the counselors' portrayal of the two roles, the judges also rated each counselor on masculine and feminine sex-role identity.

Results of the analysis indicated that there were no differences between the two roles played by each of the counselors, nor were there any differences in the roles played by the four counselors for the criteria of physical attractiveness, genuineness, empathy, and clarity of expression. The results also indicated that one of the specified criteria for sex-role identity was not satisfied. Therefore, further training emphasizing role differences was deemed necessary.

Retraining of the counselors was accomplished in 3 hours, using training methods similar to those described previously. Videotapes of each counselor role playing both the feminine and masculine roles were then rated, using the established criteria by a male graduate student (blind to the purpose of the study) and the investigator. Because the first check established the major differences between the two roles and failed to indicate a counselor effect, the second check, a clarification of one criterion, was less rigorous than the first. The results of the second counselor check indicated that the ratings of the two judges were reliable and that the specified criteria for differences between the masculine and feminine roles were met.

Procedure

Stratified by sex, subjects were randomly assigned to one of four treatment conditions: (a) masculine male counselor, (b) masculine female counselor, (c) feminine male counselor, and (d) feminine female counselor. The random assignment of subjects, however, was constrained by the predetermined counterbalanced order of the counselors' sex-role portrayal. When the subjects arrived for the "counseling" interview, they were told that the purpose of the study was to examine counselor functioning in the initial interview. The subjects were also informed that they would have the opportunity to talk about themselves and that they should disclose as much as they felt comfortable with on any subject that related to how they felt about themselves.

The 20-minute interviews were audiotaped and observed. A male graduate student assessed the clients' involvement in the counseling session and monitored the counselors' sex-role portrayal. Ten interviews were eliminated during the data collection when it was determined that either the subject or counselor was not performing within the framework of the guidelines of the study. For each eliminated subject, another subject was interviewed, until there was a total of 64 interviews included in the study. At the end of the interview, the subjects completed the entire Barrett-Lennard Relationship Inventory (1962) (Form OS-M-64) (Barrett-Lennard, 1964).

Four graduate students, who were randomly selected from a pool of graduate students who volunteered to participate in the study, rated the audiotaped interviews for frequency of client affective and nonaffective self-references. The raters received 10 hours of training, rating subject self-references on audiotapes that were made for but not used in the study. Each audiotape was divided into 20 1-minute segments. For each segment, raters counted the number of positive and negative affective and nonaffective self-references. Counts were compared and discussed after each segment, and questions were resolved by referring to a comprehensive list of affective words. Interrater reliability was assessed by the method of analysis of variance suggested by Winer (1971). Interrater reliabilities computed at the end of training were as follows: positive affective, .91; negative affective, .95; and nonaffective self-references, .91. Therefore, each rater was randomly assigned 16 subject interviews to rate independently. Interrater reliabilities computed at the end of the rating process were as follows: positive affective, .86; negative affective, 1.00; and nonaffective self-references, .81.

Dependent Measures

Barrett-Lennard Relationship Inventory. The Barrett-Lennard Relationship Inventory (BLRI) (1962) was used to measure empathy. It was completed by the client after the counseling interview. It is based on the premise that "the client's experience of his/her therapist's response is the primary locus for therapeutic influence on the relationship" (p. 2). In place of the original 6-point rating scale, a true-false response format (Form OS-M-64) was administered to the subjects in this study. The revised format was less complicated to use in a one-interview-only situation (Giannandrea & Murphy, 1973; Mann & Murphy, 1975). (See Chapter 9 for a more complete discussion of this measure.)

Client Self-Reference Statements. Frequency counts were made of two possible subject response modes: (a) Affective self-references were all statements (regardless of length) made by the subject that began with "I" and included at least one specific feeling word in reference to self. Examples included such expressions as "I'm happy," "I am upset," or "I feel ... " (followed by any word). (b) Nonaffective self-reference statements were all sentences that began with "I" and referred to the individual personally. Examples included such expressions as "I went shopping." In addition, the affective self-references were classified into separate positive and negative affective categories. A positive affective response was defined as any comment in which feelings of love, happiness, liking, enjoyment, pleasurable excitement, warmth, and desire were expressed. A negative affective self-reference was coded when feelings of anger, fear, despondency, hatred, dislike, despair, and loneliness were present (Merbaum, 1963). The scoring criteria used were similar to those of Salzinger and Pisoni (1958, 1960) and Janofsky (1971).

Interjudge reliability for this method of frequency counts has been reported in three studies. Salzinger and Pisoni (1960) reported a range from .79 to 1.00, Merbaum (1963) estimated coefficients ranging from .93 to .85, and Janofsky (1971) reported a reliability coefficient of .99. The reliability of all three studies was based on the Pearson product moment correlation.

Data Analysis

In order to test the hypotheses and to determine whether client sex and counselor sex and sex role were systematically related to client perceptions of counselor empathy and client self-disclosure, a 2 (sex of counselor) × 2 (sex role of counselor) × 2 (sex of client) factorial analysis with equal cell sizes was performed for each of the dependent variables: (a) counselor empathy, (b) positive affective self-references, (c) negative affective self-references, and (d) nonaffective self-references generated by subjects.

Results

The results of the analysis of variance indicate no significant main effects or interactions for the dependent measure of empathy. Table 7.1 gives the specific details.

A Counselor Sex × Counselor Sex Role × Client Sex interaction was, however, obtained for subject nonaffective self-disclosure. Table 7.2 displays these data and shows $F(1,56) = 4.43$, $p < .05$. As indicated in

TABLE 7.1. Summary of analysis of variance for counselor sex, counselor sex role, and client sex on counselor empathy.

Source	SS	df	MS	F
A (Counselor sex)	1.27	1,56	1.27	.11
B (Counselor role)	.39	1,56	.39	.23
C (Client sex)	13.14	1,56	13.14	1.11
A × B	.14	1,56	.14	.01
A × C	.39	1,56	.39	.03
B × C	13.14	1,56	13.14	1.11
A × B × C	4.52	1,56	4.52	.38
Error	660.38		11.79	

TABLE 7.2. Summary of analysis of variance for counselor sex, counselor sex role, and client sex on clients' nonaffective statements.

Source	SS	df	MS	F
A (Counselor sex)	203.06	1,56	203.06	.21
B (Counselor role)	2209.00	1,56	2209.00	2.30
C (Client sex)	64.00	1,56	64.00	.07
A × B	1580.06	1,56	1580.06	1.65
A × C	.63	1,56	.63	.00
B × C	6.25	1,56	6.25	.01
A × B × C	42.57	1,56	4257.56	4.43*
Error	53801.75		960.75	

*$p < .05$.

Table 7.3, males talked most about themselves with feminine female counselors and least about themselves with masculine female counselors. Females disclosed most about themselves to feminine male counselors and least about themselves to masculine male counselors. No other main effects or interactions approached significance.

TABLE 7.3. Means and standard deviations by subject sex, counselor sex, and counselor sex role.

	Masculine sex role				Feminine sex role			
	Male counselors		Female counselors		Male counselors		Female counselors	
Dependent variables	M	SD	M	SD	M	SD	M	SD
Male subjects								
Empathy	11.62	2.97	11.62	3.42	13.12	2.03	12.25	3.41
Positive affective self-references	10.87	6.96	4.88	4.29	5.75	2.71	5.88	3.72
Negative affective self-references	5.75	4.53	3.38	2.72	7.00	5.07	8.00	6.53
Nonaffective self-references	108.10	33.59	78.37	23.79	94.25	34.99	117.00	54.38
Female subjects								
Empathy	12.00	2.39	11.25	2.96	10.62	3.93	11.12	5.30
Positive affective self-references	11.12	8.56	7.50	5.21	8.63	3.70	9.50	6.68
Negative affective self-references	5.38	1.69	7.25	4.65	7.88	3.91	6.63	3.34
Nonaffective self-references	90.50	20.11	93.25	19.14	108.00	19.94	98.00	25.34

Note. All $n = 8$.

Discussion

This study provides empirical data concerning the effect of counselor sex and sex role and client sex on empathy in the counseling relationship. The findings of this study do not support the prevailing sex-role stereotypes. Although some theorists have suggested that females are better equipped as helpers because they have been raised to be more empathic than males (Carter, 1971), the results of this study indicate that clients perceived no differences in empathic understanding of male and female counselors or in feminine and masculine counselors, regardless of sex. These results, although consistent with the results of several other studies that indicate no differences in levels of empathy offered by male and female counselors (Breisinger, 1976; Feldstein, 1982; Hill, 1975; Petro & Hansen, 1977; Stengel, 1976; Taylor 1972), are inconsistent with those studies that indicate that female counselors are more empathic than male counselors (Abramowitz et al., 1976; Hill et al., 1977; Rappoport, 1975). Because no studies have indicated that male counselors are more empathic than female counselors, Carter (1971) may be partially correct when she suggests that "because role expectations for boys and girls in our society differ, being a therapist is more natural for a woman" (p. 297). Indeed, empathy may be valued and rewarded in women. However, the results of this study indicate that male counselors can be trained to behave in a feminine and empathic manner. Consequently, the assumption of counselor educators that effective counselors can be trained is supported by the findings of the present study. (However, see Chapters 8, 9, and 10 for data and discussions of the possible limits of this training.)

The present study also attempted to provide empirical data concerning the theory that same-sex pairing assures empathic understanding between counselor and client. The findings of this study do not support this theory. These results are consistent with the results of several other studies that indicate that neither same-sex nor opposite-sex pairing has an effect on levels of empathy offered by counselors (Breisinger, 1976; Petro & Hansen, 1977; Taylor, 1972) or perceived by clients (Feldstein, 1982; Hoffman, 1977a, 1977b). Contradictory results of several other studies indicate that same-sex pairing increases levels of empathy offered by counselors to clients (Daane & Schmidt, 1957; Hill, 1974). The major difference between those studies that indicate that same-sex or opposite-sex pairing has an effect on levels of empathy and those that indicate that it does not appears to be a methodological one. When counselor or client behavior was controlled by either method of presentation (e.g., video- or audiotapes of counselor training), neither same-sex nor opposite-sex pairing had a significant effect. It was only when counselor or client behavior was not controlled that same-sex pairing had an effect. The implication of this finding for the more naturalistic settings in which sex pairing was effective is that counselor and/or client behavior probably varied with the sex and/or other characteristics of the participants. Indeed, empirical data to support this speculation have been provided by several other studies unrelated to empathy (Gross, Herbert, Knotterud, & Donner, 1969; Parker, 1967; Rice, 1969) of the counseling relationship. Consequently, successful counselor-client pairing appears complex. It does not appear to be a simple matter of sex pairing. (Chapter 10 also discusses this complexity.)

The third finding of this study indicates that counselor sex and sex role and client sex affect the frequency of clients' nonaffective self-disclosure. Males disclosed most with feminine female counselors and disclosed least with masculine female counselors. Females, in contrast, disclosed most to feminine male counselors and disclosed least to masculine male counselors. The finding that counselor sex and sex role affected client self-references was replicated in a later study by Feldstein (1982) in which all clients disclosed most to feminine counselors. The finding that clients disclosed most to feminine counselors in these two studies appears to be related to role expectations of counselors; counselors are expected to be warm, supportive, and reflective listeners. Client preferences of counselor sex, in the present study however, suggest the effects of sex-role expectations of clients. The finding that male clients disclosed most to feminine female counselors appears to be related to role expectations of females; females are expected to be nurturant, succorant, and understanding listeners (Greenberg & Zeldon, 1980). Male clients disclosed least to female counselors whose masculine behavior was inconsistent with the feminine stereotype. The high self-disclosure of females to feminine males may suggest a continuation by females to devalue their own sex as they continue to invest males with greater status than members of their own sex (Johnson, 1978). However, the low self-disclosure to masculine male counselors by females seems to suggest some frustration with the prevailing sex-role stereotypes.

Contrary to expectation, the results of this study do not indicate significant interaction effects for subjects' affective self-disclosure. Given that the feminine role in this study was designed to elicit subjects' feelings, it is particularly surprising that this did not occur. It may be that subjects do not vary in their initial levels of affective self-disclosure or that a 20-minute analogue interview is insufficient to assess differences in affective self-disclosure that appear over time.

An alternative explanation of the findings concerns the limitations of this study. Clients seeking help, in contrast to the subjects of this study, would usually enter counseling with specific problems. Their involvement and commitment to counseling would therefore probably be different from that of this study's psychology undergraduates who mainly discussed educational/vocational concerns. Surprisingly, however, findings of the later analogue study (Feldstein, 1982) with undergraduates indicated that client affective self-references were affected by counselor sex role and client presenting problem. Vocational clients with feminine counselors made the most intimate self-references, while vocational clients with masculine counselors made the least intimate self-references. In contrast, the effect of counselor sex role on intimacy of self-references for the personal/social concern was minimal. In both studies, it is interesting to note that, although there were differences in client self-disclosure, clients did not perceive differences in levels of empathy offered by counselors.

Finally, the results of this study, particularly those related to the effects of counselor and client sex and sex pairing on empathy, are limited by the selection of the BLRI as the only measure of empathy. Feldstein and Gladstein (1980) suggested that different types of measurement assess different aspects of the empathic process. Although the BLRI is a good general indicator of the counselor's empathic understanding, it fails to assess the counselor's affective state. (See Chapter 9 for an elaboration of this point.) Consequently, it is recommended that further studies examining the relationship of counselor and client sex and sex role and empathy use several measures of empathy to assess the different aspects of the empathic process.

8
Issues and Methods of Counselor Empathy Training

GERALD A. GLADSTEIN

As indicated in the conclusion of Chapter 1 (and documented by the studies reported in Chapters 3-7), it is extremely difficult to determine what part empathy actually plays in influencing counseling outcomes. In fact, due to empathy's multidimensions (see Chapter 1 and Gladstein [1984] for the early theorists' views and Chapter 2 for empirical evidence), it should be expected to have several parts in this process.

Likewise, in considering counselor empathy training, one needs to think about this complexity, rather than about empathy as a unitary phenomenon. Another consideration is how empathy evolves or is learned in childhood. After all, counselors are not suddenly adults without prior empathic development. These early life experiences would probably have some effect on any attempts at training. Therefore, this chapter first looks at empathy training within the broad perspective presented earlier in this book. Then, a successful training program is described. Lastly, a proposal for a unique method of increasing affective empathy is presented.

Issues Concerning Counselor Empathy Training

A multidimensional, multistage model of empathy is presented in Chapter 1. It can involve emotional contagion, identification, and role taking. It typically involves an emotional stage first, followed by some type of cognitive activity. As an interpersonal process involving a helper (counselor or therapist) and client, the sequence includes communication between the two.

Given the model, issues exist that need to be addressed if one is to gain some understanding of methods that might be used in counselor empathy training. (This statement assumes empathy can be trained. Later, it is shown that this premise may not be legitimate.) The rest of this section seeks to shed some light on these issues. The issues involve the following questions:

1. Can empathy be learned (and taught) or does it evolve as a function of normal developmental stages or maturation?
2. If it can be learned (and taught), is it the same for affective (emotional contagion, identification), cognitive (role taking), and combined affective-cognitive?
3. What variables affect this learning? What person, environmental, and/or person-environmental interaction variables are involved?
4. What experiential, modeling, and direct teaching and training approaches result in increased affective, cognitive, and/or affective-cognitive empathy?
5. Are these experiential, modeling, and/or teaching and training results a function of the recipient's age and/or sex?
6. What empirical evidence exists regarding whether helpers can increase their affective, cognitive, or affective-cognitive empathy?

Learning to Be Empathic

Childhood and Adolescence

In Chapter 1, the early theorists' views about empathic development are briefly presented and summarized. (For a somewhat longer summary of similar views, see Goldstein and Michaels [1985].) Essentially, the very young infant is capable of responding with affective empathy (usually referred to as emotional contagion), but that cognitive empathy does not occur until about 7–8 years of age. In Piagetian terms, the ego-centered child becomes decentered and able to take on the role of the other. By adolescence, the typical boy or girl has adultlike cognitive empathic abilities.

Whether these empathic changes occur due to maturation and/or learning is not clear from the early theorists. Sociologists like Mead (1934) argued that imitation and practicing role behaviors lead to increased role-taking abilities. On the other hand, Allport (1924) stated that early life conditioning makes it possible for affective empathy to occur.

In a recent publication, Bergman and Wilson (1984), reasoning from a psychoanalytic perspective, have discussed the crucial effect that the mother can have on the child's empathic capabilities. In the earliest days and weeks of life, the mother, in response to the infant's needs, initiates an empathic relationship that makes it possible for the child to be empathic. This symbiotic relationship evolves into individuation, whereby the child can, in turn, be empathic with others.

However, the literature suggests other possible explanations as to how the child becomes empathic. Several recent studies have attempted to identify variables that might produce affective-empathic children and adolescents. Feshbach (1978) reported a study of 48 pairs of mothers and fathers and their 6–8-year-old children. The parents completed question-naires concerned with child-rearing practices and their general attitudes and values toward children. The children's affective empathy scores had been obtained in two earlier studies. The data indicated that, for boys, there was only one (out of 12 possible correlates) significant correlation with the fathers' child-rearing factors: father's emphasis on competition was associated with low empathy. For the girls, there were three significant correlations with the mothers' practices (but none with the fathers'). "Thus, empathy in girls is negatively correlated with maternal conflict and rejection, with maternal punitiveness and overcontrol, and positively associated with maternal tolerance and permissiveness" (Fesh-bach, 1978, p. 36).

Apparently, these boys' and girls' affective empathy scores were differentially related to their parents' child-rearing attitudes and be-haviors. However, because this study was correlational, and not either experimental or prospective in design, caution must be used in assigning cause-and-effect connections. Nevertheless, we can speculate that how the mother raises her daughter will affect the latter's affective empathy.

Roe (1980), using the same empathy measure as Feshbach (1978) did in the above study, also attempted to identify antecedent parental behaviors. In this case, Roe studied power assertion through interviews with 42 (21 male and 21 female) of the children from whom she had obtained empathy data 3 years earlier. She identified 8 boys and 13 girls as "high empathy" and 13 boys and 8 girls as "low empathy" and analyzed their responses to the interview questions. She found "a significant relation-ship between low empathy and the subjects' reports of fear of punish-ment" (p. 993).

Yet, the relationship was more complex than it first seemed. Roe pointed out that these Greek island children grew up in an environment where mothers and fathers tended to use punishment, including spank-ing, as part of their normal child-rearing practices. However, the fathers tended to be emotionally distant from their children, while the mothers tended to be very close emotionally with them. Roe speculated that ". . . if a child has a strong prior positive relationship (bonding) with a parent, the effect of occasional use of physical punishment or power assertion by that parent will not be a major impediment to the child's empathic development" (p. 994).

As Roe appropriately pointed out, due to the design of her study, we cannot attribute causal connections. Yet, if we combine Feshbach's (1978) and Roe's (1980) findings, it appears that mothers' child-rearing practices are related to their daughters' empathy levels. Similar findings came out of a retrospective study by Barnett, Howard, King, and Dino (1980). In this instance, 72 college students, who were divided into low- and high-empathy groups based on the Mehrabian and Epstein (1972) Affective Empathy Scale, filled out a questionnaire 2 months after completing the empathy measure. Again, mothers were reported as having more impact than fathers. Furthermore, high-empathy daughters, more than sons, indicated that their mothers had discussed feelings with them and that their parents had been more affectionate. Both the daughters and sons who scored high in affective empathy rated their parents as more empathic than those who scored low in empathy.

Although this study also suffers from its retrospective design, its consistency with earlier findings suggests the importance of mothers to empathy development. While it is possible that all of these results are due to cultural stereotypes (i.e., children and adolescents report what they learned are appropriate expectations about parents), it is also possible that these connections actually exist. If so, this would suggest that as these adolescents mature into adults and enter counselor graduate training programs, their prior experiences and learnings will have an effect on attempts to increase their empathic behaviors. In fact, it would be expected that their affective and cognitive empathic abilities would be differentially influenced by these training programs.

Overview of Counselor Training Approaches

As is noted earlier in this book (see Chapters 1, 2, and 3–7), counselor training programs invariably assume that empathy is important to effective counseling and that empathy training should be included in graduate courses. As a result, considerable literature exists. For example, Ford (1979) critiqued much of this literature as part of his comprehensive review concerning research on training counselors. Methods of teaching empathy have been developed and tried out as part of research studies. Some have evolved and been put into practice without empirical verification. Because Brennan (Chapter 9) and MacKrell (Chapter 10) review much of this literature, only the major approaches and some of the frequently used specific methods are identified and highlighted in this chapter.

As Brennan (Chapter 9) indicates, studies of counselor empathy training are of two basic kinds: brief analogues and extended packaged programs. The former usually use artificial or simulated empathy measures, such as written statements by the trainees in response to written, audio, or video client statements. Brief analogues also typically have very specific behaviors, such as physical attending, taught. While multiple training techniques may be used, employing only one technique is quite common.

Extended package programs such as Carkhuff's (1980) Human Relations Training (HRT), Ivey and Authier's (1978) microcounseling (MC), and Kagan's (1975) Interpersonal Process Recall (IPR) usually involve multiple methods, including modeling, didactic instruction, feedback, and experiential exerises (Ford, 1979). These programs also rarely are shorter than 8 hours and run as long as 100 hours. Furthermore, training involves other dimensions (such as genuineness and positive regard) as well as empathy. Artificial client stimuli may be used, but real counseling sessions are equally included.

Regardless of whether brief analogues or extended packages are utilized, as noted above, four types of techniques are typically employed. *Modeling* exists in live, video, and audio presentations. Usually, people similar to the trainees are used to illustrate empathic behaviors. *Didactic instruction* can include lectures, readings, and other media for presenting information. Usually the content centers on Rogers' (1975) views of empathy, why empathy is important during counseling, and various ways of responding empathically to clients. *Feedback* provides a means for the trainee to see or hear (or both) himself or herself while attempting to be empathic. It is common for video- and audiotapes to be used for this purpose. They are typically accompanied by explicit statements by the instructor regarding the trainee's accuracy. *Experiential exercises* can refer to practicing empathic behaviors (usually followed by feedback) or to activities designed to increase the trainee's awareness of self. The latter include "tuning in" to one's own feelings so that there can be greater awareness of what these feelings are when expressed by clients.

Although this empathy training literature is extensive, and despite the innovative techniques created, there are very few well-established facts (Ford, 1979). However, thus far it appears that, in experimental analogue research using brief empathy training, modeling, role playing, and feedback techniques in combination produce initial levels of empathic skills. However, as Brennan (1979) stated, facilitative levels are typically not reached. This means that counselors-in-training usually score below 3 on a 5-point empathy scale such as Carkhuff's Empathic Understanding Scale. Ford (1979, p. 111) also noted this point and went on to say, "... there is no evidence that any one is capable of instilling sufficient cognitive, interpersonal, or technical therapist skills [including empathy] in trainees to guarantee that the trainees are (or can be) *effective* therapists."

In essence, the empirical evidence does not demonstrate that trainees can learn to be empathic to a level that will lead to effective counseling. In view of the earlier discussion, this conclusion should not be surprising. As suggested there, empathy's multifacets and stages make such a linear expectation unlikely.

Despite this conclusion, we have come a long way in creating training methods that appear to be helpful some of the time. In the following section, a training method is described that did prove to be fruitful in one study. Perhaps further testing of this program will demonstrate its usefulness in other settings.

Successful Empathy Training Program

In Chapter 5, a single-subject design study is presented that experimentally manipulated counselor empathy and communication modalities. The training procedures are only briefly described. This section contains detailed information regarding the various components and comments on why this program was successful.[1]

As indicated in Chapter 5, the goal was to train a counselor working in a counseling agency to offer low, neutral, and high empathic behaviors in three modalities: verbal, nonverbal, and verbal-nonverbal. She was required to change both the levels and modalities on command. The treatment checks showed that she was able to do this after training and during her sessions with four female adult clients seeking vocational counseling at the University of Rochester Adult Counseling Center. The counselor carried out other aspects of her counseling in her typical manner.

Why was the training successful? It was a result of combining several specific techniques in an order that led to maximum learning. *First, didactic instruction explained each condition that she was to portray.* The trainer used the *Counselor Training Manual* and went over each condition carefully with the counselor as she read the definitions. The *Manual* is reproduced here for the reader's convenience.

Counselor Training Manual

This training manual is designed especially for counselors who will take part in projects which deal with the manipulation of counselor offered verbal, nonverbal, and verbal/nonverbal, high or low empathic conditions. The verbal and nonverbal behaviors that appear in this manual are taken from the findings of researchers who work primarily in the areas of counseling and psychotherapy outcome.

I. The following compilation of behaviors along with their respective definitions shall be considered to be those which appear most frequently in the literature as communicating high levels of empathy. These behaviors, along with certain combinations of such, will be delineated.

1. 0° *Body Orientation*— This simply means that the counselor is sitting comfortably near the client and directly facing him/her.

2. *Eye Contact*— Eye contact may be defined as maintaining a comfortable gaze, eye-to-eye with the client. The counselor's eyelids should be relaxed and blinking should occur at natural intervals. It is important to avoid staring, glancing, or giving critical, cold eye responses.

---

[1]This material is based upon Morocco's (1981) dissertation, as noted in Chapter 5.

3. *Leaning Forward*— Here, the counselor while maintaining a 0° body orientation toward the client, leans forward about 45°. This leaning into the client's "space" should be done by maintaining a comfortable distance. Leaning too far forward into the client's personal space may be perceived as an intrusion which could produce counterproductive effects.

4. *Smiling*— Smiling has been found by some to be the single most effective behavior to communicate warmth. This may be done by a "soft" smile with eyebrows slightly raised and a slight cocking of the head. Again, it is important to emphasize the naturalness of eliciting this response. Exaggerated mouth and/or eye behavior may be perceived negatively.

5. *Affirmative Head Nodding*— In this instance, the counselor simply raises and lowers his/her head about 3 to 5 inches. This should be done with a smooth, flowing movement and at a comfortable pace. The message to be communicated here is understanding, not necessarily agreement.

6. *Arm Positions*— Arms may be left in almost any comfortable position, or in motion. Folding the arms and placing them on the chest should be avoided because this usually communicates a certain amount of defensiveness.

7. *Leg Positions*— Again, most comfortable positions would be appropriate. If one feels the need to cross his or her legs, it should be done knee to knee as opposed to ankle to knee. The latter condition creates a psychological distance and barrier between the client and the counselor. It should therefore be avoided.

8. *Combinations*— Each of the behaviors defined above has been shown to communicate a certain amount of empathy. Some behaviors are considered more potent than others. It is highly recommended that the counselor engage in many combinations of these different behaviors to communicate maximally, a high nonverbal empathic condition.

9. *Frequency of Occurrence*— A critical balance in the time allowed between eliciting these nonverbal behaviors will need to be established. Within certain limits, the counselor's personal comfort zone will be taken into consideration. The optimal frequency between responses should be between 15–20 seconds on the average. These responses should not appear rehearsed or artificial, but should be congruent with the flow of the interaction.

II. *Verbal High Empathic Conditions*

It will be important within this mode that the counselor communicate accurately with the client's deeper as well as surface level feelings. The counselor must establish to the client that s/he is tuned in to and together with the client. The counselor must therefore respond with full awareness and an accurate empathic understanding of the deepest feelings.

The two most established ways of communicating high levels of verbal empathy are reflection and restatement. Basically, reflection deals with a statement made by the counselor which reflects the affect of the client. Based on the client's responses and his/her nonverbal behavior, the counselor makes some judgment as to what the client is experiencing emotionally, and feeds this message back to the client. This may be considered a surface level response of the counselor. A deeper response which tends to communicate greater levels of empathy would include some interpretation of what the client's current situation means for him/her in the broadest sense, in terms of his/her life's circumstance.

The situations used for training purposes shall be based on Carkhuff (1969a).

Low Empathic Condition

In the low empathy condition, the verbal and nonverbal components of the counselor's communication must be present to the degree that the counselor communicates a general or superficial level of understanding of his/her client. In some instances the counselor may not respond to deeper level feelings. The distinction must be drawn between a counselor's communicating low empathy and no empathy. When a counselor is not responding empathically s/he communicates no awareness of even the most obvious surface level feelings the client has (Carkhuff, 1969b). Hence, no understanding of a client's emotions is demonstrated by the counselor. S/he may respond to a client by repeatedly asking questions, talking superficially about irrelevant personal experiences, or avoiding attempts made by the client to discuss important feelings or issues in his/her life.

III. *Nonverbal Low Empathic Condition.*

Because it is important to communicate at least an understanding of the client's surface level feelings, some nonverbal empathic behaviors must be present. The two variables which can be manipulated here to draw a distinction between high and low nonverbal empathy are the length of time between counselor nonverbal responses, and the number of those nonverbal behaviors comprising each response. An average interval between 30–35 seconds will be considered a sufficient amount of time to elapse between each nonverbal response for this condition. Also, the combination of these nonverbal behaviors should typically include not more than three at any one instance.

IV. *Verbal Low Empathic Behavior*

As previously indicated, the counselor must respond with an accurate understanding of the surface feelings in order to be minimally facilitative. The situations used for training purposes shall come from Carkhuff (1969a).

V. *The Neutral Condition*

The neutral or baseline condition will consist of the counselor's feet placed flat on the floor and arms resting comfortably on the chair. Verbal empathy will be gauged at a level 3 per Carkhuff (1969b) on the empathy scale. Facial expressions and gestures will be bland.

Second, an audiotape was used to illustrate the five levels of empathy as defined by Carkhuff's (1969) model. The counselor listened to this role-play tape so that she could identify high empathy (Level 5) and low empathy (Level 2). The typescript of the first section is reproduced here.

Client: "I just don't know what to do anymore. I lost my job, my wife isn't working, we have four kids, I don't know how we're going to get by."

Counselor:

Level 1	"What kind of work do you do?"
Level 2	"I can see you're a little concerned about this."
Level 3	"You sound confused about what's going to happen."
Level 4	"It sounds like you're confused and maybe even worried about what's going to happen."
Level 5	"It sounds as though you're confused about this and maybe even worried or afraid. You're faced with having to find a new way to provide for and take care of your family."

Each of these levels was identified by the trainer. The next section of the tape (reproduced below) did not have the client responses in ascending order but rather in random order. Again, the trainer identified the empathy level for each client response.

Situation 1

Client: "My life used to be really exciting. There were so many things I was involved in, so much I used to do. No, ... I don't know ... it seems like there's nothing to look forward to anymore."

Counselor:

Response 1 "It sounds like you're bored with the way things are going for you." (Level 2)

Response 2 "You sound pretty unhappy ... sad ... almost as though there was nothing left to do, ... maybe even nothing left to live for." (Level 5)

Response 3 "Are you married?" (Level 1)

Response 4 "Life doesn't sound very satisfying for you anymore, very complete ... like something is missing." (Level 3)

Response 5 "I hear feelings of sadness in what you're saying about your life right now ... almost a sense of desperation." (Level 4)

Situation 2

Client: "I used to think having a big house and making a lot of money would guarantee my happiness. But now, since my divorce I feel so alone. I wish I were married again, even if it meant being poor."

Counselor:

Response 1 "It's true, money can't buy happiness." (Level 2)

Response 2 "I hear some sadness and maybe some regret about how you have lived your life." (Level 4)

Response 3 "It sounds as though you're feeling lonely and wished you had someone to share your life with." (Level 3)

Response 4 "You sound regretful and maybe even a little angry about how much importance you've placed on some material things in your life. The price you've paid has been high and now it seems that you wished for a chance to try again." (Level 5)

Response 5 "What has happened to your wife?" (Level 1)

Third, the counselor was required to determine (from an audiotape) the specific empathy level associated with seven counselor responses to a client statement. These seven responses were presented in random order. The typescript of these role plays is reproduced here.

Situation

Client: "My girlfriend just moved to Texas a few weeks ago. She wants me to move out there, but I don't know what to do. It means leaving my job here, finding a new one out there, and even if I do there's no guarantee that I'll like it."

Counselor:

Response 1 "It sounds as though there's a tough, confusing decision you've got to make. This one involves a certain amount of risk, and that could be scary." (Level 5)

Response 2 "Texas has a lot of opportunities. It has many growing cities." (Level 1)

Response 3 "I can see you have a decision to make here." (Level 2)

Response 4 "You sound a little confused about this decision you're going to have to make." (Level 3)

Response 5 "This decision you have to make doesn't sound easy for you. You seem to be trying to weigh the different advantages and disadvantages." (Level 4)

Response 6 "It sounds like you're really unsure what to do." (Level 3)

Response 7 "It sounds like this will be an important decision for you, one that is confusing, scary, and will be hard to make." (Level 5)

Fourth, the counselor carried out a variety of role plays with a training assistant to practice the three levels (5, 3, 2). The assistant had the counselor switch levels on cue.

The above steps focused on the *verbal* modality. Instruction was followed by modeling that was followed by practice, that was followed by feedback. In effect, a carefully designed training sequence was utilized. The exact same sequencing was then used for the *nonverbal* modality. However, here a videotape (without sound) was used to model the desired behaviors and to present the practice exercises. For the combined *verbal-nonverbal* modality, another videotape was used, including sound. The exact same procedures were followed. The entire training program took 4 hours.

Several other comments need be made here as to why this training succeeded. This counselor had a master's degree in counseling that included 2 years of supervised experience in personal/social and vocational counseling. She already knew, in general terms, what empathy is and was familiar with Carkhuff's (1969) model. However, she had not had specific empathy training. Thus, it can be inferred that she had the suitable intellectual background and positive attitude for developing high-level empathic behaviors. In essence, the trainee and training program interacted in such a way as to produce high empathy. The fact that she was able, on command, to vary her empathic levels suggests that she was truly controlling her empathic behaviors.

When the above results are compared with the typical results reported in the literature (as briefly summarized above and in more detail in Chapters 9 and 10), several distinctions stand out. First, most research has been carried out with new or inexperienced trainees. In fact, most are counselors-in-training. Second, many programs do not include multiple training procedures. Third, very few programs separate the verbal and nonverbal empathy behaviors and then combine them in serial, stepwise training. And finally, this program only was used with one trainee, whereas most studies report on groups of trainees. Hence, it is crucial that this training program be tested with many other trainees so as to make a fair comparison with the results from other studies.

Increasing Affective Empathy: A Proposal

The successful program described above can be criticized on still another basis. It only taught empathic verbal and nonverbal skills. These were measured by raters judging the counselor's behaviors as presented in audio- and videotapes. However, as discussed earlier, empathy also involves affective components. In Barrett-Lennard's (1981) model, these occur in the first, or empathic resonation, stage. This training program did not attempt to tap this area. In fact, as Brennan points out in Chapter 9, very few studies have. Yet, as Stewart (1956) and Hackney (1978) have argued, it is this aspect of empathy that is so crucial in the counseling interaction. Therefore, this last section presents the rationale and a plan for increasing counselor's affective empathy.[2]

The rationale starts from the premise that we can draw upon the humanities for insights regarding affective empathy. For example, as pointed out by Gladstein (1984), the early aesthetic empathy writers such as Lipps, Groos, and Lee described the inner feelings that occur as the empathizer loses himself or herself while contemplating an object or person. Likewise, we can look to motion pictures as a basis for ideas. For example, as far back as 1917 Munsterberg (1970) described the unique psychological elements that lead people to empathize (i.e., emotionally identify) with film characters. In recent times, the film literature has focused on the audience's emotional responses and how the writer, director, and film editor can produce these responses. Their ideas have implications for understanding the empathic relationship between a counselor and client.

The aesthetic experience of film always involves the transmission of emotion to the audience via the human technology of speech, facial

---

[2]This section is adapted from material in Gladstein, G. A., & Feldstein, J. C. (1983). Using film to increase counselor empathic experiences. *Counselor Education and Supervision, 23,* 125–131. Reproduced by permission of the © American Association for Counseling and Development.

expression, gestures, touch, and spatial distances, and the nonhuman technology of scenery, sound, and lighting, so that audiences may feel along with the film characters (Bobker, 1979; Eidsvik, 1978). The editing process itself, according to Rosenblum and Karen (1980), also has a significant effect. Viewers lose themselves in the film to the extent that they are not conscious of their surroundings. These ideas closely parallel Lipps's beliefs about empathy.

Using these ideas, it appears that there are several striking psychological similarities between the aesthetic experience of the film audience and the early empathic stages experienced by the counselor. Therefore, counselors can use their film-viewing experiences to obtain a better grasp of what the first stages of empathy in counseling should feel like.

For example, watching Hoffman portray the abandoned husband in *Kramer vs. Kramer,* audience members experience his anger, frustration, pain, and tension. The counselor's own feelings of frustration and tension may be accompanied by contractions of the muscles, changing breathing patterns, tears, or perspiration. Viewer identification is triggered by an unconscious and imaginative association with either the character or the situation and a familiar inner activity, sentiment, or attitude. The actual experience of the film character does not have to be identical to their own in order for the counselors' imaginations to make the associations to familiar inner activities. Their imaginations can find affective similarities with widely diverse film characters and situations, hence expanding the breadth of their emotional experiences. Therefore, counselors do not have to be male, separated, or divorced with children to experience Hoffman's anguish. Consequently, counselors can learn about a variety of human experiences from film without having to endure the experiences themselves. Munsterberg (1970) described this emotional reaction as the "feelings of the persons in the play that are transmitted to our own soul" (p. 53). At that moment in time, counselors are able to see, to respond, and to understand as the film character.

Whereas emotional reaction is an unconscious matching of feelings between the audience and film characters, role taking is a conscious inferential process based on both knowledge and the accurate perception of cues offered. Memory and imagination are the functions of the mind that are important to this stage of empathy. Memory adds the dimension of the past, and imagination anticipates the future. The film elements that capitalize on these include such editing techniques as flashbacks, flash forwards, and dream sequences. Consequently, role taking often results in the audience experiencing feelings entirely different from or even opposite to what is expressed by the film's characters. For example, as audience members, counselors see a laughing, happy boy (Hoffman's son in *Kramer vs. Kramer*) playing on a jungle gym, unaware that he is about to fall off. The counselors not only experience the child's joy (emotional reaction) but because of prior cues (i.e., film techniques), feel fear and horror about which the child knows nothing. The creation of a psychological distance from the film character results in a clearer interpretation of the broader situation. This cognitive process mirrors role taking during counseling.

To understand and appreciate the film creator's purpose, counselors as members of the audience need to be able to differentiate their own value judgments from the beliefs and values of the film characters. They must suspend their personal beliefs and values. Munsterberg (1970) argued that this is of fundamental importance to film viewing; however, it is often difficult if not impossible to distinguish projection from the empathic response. As film goers, counselors engage in projection if they are feeling angry and then allow this mood to influence their perceptions of the film characters, so that they perceive them, too, as angry. As a consequence, they may engage in cognitive or affective distortion. If counselors, as audience members, feel angry after witnessing a film actor's manifestations of anger, however, they are being empathic. The example of the angry audience that correctly perceives an actor's anger (e.g., Hoffman's anger in the early scenes of *Kramer vs. Kramer*) clearly illustrates the difficulty in differentiating projection from empathy. In counseling sessions, counselors must also suspend their own beliefs and values so as to avoid projection and increase empathy.

Within the context of this rationale, counselors can learn the early stages of empathy in counseling from their film-watching experiences, and counselor educators and supervisors can use films to help counselors increase empathic experiences.

Several methods can be used to demonstrate the creation of empathy's first stage, emotional reaction. First, commercial films can be shown in whole or in part, and most colleges and universities have access to inexpensive 16-mm copies. Many of these films can also be seen on television or on videotapes.

Second, minicourses concerned with this topic can be offered. For example, this author has taught a course entitled "Counseling and Film," which met four times for a total of 6 hours. The first two sessions involved discussions of readings from the film literature. Chapters from Bobker's (1979) *Elements of Film* and Eidsvik's (1978) *Cineliteracy* served as starting points. Concepts about lighting, sound, acting, editing, and directing were illustrated by selected film excerpts. The third session focused on the nature of empathy and how film creators produce this in film audiences. Again, excerpts were used to give class members an empathic experience. The final session centered on possible uses of film by counselors to increase their own empathic responses. Student evaluations from the two times that this course was offered were extremely positive. They found it emotionally as well as intellectually informative, stimulating, and challenging.

Third, supervision can be supplemented by using films. This can be similar to the way in which supervisors have used novels and poems in the past. Sometimes it is difficult to help a counselor perceive an attitude or value that is interfering with successful counseling. By discussing through analogy the novel's character or story events, the supervisor can more easily discuss an area that the counselor at that point is unable to approach. This technique is even easier to use with film. Most counselors view many films (on TV or at theaters) and are used to this medium. Supervisors can discuss the counselor's empathic emotional reactions to the characters. If no mutually viewed film comes to mind, the supervisor can suggest a current film that contains the desired experience.

Although this plan appears fruitful, it has not been fully tested. Either in its entirety or in parts, empirical research needs to be carried out. Such a course of action could take us into new realms of knowledge concerning empathy training that is badly needed.

Summary

This chapter identifies six issues (stated as questions) regarding empathy training. After discussing what is known about empathy development in childhood and adolescence, it appears that although it is known that children increase their affective and cognitive empathy abilities as they get older, it is not clear how or why this occurs. Apparently, mothers do affect their daughters' empathic development.

It is also known that adults vary widely in their affective and cognitive empathic abilities (see Chapters 1, 2, and 4). When some of these adults enter counseling training programs and are exposed to the many existing brief analogue and extended training packages, the evidence suggests that their cognitive empathy skills can be increased. However, the same research indicates that these counselors' empathy skills do not usually reach the facilitative levels thought necessary in counseling.

In an attempt to counter this situation, one successful training program is presented in detail. However, much more empirical research needs to be carried out to determine if its benefits occur with other counselors and in other settings. With the same intention, a rationale and plan for increasing counselor affective empathy is laid out.

All of the above clearly shows that there is much to learn about counselor empathy training. The two studies reported by Brennan and MacKrell in the next two chapters raise additional questions and provide further insight into this topic.

9
Effects of Four Training Programs on Three Kinds of Empathy

JOHN BRENNAN

Within the counseling/psychotherapy field, the extent to which empathy is a communication skill, an inner experience of the counselor, or the client's perception is controversial (Gladstein, 1983). The empathy training literature has, however, taken the position that empathy is a behavioral communication skill, emphasizing skill acquisition and performance. Behavioral training technology has been developed to equip trainees with a repertoire of counseling skills. The inner experience of the trainee has been neglected, however, by the empathy training literature (Hackney, 1978; Mahon & Altman, 1977). Partly, this neglect is due to the lack of an adequate conceptualization of empathy that links the complex nature of empathy with the available training technology. A view of empathy is needed that takes into account the counselor's inner experience, but is still pragmatic enough to relate to the available training technology.

Barrett-Lennard's model (Barrett-Lennard, 1981) appears to meet both of the above needs. Human Relations Training (HRT) is a popular and well-researched package of the technology that trains for empathy as a skill (Carkhuff, 1980). Tune-In is an audiotape-led empathy training program, part of which focuses on sensitizing trainees to their inner experiences (Tubesing & Tubesing, 1973). However, no study has been conducted on the effects of using both of these training programs to produce the three types of empathy presented by Barrett-Lennard.

The purpose of the study reported here was to investigate the additive and separate effects of HRT and Tune-In on the development of empathic resonation, expressed empathy in trainee counselors, and received empathy in their clients.

Review of Literature

Empathy Cycle

In Barrett-Lennard's view, empathy in counseling is a developmental phase cycle involving both the counselor and client, affect and cognition, and inner experience and communication skill. Specifically, the phases are empathic resonation, expressed empathy, and received empathy. Barrett-Lennard offered these comments concerning empathic resonation:

The extent to which this process (empathic resonation) then does happen depends ... on A's actual capacity to responsively "tune in" to the particular qualities and content of this experiencing ... thus, at best, to know experientially what it is like to *be* the other person at the time. A's actual empathy will vary partly as a result (figuratively) of having a finite range of "natural frequencies," such that there are aspects of B's experiencing to which he/she can resonate readily, clearly and strongly, and other aspects where such reverberation occurs lightly or incompletely—or that are sensed only in a partial and effortful way. (p. 93)

A "reads" or resonates to B in such a way that directly or indirectly expressed aspects of B's experience become experientially alive, vivid, and known to A. (p. 94)

Suggested here is that empathy is an inner experience of the counselor that demands sensitivity to the other and self-awareness.

The second phase, expressed empathy, is the expression of that inner experience to the client. "A expresses or shows in some communicative way a quality of felt awareness of B's experiencing" (p. 94). Implicit is that Phase II is a behavioral skill and, in fact, Barrett-Lennard suggested that this phase of empathy can be measured behaviorally, with instruments such as Carkhuff's Empathic Understanding Scale (Carkhuff, 1969a, b).

Phase III, received empathy, is the client's felt experience of the empathic relationship with the counselor. It is a perception and an inner experience and may differ measurably from Phase II empathy according to the client's perceptiveness. Indeed, while the model emphasizes that empathy is developmental, it does not contend that the phases must correlate with each other. For example, the counselor's capacity for empathic resonation may be greater or less than his or her capacity for empathic expression and may not be related at all to the client's perception and judgment (Barrett-Lennard, 1981).

In addition to the definitions, Barrett-Lennard touched on some implications of his model for empathy training.

Especially in a learning/training context, goals may include developing capacity for expression of empathy, providing one is able to detect expression) (Phase 2) of inner empathic understanding (Phase 1) as distinct from behavioral expressions of a different origin that instrument similar forms of response while largely bypassing Phase 1 empathy. Positively speaking, assisted learning procedures should be open and sensitive to different possible ways that a Phase 1 level empathic process might be expressed communicatively. (p. 96)

The present study, in identifying empathy as three dependent variables, is guided by Barrett-Lennard's recommendations.

Training for Specific Types of Empathy. All of the studies of HRT include as training objectives either the skill of empathic understanding or the ability to offer empathy as a facilitative condition. Some studies (Berenson, Carkhuff, & Myrus, 1966; Rye, 1970; Selfridge et al., 1975) have tested the effectiveness of some kind of sensitivity training experience and have done so to evaluate its additive effects on empathic skill.

Few studies have attempted to train for empathic resonation. Lesh (1971), for example, used Zen meditation techniques to produce small changes in trainees' affective sensitivity. Danish (1971) and Danish and Kagan (1971) also found small changes in affective sensitivity following a 10-day *T* group. Another popular training program, the Interpersonal Process Recall method, has resulted in success in training for affective sensitivity (Kagan, 1978).

The training methods reported by these studies have apparent promise for training for empathic resonation, but in each study, the researcher's choice of empathy measures suggests a limited, skill-oriented concept of empathy. Where the conceptual framework of the study has included a component concerned with the counselor's experience, the training method has not produced the expected result. Corcoran (1980) used an experiential focusing technique to increase the "empathic experience" in trainees when their clients experienced certain emotions. In a similar study, Aylward (1981) used biofeedback techniques in an attempt to increase counselor-perceived empathy in an initial counseling interview. Neither study reported success for either of the training methods.

Levels of Empathy Attained. A persistent problem with studies of HRT concerns the final level of empathy attained by the trainees. While there is substantial evidence that training produces statistically significant gains in trainee empathy, there is some question as to the value of the final level to counseling outcome. First, there is still the broad un-answered question concerning the relationship between empathy and counseling outcome. Gladstein (1970, 1977) reviewed studies of empathy and counseling outcome and concluded that the evidence concerning the relationship is contradictory and inconclusive. Second, and more to the point of this study, is that few studies of the HRT program have increased trainee final level of empathic skill performance to a facilitative level (3.0 on the Carkhuff Empathic Understanding Scale (EU). Of the few studies that have, trainees' initial levels were already just below the facilitative level. Perry (1975), for example, trained experienced pastoral counselors whose initial mean score on the EU was 2.49. In a 100-hour training program, lay counseling trainees reached a mean of 4.58 on the 9-point Accurate Empathy (AE) measure (Carkhuff & Truax, 1965). The facilitative level for the AE Scale is 5.0 (Mitchell, Bozarth, & Krauft, 1978). A 20-hour program reported by Berenson et al. (1966) yielded a posttraining group mean of 2.47 on the EU for volunteer college students. A 15-hour program yielded a mean of 2.5 for psychiatric inpatients (Vitalo, 1971). Other reviewers (Bath & Calhoun, 1977; Ford, 1979) have raised this concern and urged that researchers develop better predictors of success in training and thus increase the final group mean by matching trainee needs to training program components and training to criterion level.

Studies Related to Empathy

This section of the literature review examines those studies, published and unpublished, that are concerned with Barrett-Lennard's view of empathy and that concern the problems of measuring it.

Empathic Resonation. According to Barrett-Lennard, empathic resonation involves both cognitive and affective inner experiences. That it is cognitive is supported by studies by Krebs (1975) and Stotland et al. (1978). In these studies, subjects were instructed to use a cognitive process (i.e., imagine-him or imagine-self) to produce emotional arousal. No emotional arousal occurred in subjects who were instructed merely to observe the model. Developing the idea further, Coke, Batson, and McDavis (1978) found that emotional arousal facilitates the observer in taking the perspective of the other, a cognitive process. Furthermore, recent evidence offered by Batson et al. (1981) suggests that it is this affective part of empathy that is a source of altruistic motivation for helping others.

The studies of empathy as emotional arousal have typically relied on physiological instruments to determine very crudely the level of arousal (Krebs, 1975; Robinson et al., 1982; Stotland et al., 1978). While these measures can detect the presence and intensity of emotion, they cannot identify the kind of emotion (Krebs, 1975). Clearly, in the case of empathy, it is critical that the observer experience and correctly label feelings similar to those of the client.

Feldstein and Gladstein (1980) suggested that the nonverbal realm might provide some clues as to feelings that the counselor might be experiencing when empathizing. One approach involved the use of a foot pedal to signal the presence of unexpressed feelings (Kagan et al., 1967). A refinement of this method was developed by Loesch (1975). Loesch used four push buttons, each of which corresponded to one of four nonverbal feeling dimensions: frustration, anxiousness, negativeness, and positiveness. A limitaiton of these measures is that while they detect the presence of emotional arousal, they do not discriminate among all possible emotions. For example, sadness, a frequently occurring emotion in counselees, cannot be identified by the Loesch method. Therefore, while they may be useful in establishing that the counselor has had some kind of emotional experience, they cannot accurately identify the full range of emotions.

Barrett-Lennard (1962) published a Relationship Inventory that included an empathy scale that came in two forms, namely the counselor's perceptions and feelings about the client (MO) and the client's perceptions and feelings about the counselor (OS). Barrett-Lennard (1981) believes that the MO is a measure of empathic resonation. In the 1962 study, the MO was administered to therapists after five interviews. Split-half reliability for the empathy scale of the MO was 0.96. Two decades of studies investigating the validity of the Barrett-Lennard empathy measures have usually found that the OS and the MO do not correlate with each other, or with other measures of empathy (Kurtz & Grummon, 1972; Lake et al., 1973; Lambert et al., 1978), and perhaps do not measure empathy at all but rather overall satisfaction with the relationship (Lanning & Lemons, 1974). This suggests that the two forms may perhaps be measuring two kinds of empathy. Feldstein and Gladstein (1980) in examining the construct validity of the empathy scale of the Relationship Inventory judged that "the affective state of the counselor is only hinted at in any of the items" (p. 53). However, items in the MO do appear, at face value, to relate to empathic resonation: for example, "sometimes I think that he feels a certain way, because that's the was I feel myself," and "I usually sense or realize how he is feeling" (Barrett-Lennard, 1978, p. 45). Furthermore, support for the construct validity of the MO is offered by Robinson et al. (1982), who correlated physiological measures of empathy with scores on the MO.

Thus, the MO form of the Relationship Inventory appears to have adequate reliability but its validity remains somewhat questionable. Nevertheless, it is the only available written measure of empathic resonation. Given the inadequacies of the nonverbal measures, the written measure was chosen for the present study.

Expressed Empathy. Empathic understanding is a communication skill. Its purpose is to convey to the client the counselor's understanding of the client's expression of his or her expreience. This experience is assumed to have content and feelings. The communication occurs both verbally and nonverbally. When it is accurate, it is assumed to set up conditions for client self-exploration and eventual change, though the research evidence is equivocal on this assumption.

The measurement of empathic understanding has been approached in two ways. In the first approach, frequency of empathic responses has been considered the important dimension (Gormally & Hill, 1974; Ivey & Authier, 1978). The advantage of frequency of responses is that it is easily quantifiable. Its limitation is that it supplies no information about the quality of the response.

The second approach has been to evaluate the accuracy of the empathic understanding response by having objective judges rate it. The main example of this measure is Carkhuff's Empathic Understanding Scale (Carkhuff, 1969a, b). Controversies surrounding this instrument concern its construct validity (Feldstein & Gladstein, 1980). (See Chapters 2, 3-6, and 10 for additional comments concerning this measure.) Part of the controversy concerns whether an objective judge or the client is in the best position to evaluate the accuracy of the counselor's empathic response. The advantage of the objective judge is that he or she can be trained to rate reliably and accurately according to the scale's criteria. The client, however, as the recipient of the empathy, would seem to be the best judge of the value of the counselor's response. However, we cannot know how reliable the client's ratings are, nor if they are valid; perhaps the client is rating counselor effort or global "good guy" quality. Another question raised by Fridman and Stone (1978) is whether the raters should focus on the counselor's response, the client's response to the counselor's empathic communication, or the sequence of client-counselor-client statements. Their study found no differences when rater focus was varied.

A further problem in rating the EU is the difficulty in obtaining high interrater reliability (Butler & Hansen, 1973; Fridman & Stone, 1978; Kurtz & Grummon, 1972; Rappaport, Gross, & Lepper, 1973). The evidence from these studies suggests that perhaps obtaining high interrater reliability on the EU is difficult when audiotapes are used. One method of avoiding this difficulty is, where practical, to use a single trained rater. (However, very high interrater reliabilities have been obtained. Differences in rater training may be the explanation. See Chapter 5 for an example of extremely high reliability.)

Another limitation of the EU is that it does not provide the judges access to the nonverbal, visual channel of communication. That this is a serious limitation is suggested by a study by Haase and Tepper (1972) in which they analyzed the relative contribution of verbal and nonverbal behaviors to the judged level of empathy. Nonverbal effects accounted for twice the variability of the verbal in the communications. However, in a more recent study, Young (1980) suggested that the effect of the counselor's nonverbal gestures is strongly influenced by client subjective factors, such as global impressions and attitude towards counseling. Both studies were analogues, however, and further investigations are necessary to clarify the issue. Finally, the EU's construct validity has been called into question in several studies in which statistically significant correlations of the EU with other empathy measures were not observed (Kurtz & Grummon, 1972). In reviewing the construct validity of the EU, Feldstein and Gladstein (1980) advised that since the EU ignores the nonverbal communication and affective experience of the counselor, it should not be used alone in research. In addition, though not specific to the EU, unanswered questions concern at what point in an interview ratings should be taken; are trained raters more accurate than untrained raters and does the sex of the rater have effects? The research evidence on these issues, reviewed by Lambert et al. (1978), is inconclusive.

Another frequently used measure of expressed empathy is the Accurate Empathy (AE) Scale (Traux & Carkhuff, 1967). The AE is the forerunner of the EU; the essential difference between the two is that the AE is a 9-point scale while the EU has 5 points. Since the EU is a smaller scale, there is less random error and it is therefore preferred (Kurtz & Grummon, 1972).

To summarize, the best available measure of expressed empathy is the EU. However, the research has not yet indicated clearly the optimal conditions for its use.

Received Empathy. Prior to Barrett-Lennard's conceptualization of the empathic process, received empathy was viewed as the client's perception of counselor-offered empathy. Interest in this view stemmed from the Rogerian assumption that the client's experience was the only truly meaningful phenomenon worthy of investigation. Instruments such as the OS form of the Relationship Inventory and the Truax Relationship Questionnaire (Truax & Carkhuff, 1967) were developed to assess the client's experience of counselor-offered empathy. Client perception of empathy seems to be more highly related to satisfaction with counseling outcome than any other variable (Gladstein, 1977). The Barrett-Lennard model links the three kinds of empathy by postulating that they are the phases of an empathy cycle.

The implications for training of the above considerations are that in order to evaluate the effectiveness of the programs, more than the client's perception of empathy must be measured. However, because it is related to outcome of counseling and because it is theoretically influenced by the previous phases of empathy, this perception should be included in measuring effectiveness of empathy training.

Thus, because received empathy is an important part of the empathy cycle, it is measured in this study. The use of the OS form of the Relationship Inventory has been frequently reviewed. Gladstein (1977) concluded that there is some evidence linking the instrument with positive counseling outcome. Kurtz and Grummon (1972) found correlations between the OS and outcome measures to be higher than any of the other empathy measures. Gurman (1977) and Lambert et al. (1978) arrived at similar conclusions. Received empathy was measured in the present study by the OS form of the Relationship Inventory because it has been linked with positive counseling outcome.

Empathy Training of Community College Students

A wide variety of populations have received various forms of empathy training (Carkhuff, 1980; Ford, 1979; Reddy & Lippert, 1981). However, only one study has investigated the effects of empathy training on community college students. Armstrong (1982) compared the relative effectiveness of structured and unstructured group experiences on empathy development in first-year human services students in a community college. He found no differences between the two methods and that both were significantly more effective than a control condition. That there has been only one reported study is surprising, given the importance of empathy in the helping process and the large numbers of human services students at the community college level. The present study, therefore, by expanding the experimental data base concerning empathy training at the community college level, should assist in faculty curriculum planning and stimulate further research with this important population.

Methodological Issues

Previous research and reviews of research (Brennan, 1979; Ford, 1979) indicate that studies concerned with the effects of training programs have been deficient in several respects. First, they have either traded off external validity, as in the case of analogue studies, or internal validity, as in the case of the HRT studies. In the latter cases, training procedures have not been clear, placebo groups have not been included, and, until recently, coached client training and performance has not been monitored. Furthermore, measures taken under naturalistic conditions correlate more highly with follow-up performance than written tests.

These points suggest that a combination of the Tune-In program and the HRT program should affect the development of empathic resonation, expressed empathy, and received empathy more than either training program alone and more than a lecture-discussion. Also, the HRT program alone should improve expressed empathy and received empathy but not empathic resonation. Similarly, Tune-In should result in improved empathic resonation but not expressed or received empathy. Finally, Tune-In and HRT, both separately and in combination, should effect empathy development to a greater extent than lecture-discussion.

Research Questions and Hypotheses

The primary research question was: What are the effects of Tune-In and HRT, separately and in combination, on the development of empathic resonation and expressed empathy in trainees and received empathy in their clients? A secondary question was: Can the combined programs produce performances of expressed empathy at the facilitative (i.e., 3.0 on the EU Scale) level?

The nine hypotheses under investigation in the study were as follows:

1. Tune-In has a greater effect than HRT on empathic resonation.

2. Tune-In has a greater effect than lecture-discussion on empathic resonation.
3. HRT plus Tune-In have a greater effect than lecture-discussion on empathic resonation.
4. HRT has a greater effect than Tune-In on expressed empathy.
5. HRT has a greater effect than lecture-discussion on expressed empathy.
6. HRT plus Tune-In have a greater effect than lecture-discussion on expressed empathy.
7. HRT has a greater effect than Tune-In on received empathy.
8. HRT has a greater effect than lecture-discussion on received empathy.
9. HRT plus Tune-In have a greater effect than lecture-discussion on received empathy.

Methodology

The study was designed to investigate experimentally the effects of HRT and Tune-In, singly and in combination, on the development of empathic resonation, expressed empathy, and received empathy. The levels of the independent variable were the two training programs singly and in combination and a lecture-discussion program. The dependent variables were the kinds of empathy.

Experimental Design

According to the classification system of Campbell and Stanley (1966), the design was a posttest-only experimental design with four treatment groups (Design 6). Basic to the choice of this design was the assumption that true randomization is possible. The authors also emphasized the experimental superiority of Design 6 over Design 4 (pretest and posttest) as long as randomization is possible. This alleged superiority, coupled with the advantage of not having to subject the trainees to a pretesting, made the posttest-only design more attractive for the present study.

Subjects

All subjects were students at a community college in upstate New York. The students were recruited through announcements in the departments of Human Services, Psychology, Sociology, Criminal Justice, Nursing, and Speech and Theater, and through posters displayed throughout the campus. Seventy-nine subjects indicated interest in the research by signing a Statement of Interest form or by contacting the researcher by telephone. After being informed what their involvement would be, 45 voluntarily signed a consent form. Thirty-two subjects who had signed consent forms presented themselves at the training site. Twenty-four were female and eight were male.

Measures

To measure empathic resonation, the MO form of the Barrett-Lennard Relationship Inventory was modified. In place of the original six-point rating scale, a true-false format was administered to the trainees. The decision to use this format was made because the revised format was less complicated to use in a brief simulated interview (Ham, 1980/1981). A similar modification was made for the OS form of the Relationship Inventory to measure received empathy. To measure expressed empathy, the Empathic Understanding Scale (Carkhuff, 1969a, b) was used.

Trainers

Trainers were three males in their early thirties. Two of the trainers had several years of experience in leading personal growth and interpersonal skill training groups, had taught undergraduate level students, and had master's degrees in helping professions. The third trainer was an advanced doctoral candidate studying empathy. Prior to training, the HRT trainer was rated by the experimenter on the EU Scale in a simulated 10-minute interview with a coached client. The trainer's mean score was 3.2 with a .49 standard deviation. This mean score just exceeds the minimally facilitative level of 3.0.

Coached Clients

Five experienced actors, one male and four females, were recruited from local theater groups. Each was paid $25 and trained to meet role fidelity and role consistency criteria similar to a procedure reported by Larrabee and Froehle (1979). The coached clients were instructed to use their own personal data relevant to the role while meeting the following criteria.

1. Describe a personal or interpersonal problem. Problems chosen included a conflict with a roommate, a pressing decision regarding application to a fraternity, poor academic performance related to time management, and the breakup of an intimate relationship.
2. Express discomfort about the problem.
3. Talk about external pressure compounding the problem.
4. Ask for help.

Treatment Conditions

HRT. The HRT program was used to train for expressed empathy. After a brief overview of the HRT model, the skills of attending and responding were presented. These skills were broken down into parts, outlined in the trainer's guide by Carkhuff et al. (1980). Attending meant attending (a) physically, (b) by observing, and (c) by listening. Responding meant responding to (a) content, (b) feeling, and (c) meaning. Each part was explained and illustrated by the trainer and then discussed. The trainer then demonstrated the use of the skill in a simulated interview with a volunteer trainee. All trainees then wrote responses with the group and then practiced the skill by role playing in triads, with the first person playing counselor, the second playing counselee, and the third playing observer. At the conclusion, the observer gave feedback to the counselor and then roles were reversed until all trainees had played the role of counselor. Personalizing and initiating skills were then presented and practiced in a similar manner. Finally, a film of Carl Rogers counseling a client (Shostrom, 1977) was shown to further model expressed empathy.

Tune-In. The total Tune-In program (Tubesing & Tubesing, 1973) consists of eight sessions. The first three sessions of the program were used to train for empathic resonation. The first session included a lecture and nonverbal exercise for locating and labeling feelings in one's body. The second session contained a lecture on the differences between thinking and feeling and how they may conflict. The effects of the conflicts on one's self-concept were then discussed, followed by an exercise in identifying conflicts between thoughts and feelings. The third session included a lecture on suppressing feelings, verbal and nonverbal ways of expressing feelings, and barriers to the expression of feelings. Group exercises included sharing feelings verbally and nonverbally and written exercises assessing one's level of self-disclosure. The trainer presented the lecture material and either demonstrated or participated in the exercises.

HRT–Tune-In Combined. This group received 6 hours of Tune-In training, led by the Tune-In trainer, and 6 hours of HRT training, led by the HRT trainer. Total training time was 12 hours. The HRT training was abbreviated by omitting the film and the personalizing and initiating skills, judged to be less related to expressed empathy. The Tune-In program was abbreviated by eliminating every other lecture and group exercise.

Lecture-Discussion. This program was designed to represent the traditional classroom approaches to training for empathy. The format was lecture-discussion, plus a film (Whitley, 1974) in which Carl Rogers talks about what empathy means to him and reports on his research concerned with empathy. Topics included definitions of empathy, empathy and development, empathy in education, empathy and altruism, empathy and counseling, and measuring empathy. Both theoretical views and research findings were presented and trainees were encouraged to develop and share their own views. Duration of each training program was 12 hours, including testing (2, 6-hour days over 3 weekends).

Procedure

Thirty-two subjects were present at the beginning of the training. Subjects were stratified according to sex and then randomly assigned to the four treatment conditions. Due to attrition, and to preserve equal representation of sex across groups, data on 28 subjects were collected at posttest. Training occurred over 3 successive Saturdays, to enable the HRT and Tune-In training specialists to lead their respective parts of the combined program. Each subject interviewed for 12 minutes a coached client of the same sex at posttest. Subjects were assigned randomly to the available interview time slots.

All test interviews were recorded on audiotapes. Immediately after each interview, the coached clients completed the OS form of the Relationship Inventory and the subjects completed the MO form. The posttest interviews took place immediately following the completion of training.

Raters and Rater Training

Each of the 28 12-minute posttest audiotaped interviews was divided into three equal segments. The 84 segments were then coded and rated by the researcher. A random check was made by an independent scoring by another trained rater. The researcher and second rater were trained according to the procedures outlined by Fridman and Stone (1978). Interrater reliability for the 10% random check resulted in a +.81 correlation coefficient.

Analysis of Data

The means were subjected to a statistical test recommended by Myers (1972) for nonorthogonal comparisons. The necessary comparisons were not orthogonal because the sum of cross-products of coefficients did not equal zero. In other words, the comparisons were not completely independent of each other. However, the method described by Myers is essentially the same as for orthogonal contrasts.

Results

Table 9.1 summarizes the data collected in the study.

Outcomes Concerning Empathic Resonation

Hypothesis 1: *Tune-In has a greater effect than HRT on empathic resonation.*
   Inspection of Table 9.1 shows a mean of 10.00 for Tune-In and a mean of 12.00 for HRT. This difference is not significant.
Hypothesis 2: *Tune-In has a greater effect than lecture-discussion on empathic resonation.* Inspection of Table 9.1 shows a mean of 10.00 for Tune-In and a mean of 11.43 for lecture-discussion. This difference is not significant.

TABLE 9.1. Means and standard deviations of four treatment groups on three empathy measures.

| | Treatment groups | | | | | | | | | |
| | HRT | | Tune-In | | HRT–
Tune-In | | Lecture-
Discussion | | All
subjects | |
Empathy	M	SD	M	SD	M	SD	M	SD	M	SD
Empathic resonation (MO)	12.00	1.53	10.00	2.08	13.86	1.57	11.43	2.82	11.82	2.07
Expressed empathy (EU)	1.85	.65	1.48	.20	1.51	.46	1.48	.36	1.58	.45
Received empathy (OS)	10.29	5.47	12.57	3.10	12.10	3.08	11.86	4.74	11.72	4.23

Note. $N = 28$.

Hypothesis 3: *HRT plus Tune-In have a greater effect than lecture-discussion on empathic resonation.* Inspection of Table 9.1 shows a mean of 13.86 for HRT plus Tune-In and a mean of 11.43 for lecture-discussion. Table 9.2 shows that this difference between the two means is significant and in the predicted direction.

Outcomes Concerning Expressed Empathy

Hypothesis 4: *HRT has a greater effect than Tune-In on expressed empathy.* Inspection of Tables 9.1 and 9.3 shows a mean of 1.85 for HRT and a mean of 1.48 for Tune-In. The differences between the two means is not significant.

Hypothesis 5: *HRT has a greater effect than lecture-discussion on expressed empathy.* Inspection of Tables 9.1 and 9.3 shows a mean of 1.85 for HRT and a mean of 1.48 for lecture-discussion. The difference between these means is not significant.

TABLE 9.2. *F* statistics for differences between experimental group means on empathic resonation.

Source	df	Mean squares	F
Treatments			
Tune-In vs. HRT	1	14.00	3.29
Tune-In vs. lecture-discussion	1	7.14	1.68
HRT–Tune-In vs. lecture-discussion	1	20.64	4.85*
Error	24	4.26	

*$p < .05 = 4.26$.

TABLE 9.3. F statistic for differences between experimental group means on expressed empathy.

Source	df	Mean square	F
Treatments			
HRT vs. Tune-In	1	.19	.04
HRT vs. lecture-discussion	1	.19	.04
HRT–Tune-In vs. lecture-discussion	1	.02	.003
Error	24	4.83	

$p < .05 = 4.26$.

Hypothesis 6: *HRT plus Tune-In have a greater effect than lecture-discussion on expressed empathy.* Inspection of Tables 9.1 and 9.3 shows means of 1.51 and 1.48 for HRT–Tune-In and the lecture-discussion program, respectively. This difference in favor of the combined program is not significant.

Outcomes Concerning Received Empathy

Hypothesis 7: *HRT has a greater effect than Tune-In on received empathy.* Inspection of Tables 9.1 and 9.4 indicates a mean of 10.29 for HRT and a mean of 12.57 for Tune-In. This difference is not significant.

Hypothesis 8: *HRT has a greater effect than lecture-discussion on received empathy.* Inspection of Tables 9.1 and 9.4 shows a mean of 10.29 for HRT and a mean of 11.86 for lecture-discussion. This difference is not significant.

Hypothesis 9: *HRT plus Tune-In have a greater effect than lecture-discussion on received empathy.* Tables 9.1 and 9.4 show means of 12.1 and 11.86 for the combined program and the lecture discussion program, respectively. This difference is not significant.

TABLE 9.4. F statistic for differences between experimental group means on received empathy.

Source	df	Mean squares	F
Treatments			
HRT vs. Tune-In	1	1.14	.06
HRT vs. lecture-discussion	1	.78	.04
HRT–Tune-In vs. lecture-discussion	1	.12	.01
Error	24	17.87	

$p < .05 = 4.26$.

Anecdotal Feedback

The trainers for the Tune-In and lecture-discussion programs reported that the subjects in their groups appeared to be interested and to experience success in the various learning activities. Both these trainers stated that they felt satisfied with their own performance in the role of trainer. The trainer for the HRT program compared the subjects in the experiment to those in an earlier pilot study. He stated that the pilot-study subjects impressed him as being superior in ability and motivation to those in the experiment. As a trainer, he felt disappointed with the level of responsiveness of the subjects in the experiment and stated that he did not enjoy them as much as he did the subjects in the pilot study. He also remarked to the experimenter that he could not imagine teaching at the community college level because the students do not challenge him.

Posttraining comments of subjects to the trainers and the experimenter included: "it was interesting," "can we get the results (of the experiment)," and "wish we could have more of this type of training." Feedback from the actor and actresses included: "some (trainees) were really good and others were terrible," and " some of the questions (on the OS) didn't apply because there wasn't enough time to judge."

Summary

These results provide mixed support for the hypotheses of the study. The results produce support for the superiority of the HRT–Tune-In in training for empathic resonation. There is no evidence, however, of any significant difference among the other programs in training for expressed empathy and received empathy. In addition, anecdotal feedback was that the HRT trainer felt disappointed in the level of responsiveness of his trainees and the coached clients experienced some difficulty with the measure of received empathy (the OS).

Discussion

This discussion of the results of the study includes concerns about the absence of treatment effects, the secondary research question, the extent to which the data support the Barrett-Lennard empathy cycle, the experimental design, the instrumentation, and the relationship of this study to correspondent studies.

Outcomes Concerning Empathic Resonation

The hypothesis concerning the combined program (HRT plus Tune-In) was supported, but the hypotheses concerning the superiority of Tune-In over HRT and Tune-In over lecture-discussion were not supported. Possible explanations for the lack of support of the latter hypotheses include:

1. Subjects in Tune-In plus HRT felt more confident about their empathy because they had had training in both resonating and communicating with clients. The Tune-In group, although trained to resonate, perhaps felt inadequate in the posttest interview because they had not been trained in how to communicate their empathy to the client. Consequently, they may have been reluctant to rate themselves as being high on empathy.
2. Alternatively, the finding that Tune-In alone was not superior to either lecture-discussion or HRT suggests that Tune-In might train for empathic resonation only when combined with HRT.

Outcomes Concerning Expressed Empathy

An explanation for failure of a significant difference among treatment groups might be a possible interaction effect between the trainer and subjects. In the light of the informal posttraining feedback of the trainer, these results suggest that the trainer's attitude towards the subjects may have negatively influenced their performance in the posttest interview. Assuming that the training itself would have been effective, possibly the trainers' expectations of the subjects' potential had a detrimental effect on their motivation during training, which subsequently lowered their performance on the EU.

Outcomes Concerning Received Empathy

By way of explanation for the lack of statistical support for the three hypotheses concerning received empathy, it is possible that all programs are equally effective in training for received empathy. The range of means (10.29–12.57) is at the high end of the scale, indicating that clients felt empathy from counselors in the study.

Secondary Research Question

A secondary research question asked if the HRT plus Tune-In program could produce performance of expressed empathy at the minimally facilitative level (3.0 on the EU Scale). Clearly the posttest mean score of 1.51 falls considerably short. Because of a possible trainer effect, this study may not have been a fair test of the question. However, the assumption that a score of 3.0 measured during the first quarter of a counseling interview is an appropriate training objective is called into question by a recent study by Edwards, Boulet, Mahrer, Chagnon, and Mook (1982). In this study, two initial interviews by Carl Rogers, an acknowledged expert in empathy, were analyzed in their entirety, using the EU Scale. It was found that Rogers manifested moderate levels of empathy throughout both interviews. In one of the interviews, however, his mean score on the EU for the first quarter was only 2.6. His mean scores for the entire interviews were 3.0 and 3.1, respectively. First of all, perhaps it is unrealistic to expect that subjects naive to counseling can be trained in a few hours to express empathy at the same level as highly skilled experts. Second, it may be even more difficult to achieve these results when measures are taken in the first quarter of the initial counseling interview. Perhaps, for novice trainees, a more attainable objective for empathy training is a score of 2.5 on the EU Scale. With a standard deviation of .5, this objective would ensure that some facilitative levels are reached some of the time during posttesting. In other words, the trainees acquire the skill of expressing empathy at a facilitative level, but are not yet consistent in their use of it. This experimenter's observations of trainees who have evidenced ability to produce a 3.0 response are that they use it only sporadically and are sometimes easily trapped into advice giving and interpretation. Alternatively, Ivey and Authier (1978) have suggested that frequency counts of expressed empathy statements have more promise because they differentiate those trainees who have acquired the skill, but who perhaps are not using it often enough, from those who have not yet mastered it.

How Data Support the Empathy Model

In Barrett-Lennard's view, empathy in counseling is a developmental phase cycle involving both the counselor and client, affect and cognition, inner experience, and communication skill. Specifically, the phases are empathic resonation, expressed empathy, and received empathy. A secondary objective of this study was to investigate the validity of this empathy cycle. Had all hypotheses been supported, the Barrett-Lennard model of empathy would have had support for its validity. However, the training programs, whose objectives and activities were different, did not for the most part differentially affect trainee empathy, except for empathic resonation. We do not know if the training did not have effect because of the training itself or because the instruments did not measure what they purport to measure. In the case of empathic resonation, the finding that the combined program was superior to the other programs in affecting scores on the MO, but on no other instruments, seems to suggest that empathic resonation is a valid and separate aspect of empathy. The fact that there were no differences among treatments on expressed and received empathy neither supports nor rejects these two phases of the empathy cycle.

Relationship of This Study to Corresponding Studies

The purpose of this study was to compare the effects of various training approaches on three kinds of empathy. Previous studies of empathy training have used a variety of instruments to measure results and have trained a wide range of populations. In essence, the findings of the present study differ from the findings of previous research in two important ways. First, the results of the present study fail to support the bulk of the previous research findings that HRT is a superior method of training for expressed empathy. Second, the present study differs from the previous research by demonstrating the effectiveness of a feelings-focused module combined with a skill-oriented module in training for empathic resonation. In addition, the results of the present study are similar to results obtained in previous research in as much as the HRT programs failed to produce performance of expressed empathy at the facilitative level.

Limitations

A major limitation of this study concerns its external validity. A conservative position is that the results of the study cannot be generalized to all community college students, because the study's trainees did not represent a sample of a population because they were not randomly selected. Furthermore, because measures were taken under simulated counseling conditions, they cannot be generalized to actual counseling conditions. Perhaps, for example, the actors and actresses were not able to capture the subtleties of nonverbal communication or the intensity of feeling that the in vivo client experiences. Knowing also that the interview is a simulation may have taken the edge off the trainee's empathic resonation.

While the instruments are the best available, they have many limitations (previously documented) that caution conclusions. The MO, for example, measures only the counselors' perceptions and remembrances of their empathic resonation. It does not provide information about how empathic resonation varied across client responses. Similarly, the OS concerns the client's perception of the counselor's overall empathy, which does not provide information about how it might have varied. The rater on the EU Scale did not have access to the visual nonverbal component of the counselor's response, and so it is not certain how effectively trainees had learned these behaviors. Finally, although the three trainers were fairly evenly matched for age, sex, education, and years of interpersonal skill training experience, they were not matched for other variables that may have influenced trainee performance, for example, ethnic background, interest, attractiveness, or personality variables.

Conclusions

The investigation of the hypotheses resulted in a number of findings that in turn generated the following conclusions:

1. No evidence has been offered to support the thesis that there are differences among the training programs in their ability to train for expressed empathy in trainees and received empathy in clients.

2. Evidence has been offered to support the thesis that an abbreviated form of the HRT program combined with the first three sessions of the Tune-In program is more effective in training for empathic resonation than either of these programs singly and is more effective than a lecture-discussion program.
3. Evidence has been offered to question the effectiveness of the HRT program in training for a facilitative level of expressed empathy.
4. Evidence has been offered to support the validity of the empathic resonation phase of the empathy cycle. The evidence neither supports nor rejects the validity of the expressed and received phases of the empathy cycle.

10
Supervision Method and Supervisee Empathy

SUSAN MACKRELL

In the previous two chapters, studies are reported that illustrate different approaches to training counselors and students in empathy. However, neither concerns the supervisory process. Yet, the counseling/psychotherapy field assumes that it is the face-to-face supervision encounter that is extremely important in learning skills and attitudes—probably more important than initial skill acquisition in isolation.

In reviewing the literature in this area, it became apparent that investigators have been exploring counselor training and supervision on, at least, two different dimensions. The first dimension is concerned with the relationship between the supervisor and the trainee. More specifically, this literature investigates the effect of the supervisor's facilitative conditions on the trainee. This literature questions the effect of supervisory strategies or training modes on the development of empathy in counselor trainees.

The second dimension was the focus of this study. Several researchers have explored the relative effectiveness of didactic, experiential, and the integrated didactic-experiential styles of supervision on the development of trainees' facilitative conditions. These studies found the didactic approach to supervision to be significantly more effective than the experiential approach in increasing empathy levels of trainees.

Other researchers explored the level of trainee sophistication, but did not isolate styles of supervision. Some separated the didactic and experiential approaches, but only investigated their effectiveness in relation to low-functioning, inexperienced trainees. Therefore, one purpose of the present study was to explore the two sets of variables by investigating the differential effects of didactic and experiential styles of supervision on the improvement of empathic understanding by trainees functioning at low and moderate levels of sophistication on this skill prior to training.

In addition, some research suggests that accuracy of empathic responding may be related to sexual similarity of client and counselor and that female counselors may be more empathic than male counselors.

However, the literature is not consistent in this area, with research yielding results that contradict the above findings. Although this research is not related directly to the training of counselors, it does have some implications for the supervision dyad. Thus, the second purpose of the present research was to gain some understanding of the importance of the sex variable in the supervision interaction by exploring the effects of didactic and experiential supervision on both low and moderate female and male subjects who have received training from the same-sex supervisor.

Summary of Literature

The above-mentioned two dimensions have been used to organize the summary of the research literature presented here. It should be noted that the literature is quite extensive and that some of the subtleties of the research designs and findings may not be apparent in this summary/ critique. (For a fuller anlaysis, see MacKrell [1983].) The intent here is to identify the main elements and their significance to this study.

Dimension I: Supervisory/Trainee Relationship

In summarizing the findings of eight studies, a pattern seems to emerge. Those studies that found a positive correlation between supervisors' levels of facilitative conditions and trainees' demonstration of these same conditions did *not* isolate empathy in their investigation (Pierce, Carkhuff, & Berenson, 1965; Pierce & Schauble, 1970, 1971a, 1971b). Also, these studies measured the supervisors' levels of facilitation through ratings of taped *therapy* sessions *not supervision* sessions. This approach leaves doubt as to the actual facilitative levels present in the supervision sessions and suggests that by measuring facilitation we are looking at a more global phenomenon, not necessarily reflected through empathy alone. The findings of Wedeking and Scott (1976), Seligman (1978), and Karr and Geist (1977) lend some support to this conjecture. These researchers assessed the supervisors' empathy levels during supervision through objective ratings and did not find a significant correlation between these levels and the empathy levels of trainees in counseling. In addition, Seligman (1978) and Karr and Geist (1977) found that trainee perceptions of supervisor-offered conditions, including empathy, were not significantly correlated to their own level of functioning in therapy. This suggests that perhaps the presence of empathy in the supervisory relationship is not necessary for the development of this quality in trainees and that some other process is intervening to facilitate empathic responding in trainees.

It must be noted that of the eight studies reviewed, seven were of a pre-experimental nature with no controlled experimental manipulation. All that can be said is that the subjects received some form of unspecified supervision for varying lengths of time. Given the lack of internal validity within the studies and the differences between the studies as to level of trainee and supervisor experience and length of training, the results must be accepted cautiously.

Dimension II: Process of Supervision

In summarizing the nine studies from this second dimension, it appears that an integrated didactic-experiential approach to supervision can be beneficial in improving empathic responding for trainees at various levels of skill development (Butler & Hansen, 1973; Carkhuff & Truax, 1965). However, two studies found the didactic approach to be more helpful in improving the empathic responding skills of inexperienced subject trainees (Birk, 1972; Payne, Weiss, & Kapp, 1972). An understanding of this didactic approach to supervision has been expanded through several behavioral studies. It has been found that positive reinforcement is more beneficial in the development of empathy than negative statements (Blane, 1968). Also, the immediacy of this reinforcement, coupled with instruction, seems to create a growth-producing learning situation (Carlson, 1979). In addition, immediate modeling of facilitative responses (Silverman & Quinn, 1974) and the use of programmed instruction (Saltmarsh, 1973) have been suggested as effective techniques in the development of trainee empathy in supervision. Finally, two researchers (Bradley, 1974; Kingdon, 1975) exploring another form of didactic supervision, the Interpersonal Process Recall (IPR) technique (Kagan et al., 1967), found that this approach was no more beneficial than traditional supervision techniques in the improvement of trainees' empathic responding skills.

The Effect of Sex Variables in Supervision and Counseling Process

The empirical literature has consistently neglected the investigation of the sex variable in the development of empathic skills by counselor trainees. Only one study (Robinson, Froehle, & Jurpius, 1979) was found that specifically focused on the sex variable in the trainee-supervisor dyad and this study did use empathy as a variable. These investigators, in an experimental study, examined the effect of written versus videotaped model presentation and the effect of a male versus a female model on counselor trainee's production of counselor tacting response leads (CTRL). It was found that both male and female models were equally effective in promoting initial learning with respect to produced CTRL. These findings seem to indicate that, at least in the modeling component of supervision, there is no apparent difference between using male and female demonstrators.

Although the Robinson et al. (1979) study was the only research found on the sex variables in supervision, several studies, reporting conflicting findings, do exist in the counseling literature that may be related to the supervision dyad. Because Feldstein in Chapter 7 of this book has reviewed this literature, only a brief summary is presented here. Conflicting results have been found related to which sex is more empathic and to the importance of same-sex pairing in the counseling dyad. Some researchers have found that female counselors are more empathic than male counselors. However, others found no significant differences between the empathic ability of male and female counselors. It has also been found that accuracy of empathic responding may be related to sexual similarity of the client and counselor. Yet, others found no significant differences in empathic responding in same-sex or cross-sex counseling dyads.

These inconsistent findings suggest that the sex variable may be an important factor in the counseling encounter and, thus, may be of equal importance in the development of empathic understanding in the supervision dyad, which is often similar to a counseling situation. In addition, these findings support the need for experimental research on the effect of sex variables in both the counseling and supervision interaction.

Research Questions and Hypotheses

The present study was designed to explore systematically several of the supervision variables identified in the above summary of the literature. The primary area of investigation involved the differential effect of didactic and experiential styles of supervision on the improvement of empathic understanding by trainees functioning at low and moderate levels of sophistication prior to training. A secondary area for consideration centered around the sex variable in the supervision process. Specifically, would low and moderate, male and female, trainees differentially improve in empathic understanding after receiving didactic or experiential training from the same-sex supervisor?

The hypotheses (for the first research question) were as follows:

1. Subjects will improve in empathic understanding after receiving supervision.
2. Didactic supervision will be more effective in the improvement of empathic understanding than experiential supervision for trainees with low-level skill development.
3. Experiental supervision will be more effective in the improvement of empathic understanding than didactic supervision for trainees with moderate-level skill development.

Since only one study was found that investigated the importance of sex variables in the supervision process, this area was explored without any specific hypotheses.

Methodology

A pretest-posttest experimental design using a supervision analogue was used in this study.

Subjects

Subjects were 72 graduate students (36 males and 36 females) enrolled in a master's level Counselor Education Program at a small, Catholic university, who were recruited to participate in the study on a voluntary basis. The female subjects ranged in age from 24 to 42 years; 2 of the subjects were black and 34 were white; and they had completed an average of six graduate courses toward their master's degree. The male subjects ranged in age from 22 to 38 years; 3 were black and 33 were white; and they had completed an average of five graduate courses toward their master's degree. Data concerning the female subjects were collected during the fall 1981 semester. Data concerning the male subjects were collected during the spring 1982 semester.

Supervisors

Two female and two male counselors were trained in both the didactic and experiential styles of supervision. One female supervisor, age 37, held a Ph.D. in Counselor Education and had 4 years of supervisory experience in a university setting. The other female supervisor, age 34, possessed a Sixty-Hour Specialists Certificate in Counseling and had 6 years of supervisory experience in an agency setting. One male supervisor, age 45, held an Ed.D. degree in Counselor Education and had 7 years of supervisory experience in a university setting. The second male supervisor, age 40, held a Sixty-Hour Specialists Certificate in Counseling and had 10 years of supervision experience as director of a university counseling center.

The criterion for the supervisors' ability to deliver each condition was met when two independent judges agreed as to which strategy was being used by the supervisors in simulated role-play situations. During the course of the study, random supervisory sessions were monitored (through a one-way mirror) by the experimenter to ensure consistency.

As a check on the supervisors' level of competence, after completion of the study, the two pretrained raters were asked to evaluate three randomly selected taped supervision sessions for each supervisor by condition. Thus, 24 supervision sessions were rated, three didactic and three experiential for each of the four supervisors. The rating system consisted of a scale from 1 to 5, with a 1 indicating that the supervisor almost never delivered the appropriate condition and a 5 indicating that the supervisor almost always delivered the appropriate condition. An average rating of 3 for each supervisor by condition was established as the minimal

TABLE 10.1 Mean ratings for supervisor competency.

| | Supervision condition | | | |
| | Didactic | | Experiential | |
Sex of supervisor	Session I (M)	Session II (M)	Session I (M)	Session II (M)
Female	4.3	4.6	4.0	4.6
Male	4.3	4.0	4.3	4.3

acceptable competence level for this study. The results of this rating procedure are presented in Table 10.1.

Supervisory Conditions

For the *experiential* style of supervision, an informal discussion atmosphere was encouraged. The supervisor was instructed to ask the supervisee for relevant personal life experiences in the present or past that may be similar to that of the client. Supervisors, via their empathic behavior, explored the supervisee's dominant emotional quality while interviewing the client and, when appropriate, utilized the supervisory relationship as an experience wherein the supervisee was able to relate himself or herself in relationship to the client. Thus, emphasis was placed on the parallelism between the supervisory and the counseling relationship (Birk, 1972). Examples of experiential supervision were statements by the supervisor such as, "I detect some anger in your voice" and "You seem to be avoiding the issue." In addition to reflecing on the trainees' affect, the supervisor continuously encouraged the students to relate situations to themselves. For example, the supervisor would say, "You seem anxious—is the client's situation similar to something you may have experienced?"

For the *didactic* supervision, the supervisor maintained a structured approach in which he or she gave direction to the sessions. He or she specified for the supervisee those remarks that appropriately communicated empathic understanding. For weak and inappropriate responses made by the supervisee, the supervisor suggested more effective responses. The supervisor questioned the supervisee to test his or her recognition of appropriate and inappropriate responses made during the counseling sessions and positively reinforced the supervisee's accurate recognition of appropriate and inappropriate responses (Birk, 1972). Examples of didactic supervision were statements such as, "Yes, you seem to be with the client" and "Good, you are taking the client deeper into feelings." Examples of supervisor responses to inaccurate trainee statements were, "I think you're missing it—let's listen again and see if you can pick out the client's feelings" and "Can you phrase some alternative responses that are closer to the client's feelings?"

Client-actors

Three female and three male Theater Arts majors were recruited to participate as coached clients in the study on a voluntary basis. Two of the female actresses were juniors in college and both were 20 years of age. The other female actress was in her senior year of college and was 21 years old. The male actors were all in their junior year of college, two were 21 years old and one was 22 years old. All six client-actors were white.

Videotaped Client Stimulus Material

A typescript was made of six different client problems (three male, three female) and each client-actor was assigned one of these scripts that consisted of 10 client statements centered around a specific concern that had the flow of a counseling session. The client-actors were coached in expressing their statements with affect and gestures consistent with the content material. A videotape was then made of each client delivering, with appropriate affect and gestures, her or his client material with a 45-second pause included after each statement. Thus, the stimulus material consisted of the six simulated, videotaped counseling sessions with 45-second time periods for the subject to make his or her counseling responses.

A treatment check was done, by this researcher, on each videotape to ensure that the simulated role plays were, in fact, reflective of an in vivo counseling situation. This was a subjective evaluation in which the experimenter, having 10 years of counseling experience, viewed the videotapes and determined that the presented situations were typical of problems encountered in actual counseling sessions.

Measures

The Empathic Understanding Scale in Interpersonal Process (EU) was used to assess empathy levels (Carkhuff, 1969a, b). This 5-point scale was used by two independent judges to rate the subject's level of empathy in both written and oral response modes. Although Butler and Hansen (1973) found no equivalence between level of facilitative functioning between written and oral responses, Abramowitz et al. (1976) and Therrien and Fischer (1978) reported data that indicated that written responses represent a valid assessment of a counselor's oral level of functioning. The present research, using the Pearson product moment correlation, resulted in a .80 correlation for the female subjects and a .91 correlation for male subjects between written and oral response modes, supporting the Abramowitz et al. (1976) and Therrien and Fischer (1978) findings. (See Chapter 9 for a discussion of this scale's reliability and validity.)

Raters

One male and one female master's level counselor familiar with the Empathic Understanding Scale were previously trained during the fall 1981 semester. These individuals were retrained in the rating procedures for the purposes of this study. The previous training resulted in an interrater reliability, using Pearson product moment correlation, of .94 for the written response mode and .90 for the oral response mode. During this phase of the study, an interrater reliability of at least .90 was established as the minimal acceptable level. This was met, with raters achieving a reliability of .92 on the written response mode and .91 on the oral response mode.

Procedure

During the 1981–1982 school year, all graduate students enrolled in the Counselor Education Program were asked to make written responses to 10 audiotaped standard client statements (Carkhuff, 1969a,b). The male students responded to male client statements and the female students responded to female client statements. These responses were rated by two independent judges using the 5-point Carkhuff (1969a, b) scale, and an average score was determined for each participant. The ratings were then used to stratify the pool of subjects on level of empathic understanding. Those individuals scoring 2.5 and below were considered low in empathic responding; those above the 2.5 level were considered moderate in empathic responding. The 2.5 division point was considered appropriate, since any individual scoring above 2.5 would have sufficient skill development to elicit, periodically, Level 3 interchangeable empathic responses. It was decided that any subjects averaging above a 3.5 in empathic understanding would be considered high responders and would not be used in the study. This level, however, was not achieved by any subjects in either the written or oral response modes.

At this point, the researcher visited all the graduate classes and asked for volunteers to participate in the study. Those who agreed to participate were assigned times to report for the experiment. Prior to the treatment, the subjects were stratified on their level of empathic responding and randomly assigned to a supervisor and a treatment condition (didactic or experiential supervision). Male subjects interacted only with male supervisors and viewed the male videotaped simulated counseling sessions. Thus, 18 low males and 18 moderate males were randomly assigned to a treatment condition (didactic or experiential supervision) and randomly assigned to one of the two male supervisors. Similarly, the 18 low and 18 moderate female subjects were randomly assigned to a treatment condition and a female supervisor, and viewed the female videotaped counseling sessions.

No control group was used in this study, since the research questions were not directed at whether supervision was more effective than no supervision in improving empathic understanding. Instead, the study was focusing on variables that may facilitate this improvement within the supervision process. In addition, several investigators have found that receiving supervision is significantly more beneficial in facilitating growth than not receiving some form of supervision (Berg & Stone, 1980; Blane, 1968; Butler & Hansen, 1973; Dalton, Sunblad, & Hylbert, 1973; Stone & Vance, 1976).

Treatment Steps

1. Each subject reported to the treatment room and was told by the experimenter that he or she would be involved in three videotaped, simulated counseling sessions. During these sessions, the subject was asked to make "feeling level, empathic responses" to the client statements. Each simulated counseling session consisted of 10 client statements with 45 seconds separating each statement. In this interval, the subject was instructed to make his or her response. These sessions were audiotaped.
2. Immediately following Counseling Session I and Counseling Session II, each subject received 15 minutes of the preassigned style of counseling supervision (with the same-sex supervisor), centering around their audiotaped responses.
3. No supervision was received after Counseling Session III.
4. The total treatment time for each subject was approximately 1 hour and 15 minutes.

Each subject viewed the three videotaped, simulated counseling sessions in a randomized order and their empathy levels were assessed using the Carkhuff Scale (1969a, b) by rating their taped responses from Counseling Session I and Counseling Session III. As in the written response rating, the two independent judges rated all 10 of the responses (for one half of the subjects) on each session and arrived at an average score for each participant on Counseling Session I and Counseling Session III. Subjects' improvement in empathic understanding from Counseling Session I to Counseling Session III served as the dependent measure in this study.

Analysis

Subjects' responses from Counseling Session I and Counseling Session III were rated by two independent judges on the Empathic Understanding Scale to determine improvement in empathic responding over time. A Univariate Repeated Measures Analysis of Variance was conducted on the data to determine at the .05 significance level all possible main effects (time, skill level, treatment, and sex) and interactions. According to Finn and Mattson (1978), this procedure is appropriate to use whenever each subject in a study is measured with the same instrument at more than one point in time. In addition, Lord (1967) suggests that this method of analysis is appropriate, since the research questions necessitate maintaining the initial differences in skill level of the subjects. Finally, a t procedure was conducted to determine at the .05 level of significance which specific means differed significantly from each other (Bruning & Kintz, 1977).

Results

A univariate repeated-measures analysis of variance resulted in a nonsignificant F (Table 10.2) for the four-way interaction of time $\times$ sex $\times$ skill $\times$ treatment. However, an F of 20.4951 ($p < .001$) was found for the interaction of time $\times$ skill $\times$ treatment (Table 10.2), indicating that, over time (Counseling Session I to Counseling Session III), initial skill level (low or moderate) interacted with supervision condition (didactic or experiential) resulting in differential improvement of empathic understanding by the subject trainees. A t procedure was conducted to assess the specific interaction effects of trainee skill level and supervisory condition (Table 10.3). Regardless of sex, both low ($p < .001$) and moderate ($p < .05$) trainees showed significantly more improvement in empathic understanding after receiving didactic supervision as compared to trainees receiving experiental supervision. Also, low-level trainees showed significantly more improvement when compared to moderate-level trainees after receiving didactic supervision ($p < .001$), but no significant difference was found in the improvement of empathy levels

TABLE 10.2. Univariate repeated-measures analysis of variance for empathic understanding scores by time (Counseling Sessions I and III), trainee sex, trainee level of skill development (low and moderate), and supervision method (didactic and experiential).

Source of variance	df	Sums of squares	Mean squares	F
Time	1	6.588	6.588	80.058**
Sex	1	.002	.002	.022
Skill	1	2.531	2.531	30.758**
Treatment	1	4.795	4.795	58.261**
Sex $\times$ skill $\times$ time	1	.405	.405	4.921*
Sex $\times$ treatment $\times$ time	1	.157	.157	1.905
Skill $\times$ treatment $\times$ time	1	1.687	1.687	20.495**
Sex $\times$ skill $\times$ treatment $\times$ time	1	.013	.013	.156
Error (within cells)	64	5.261	.082	

*$p < .05$.
**$p < .0001$.

TABLE 10.3. t Test for differences between experimental group means on improvement of empathic understanding.

Trainee skill level and supervisory condition	t Score
Skill × treatment	
Low didactic/low experiential	7.499*
Moderate didactic/moderate experiential	2.470*
Low didactic/moderate didactic	6.369***
Low experiential/moderate experiential	.851
Skill × skill	
Low males/moderate males	3.239**
Low female/moderate females	1.998*
Moderate males/moderate females	1.570
Low males/low females	.909
Sex × skill × treatment	
Low female didactic/low female experiential	8.516***
Moderate female didactic/low female experiential	1.171
Low male didactic/low male experiential	4.789***
Moderate male didactic/moderate male experiential	2.451*

*$p < .05$.
**$p < .01$.
***$p < .001$.

for low and moderate trainees after receiving experiential supervision (Table 10.3).

In addition to the interaction of time × skill × treatment, a significant F ratio (Table 10.2) was found for the interaction of time × sex × skill ($F = 4.9212, p < .05$). A t procedure (Table 10.3) indicated that, regardless of treatment, low males improved significantly more than moderate males ($p < .001$) with a similar effect found for female subjects ($p < .05$).

Significant main effects (Table 10.2) were found for improvement over time ($F = 80.058, p < .001$), initial skill level of subject trainee ($F = 30.758, p < .001$), and received treatment condition ($F = 58.261, p < .0001$). These main effects indicate that subjects improved significantly from Counseling Time I to Counseling Time III (Table 10.4), and that trainees who were rated as low on empathic understanding, regardless of sex or treatment, showed consistently more improvement on this skill than did moderate trainees (Table 10.5), with low subjects exhibiting a mean improvement score of .490 and moderate subjects exhibiting a mean improvement score of .115 (Table 10.5). In addition, subjects who received didactic supervision, regardless of sex and skill level, improved consistently more than trainees who received experiential supervision (Table 10.5), with a total mean improvement score of .560 for those subjects who received didactic supervision and .044 for subjects who received experiential supervision (Table 10.5). Also, a nonsignificant F ratio was found for sex (Table 10.2), indicating that this variable did not contribute

TABLE 10.4. Mean empathic understanding scores by level of skill development and supervision condition for Counseling Sessions I and III.

	Supervision condition					
	Didactic		Experiential		Totals[a]	
Skill level	Session I (M)	Session III (M)	Session 0 (M)	Session III (M)	Session I	Session III
Female data (N = 36)						
Low	2.08	2.83	2.20	2.26	2.14	2.55
Moderate	2.72	2.97	2.78	2.90	2.76	2.94
Total	2.39	2.90	2.49	2.58	2.45	2.75
Male data (N = 36)						
Low	1.58	2.62	1.98	2.08	1.78	2.35
Moderate	2.96	3.14	2.89	2.80	2.93	2.97
Total	2.27	2.88	2.43	2.44	2.35	2.66
Combined male-female data (N = 72)						
Low	1.83	2.73	2.09	2.17	1.96	2.45
Moderate	2.84	3.06	2.86	2.87	2.85	2.96
Total	2.33	2.89	2.47	2.52	2.40	2.70

[a]Average score across conditions.

TABLE 10.5. Mean empathic understanding improvement scores by trainee level of skill development and supervision condition.

	Supervision condition		
Skill level	Didactic (M)	Experiential (M)	Totals[a]
Female data (N = 36)			
Low	.761	.059	.410
Moderate	.257	.113	.185
Total	.509	.086	.297
Male data (N = 36)			
Low	1.040	.098	.570
Moderate	.183	−.093	.045
Total	.612	.003	.307
Combined male-female data (N = 72)			
Low	.901	.078	.490
Moderate	.220	.010	.115
Total	.560	.044	.302

[a]Mean improvement across conditions.

TABLE 10.6. Means and standard deviations for empathic understanding scores by level of skill development, supervision condition, and sex of trainee for Counseling Sessions I and III.

	Supervision condition							
	Didactic				Experiential			
	Session I		Session III		Session I		Session III	
Sex and skill level	M	SD	M	SD	M	SD	M	SD
Low males	1.58	0.373	2.62	0.359	1.98	0.337	2.08	0.477
Low females	2.08	0.300	2.83	0.314	2.20	0.147	2.26	0.230
Moderate males	2.96	0.240	3.14	0.246	2.89	0.254	2.80	0.468
Moderate females	2.72	0.191	2.97	0.352	2.78	0.284	2.90	0.233

to the differential improvement of empathic understanding by subject trainees. Table 10.6 reports all experimental group means and standard deviations.

Finally, in addition to the results regarding the hypotheses, another unexpected finding was observed. It was the impression of this researcher that a number of subjects, expecially low-level trainees, actively resisted the experiential mode of supervision by indicating that they were less concerned with exploring their own feelings and more interested in understanding how to respond to the client.

Discussion

It was hypothesized in the present study that: (a) subjects would improve in empathic understanding after receiving supervision, (b) didactic supervision would be more effective in the improvement of empathic understanding than experiential supervision for trainees with low-level skill development, and (c) experiential supervision would be more effective in the improvement of empathic understanding than didactic supervision for trainees with moderate-level skill development. Results confirmed the first and second hypotheses, but failed to confirm the third hypothesis. Subjects improved over time, with low subjects showing the greatest amount of improvement and with didactic supervision being the most beneficial in the improvement of empathic understanding for trainees at both levels of skill development.

The above findings support the earlier research of Carkhuff and Truax (1965) and Butler and Hansen (1973), who found that levels of facilitation can be increased for both low and moderate (Butler & Hansen, 1973) or inexperienced and experienced (Carkhuff & Truax, 1965) trainees. The results also confirm the research of Birk (1972) and Payne et al. (1972), who found that didactic supervision was more beneficial than experiential supervision in the development of empathic understanding for inexperienced trainees.

In addition to exploring trainee level of skill development, the present study investigated the sex variable through a research question asking whether male and female, low and moderate trainees would differentially improve in empathic understanding after receiving didactic or experiential training from the same-sex supervisor. Results yielded no significant difference between male and female subjects on the improvement of empathic understanding, regardless of their initial skill level or received style of supervision.

This finding is consistent with the work of Robinson et al. (1979), who found that both male and female models were equally effective in promoting initial learning in counselor trainees. In addition, relating the findings to the counseling literature, this study partially supports the work of both the researchers who found no difference between male and female counselors (Breisinger, 1976; Petro & Hansen, 1977; Walker & Latham, 1977) and the researchers who found results suggesting that female counselors are more empathic than male counselors (Abramowitz et al., 1976; Hill, 1975; Kimberlin & Friesen, 1980). Using a t procedure (Table 10.7), the present study found no significant difference between the empathic abilities of moderate-level male and female subjects at either Counseling Session I or Counseling Session III. However, at Counseling Session I, low-level female subjects were found to be significantly higher than low-level males in empathic understanding ($p < .01$). This difference was not found for low-level subjects at Counseling Session III. Also, adding to the information available on the supervision process, no significant difference was found between male and female subjects in their ability to learn and improve empathic responding after receiving supervision from the same-sex supervisor (Table 10.3). (See Chapter 7 for a related discussion of sex role and empathy differences.)

TABLE 10.7. t Test for differences between low and moderate male and female subjects on empathic understanding for Counseling Sessions I and III.

	t Score	
Comparisons	Session I	Session III
Sex × skill		
Low males/low females	3.33*	1.316
Moderate males/moderate females	1.963	.128

*$p < .01$.

In the present study, trainees with low-level empathic understanding skills improved over a short period of time. This improvement was facilitated more by didactic than experiential supervision. In addition, trainees with moderate empathic skills exhibited significantly less improvement (on this skill) than did low-level trainees. However, consistent with the low subjects, the didactic approach as compared to the experiential approach was significantly more effective in facilitating the growth that did occur in empathic understanding.

Given the short-term analogue nature of this study, it is not surprising that moderate trainees exhibited less improvement than low-level subjects. As is sometimes true with skill development, initial basic learning can often be quite rapid, but the process of skill refinement can be a slow, tedious process. Perhaps a study conducted over a longer period of time (a semester or year) would result in more substantial gains for moderate-level trainees.

The finding, relating to the significance of didactic supervision for moderate subjects, needs further exploration, since a t procedure (Table 10.3) resulted in no significant difference for moderate females in the improvement of empathic understanding as a result of style of supervision received, but did yield a difference for moderate male subjects, with didactic being significantly more effective than experiential supervision ($t = 2.451, p < .05$). However, once the male and female data were combined, a significant difference emerged for moderate subjects receiving didactic as opposed to experiential training (Table 10.3). This combining or collapsing of the data may mask the fact that only the male subjects in the moderate-ability group showed differential improvement as a result of treatment and that the supervisory conditions for the moderate subjects resulted in minimal differences in the improvement of empathic understanding. The didactic approach was significantly better than the experiential approach for both ability levels (Table 10.3), but the low subjects showed a more substantial difference between the two conditions ($p < .0001$) than did the moderate subjects ($p < .05$). Taking this into consideration, it is suggested that some trainees with moderate abilities, particularly females, do not respond consistently to one specific type of training and may require, instead, a supervision experience that is designed to meet changing individual needs at various points in the process. It is possible that variables other than supervision style intercede at this stage of the trainee's development to effect change in empathic understanding. It is suggested that the relationship between the trainee and his or her supervisor may be of crucial importance, or, perhaps, the trainee's supervision preference is an important aspect of the process. Although these considerations are speculation, it seems obvious that the conditions that facilitate the expansion of empathic understanding by trainees at more advanced levels needs further investigation.

As an explanation of the nonsignificant differences between male and female subjects, it is suggested that all subjects possessed relatively the same motivation and ability to profit from the supervision experience. This conjecture is reinforced by the finding of no significant difference between low males and low females or moderate males and moderate females on the dependent variable (Table 10.3). The sex variable did not contribute to the differential improvement in empathic understanding. This may have occurred because the male and female subjects in this sample were, in many ways, quite similar. All subjects were over the age of 22 and enrolled in a master's degree program in Counselor Education at a small, Catholic university. Over 90% of the participants were pursuing their degrees on a part-time basis while working as teachers or helping service professionals. Taking these similarities into consideration, it has been suggested that as more and more individuals share common experiences, the interests of men and women in general—but particularly those in the same occupation—should increasingly resemble each other (Kuder, 1976). This seems to be the case for the individuals participating in the present study. It should be emphasized, however, that all supervision and counseling dyads consisted of same-sex pairs. Perhaps, as suggested by Hill (1975), if opposite-sex pairs had participated or if sex role of supervisor and clients had been varied (Feldstein, 1979), then initial skill level and improvement scores for male and female subjects may have been less consistent. This area of supervision process needs further research and investigation.

Assuming that the subjects in this study are representative of other counselor education trainees, the results of this research suggest substantial implications for training and supervision in counselor education. Subjects in this study responded quickly and effectively to a structured, direct style of supervision in the initial stages of their development. If this finding is applied to counselor training, it suggests that students would profit from an intensive program of skill development during the first few months of their training. This could include a set of readings on the concept of empathy, a series of video- and audiotapes illustrating effective empathic responses, and continual practice sessions that would begin with the trainee recognizing various levels of empathic responding and then move to actually having the trainee develop his or her own responses to single client statements.

At this point, the supervisor (instructor) would take an active role in reinforcing accurate empathic responses by the trainee. The supervisor would take responsibility for making such statements as, "Yes, you seem to be with the client" or "That was a response that could take your client further into feelings." If the trainee's responses are not accurately reflecting content and feeling, the supervisor could demonstrate (role model) more effective responses or ask the student to try alternative responses. This approach would continue until the trainee could consistently give Level 3 responses to single statements. When this was achieved, the trainee's empathic responding ability could be integrated into short (10–15 minutes) role-played counseling sessions. Supervision would immediately follow the role play and continue as before, with the trainer praising accurate responses (i.e., "Yes, that's it," "You're with the client") and encouraging the trainee to recognize and practice alternatives to inaccurate responses. This phase of the training process would continue until the trainee exhibited confidence in his or her ability to deliver Level 3 empathic responses in a role-play situation. Thus, low-level trainees would have profited from didactic supervision and would now be at a moderate level of skill development.

The final phase of the supervision process would include a counseling practicum situation plus individual supervision. Since the present research found that moderates improve at a slower rate than low subjects and that only males improved significantly more with didactic as opposed to experiential supervision, the approach would focus on skill refinement using a flexible, integrated didactic-experiential style of training. The supervisor would continue to model and reinforce accurate responses, but would also gradually emphasize the trainee's self-awareness in the counseling process. This slow move to an experiential mode requires sensitivity on the part of the supervisor. From the present research and from this writer's past experience as a supervisor, it appears that most trainees are reluctant to explore their own feelings in the counseling process until they are fairly confident in their skills. Experiential supervision by definition moves away from empathic responding and places the emphasis on the feelings of the counselor trainee. Such experiential statements as, "I detect some anger in your voice," "You sound a bit hesitant," or "You seem to be avoiding the issue," can be very threatening if the student is not prepared to look at himself or herself in the process, but is still concerned with what to say or do next with the client.

This advanced stage of training necessitates a careful match between the trainee and the supervisor. It also requires a skilled supervisor who is sensitive to the changing needs of the student and who is capable of changing from didactic to experiential training when the student seems receptive. As noted in the results section of this chapter, a number of students, expecially low-level subjects, actively resisted the experiential mode. This indicates that experiential techniques should be incorporated in supervision with caution. If a trainee is not ready to explore his or her own feelings in the counseling situation, then an approach that demands self-exploration can be counterproductive and, perhaps, even discourage students from continuing their training.

Thus, it is suggested that a model of supervision should be designed that would initially emphasize intense skill development until the student feels relatively confident in his or her abilities. The training would then expand by encouraging trainees to explore their own affect during the counseling process. This would result in developing counselors who are skilled in delivering high-level empathic responses, and who also are aware of the importance of understanding themselves and their presence in the counseling situation.

11
What It All Means

GERALD A. GLADSTEIN

It is time now to step back from the highly detailed investigation of empathy (as illustrated in Chapters 9 and 10) and to take a broader view. What are the main ideas that have emerged from this entire book? What conclusions can be drawn? What are the implications for research and practice? These are the questions that are addressed in this last chapter.

Summary

In an effort to determine, theoretically, the role of empathy in counseling, Chapter 1 presents an analysis of the counseling/psychotherapy, social, and developmental psychology literature. As a result of this analysis, it is concluded that empathy should be *expected* to have a complex relationship to counseling outcomes. This complexity appears to be a result of different types of empathy interacting with various counseling goals, stages, and client preferences. The research studies that are presented in Chapters 2-10 all attempted to unravel some aspect of this complexity.

In Chapters 2-7, six studies are reported that are concerned with the nature of counselor empathy and its role in counseling process and outcome. Their research designs (see Table 11.1) included four experimental (two laboratory and two in vivo) and two descriptive. Of the four experimental, two used group comparison and two used $N = 1$ approaches. The six studies used seven measures of counselor empathy, including Hogan Empathy Scale (Chapters 2 and 3), the Kagan Affective Sensitivity Scale (Chapters 2 and 3), the Barrett-Lennard Relationship Inventory (Chapters 3 and 7), the Truax Accurate Empathy Scale (Chapter 4), the Carkhuff Empathic Understanding Scale (Chapters 5 and 6), the Truax Relationship Questionnaire (Chapter 6), and the Gladstein Nonverbal Empathy Scale (Chapter 6). These measures tapped affective, cognitive, and affective-cognitive empathy. They also utilized trait and state empathy dimensions as well as empathy from the counselors, clients, and independent judge's perspectives.

TABLE 11.1. Summary of empirical studies.

Author and chapter	Type of study	Variables	Subjects	Findings/comments
Ham				
Chapter 2	Descriptive	Counselor empathy (two types)	100 experienced counselors (males and females)	No relationship between counselor affective and cognitive empathy
	In vivo: questionnaire and stimulus problem solving	Counselor sex		
Chapter 3	Experimental	Counselor empathy (two types)	19 experienced counselors	Counselor-offered empathy affected by sequencing of client behaviors (disruptive affects offered empathy);
	Laboratory: counseling analogue; questionnaires and stimulus problem solving	"Client compliant/disruptive behaviors		Counselors offer more empathy with compliant client
Kreiser				
Chapter 4	Descriptive	Counselor empathy	10 experienced counselors	Counselors were not very empathic in interviews;
	In vivo: real counseling interviews, audio tapes, questionnaire	Counselor trait anxiety	5 high trait anxiety	No relationship between counselor anxiety and empathy (important methodological weaknesses weaken the findings)

Gladstein Chapter 5	Experimental	In vivo: multiple-N, multiple-I time series, audio-video tapes, questionnaires; limited number of counseling sessions	Counselor-offered empathy Verbal, nonverbal modalities Client perceptions of counseling process and outcome Client self-exploration	4 female URACC clients	Counselor high empathy led to positive client outcomes; Counselor low empathy did not lead to negative client outcomes; Combined verbal-nonverbal modalities had the greatest effects
Chapter 6	Experimental	In vivo: multiple-N, multiple-I time series, audio-videotapes, questionnaires	Counselor-offered empathy Client perceptions of counseling process and outcome Client self-exploration	3 female 2 male URACC clients	Clients perceived counseling positively; Counselors unable to maintain experimental conditions in real, ongoing counseling sequence

TABLE 11.1. (*Continued*)

Author and chapter	Type of study	Variables	Subjects	Findings/ comments
Feldstein Chapter 7	Experimental	Counselor sex	35 male	No differences in empathy for sexes or sex roles;
	Laboratory: counseling analogues; questionnaire and audiotape	Counselor sex role	39 female college students	Male and female counselors can be trained to offer either masculine or feminine behaviors;
		Client sex		Same-sex pairing of counselor/client did not lead to higher empathy
		Counselor-offered empathy Client affective and self-referent behavior		

Brennan Chapter 9	Experimental	Four types of counselor training	24 female 8 male college students	Empathic resonation best achieved by combination of two types of training;
	Laboratory: group multitreatment; questionnaire and audiotape	Three types of counselor empathy		No differences in other types of empathy as result of training types; Low levels of empathy achieved
Mackrell Chapter 10	Experimental	Two types of supervision	36 male	Didactic supervision more effective than experiential;
	Laboratory: supervision analogue; audiotape	Supervisee sex	36 female counselors-in-training (supervisees)	Didactic supervision resulted in higher level of empathic understanding for low-skill supervisees;
		Supervisee skill level		Experiential supervision did not result in higher level of empathic understanding for moderate-skill supervisees;
		Supervisee empathic understanding Interview time sequence		No differences by sex

The six studies also included a variety of counselor independent variables: anxiety level, gender, sex role, and verbal, nonverbal, and verbal-nonverbal modalities. Client independent variables were gender and compliant versus descriptive behaviors. Empathy was also a counselor dependent variable in five studies. Client dependent variables included depth of self-exploration, satisfaction, perceptions of the counseling process, and self-reference statements.

Given this multiple set of empathy measures and independent and dependent variables, it should not be surprising that it is hard to identify common findings that cut across these six studies. However, one methodological generalization does stand out. *It was difficult to study empathy and counseling as complex phenomena.* Each study had limitations. For example, Kreiser had difficulty finding highly anxious counselors to participate.

As noted above, these studies were designed to look at these variables as complex, rather than as unidimensional. For example, Ham (Chapters 2 and 3) looked at counselor trait and state empathy, Kreiser (Chapter 4) measured counselor trait and state anxiety, and Gladstein (Chapters 5 and 6) manipulated three empathy communication modalities. In effect, because each study sought to explore somewhat different but related questions and/or hypotheses, their content findings supplement rather than reinforce each other.

Within the constraint of the above statement, it appears legitimate to draw this content summary:

1. Counselors' affective and cognitive empathy are unrelated,
2. Counselors can learn to offer high, medium, and neutral empathy,
3. Counselors can learn to offer masculine and feminine sex roles,
4. Counselors who offer empathy are affected by disruptive clients,
5. High counselor empathy leads to some positive client outcome.

In view of the fact that each of these generalizations is based on only one research study, it really should be viewed as very tentative. (This point is discussed further in the following section.)

Chapter 8 presents the context for the last two studies presented in Chapters 9 and 10. Counselor empathy training is viewed from the perspective of the development of empathy in childhood, adolescence, and adulthood. After briefly reviewing the early theorists' views and the existing literature, several studies are highlighted.

From all of this information, it is evident that cognitive empathy does increase over time. Why children become more cognitively empathic is not clear. It appears that mothers do influence their daughters' empathic development. The evidence for boys is much less clear.

Thus, by the time adults arrive at graduate counselor training programs, wide variations in their affective, cognitive, and affective-cognitive empathy exist. As a result of their earlier family interactions, as

well as other environmental influences, it can be assumed that considerable differences in potential for increasing their empathy also exist.
Yet, Chapter 8 further indicates that, although many different approaches
and techniques of empathy training have been created and researched,
the evidence strongly suggests that counselors-in-training increase their
empathic skills only minimally. Very few are able to offer facilitative
empathy.

By way of a countermeasure, Chapter 8 also presents in detail a
comprehensive training program that was very successful in one research
project (as described in Chapter 5). This combined, in sequential order,
didactic, modeling, practice, and feedback in several modalities. The
counselor, in real counseling interactions, was able to vary high, medium,
and neutral empathy, as determined by verbal, nonverbal, and verbal-
nonverbal behaviors. Finally, a proposal for increasing counselor
affective empathy is presented. This involves using concepts and methods
from the film literature. Preliminary tryouts of this program indicate that
graduate students can increase their awareness of their own feelings
through the use of film. However, as with the detailed training procedures
noted above, research needs to be carried out to test the usefulness of
these ideas.

Although Chapters 9 and 10 do not report on studies using these two
counselor training programs, they do include many of the elements of the
comprehensive program described in Chapter 8. Both Brennan and
MacKrell used systematic, multiple training procedures. These were
tested out through similar research approaches. They used experimental,
laboratory, group comparison designs that included manipulation of
training (or supervisory) methods. Both also took a complex view of
training as involving several aspects.

Although each study had its own unique content findings (see Table
11.1), two common ones evolved. *Didactic techniques were effective for
teaching beginning level communicative empathic skills* (as measured by The
Carkhuff Empathic Understanding Scale). *However, the level of empathy
achieved did not reach the facilitative level.* Mean group scores on the EU
scale after training ranged from 1.48 to 2.48 in the Brennan study to 2.35–
2.97 in the MacKrell project. In effect, college students and counselors-in-
training improved as a result of didactic instruction, but were typically
unable to demonstrate high-level empathy. As noted above, other
research has shown the same thing. (These and other findings are
discussed in the next section.)

Discussion

This book begins with three fundamental questions: (a) What is
empathy? (b) How does it develop? and (c) What is its role in counseling
and similar helping processes? By now it should be very evident to the
reader that there are no simple answers to these questions.

In fact, both theory and empirical research evidence indicate that asking these questions, as stated, is *not very useful*. Based upon what is presented in Chapters 1-10, each question must be changed so that it reflects a more accurate comprehension of empathy's complexity. Therefore, this discussion focuses on these revised questions.

What Kinds of Empathy Exist?

Theorists (early and contemporary) and researchers have identified empathy in three domains: *affective* (identification, emotional reaction, emotional contagion, resonation), *cognitive* (role taking, perspective taking, predictive, communicative), and *affective-cognitive* (combinations of various types in various proportions). They have also shown that it exists as a *trait* (inactive in the person but capable of being activated) and a *state* (the activated condition as manifested in feelings, thoughts, or behaviors). Most theorists have also argued that it is different from sympathy. The latter involves feeling sorry for the other person.

When researchers have attempted to measure these various types of empathy, they have used three perspectives: (a) the empathizer, (b) the empathizee; and (c) an outsider. They have also utilized physiological (such as galvonic skin response) and behavioral (such as body orientation) indicators. *Based upon these multiple measurement approaches, the evidence overwhelmingly demonstrates that these various empathy traits and states have little relationship to each other.* Therefore, it would be more accurate and useful to refer to various kinds of empathy, just as we refer to various kinds of psychological needs (e.g., Maslow's [1962] deficiency [D] and being [B] needs.)

As an aid, these types have been categorized and labeled and matched with frequently used empathy measures. Table 11.2 includes this

TABLE 11.2. Coded types of empathy and frequently used measures.

Domain	Trait			State		
	Empathizer	Empathizee	Other	Empathizer	Empathizee	Other
Affective	ATER	ATEE	ATO	ASER	ASEE	ASO
	(1)	(2)	(3)	(4)	(5)	(6)
Cognitive	CTER	CTEE	CTO	CSER	CSEE	CSO
	(7)	(8)	(9)	(10)	(11)	(12)
Affective/Cognitive	A/CTER	A/CTEE	A/CTO	A/CSER	A/CSEE	A/CSO
	(13)	(14)	(15)	(16)	(17)	(18)

Note. Barrett-Lennard Relationship Inventory: MO = A/CSER (16); Barrett-Lennard Relationship Inventory OS = A/CSEE (17); Carkhuff Empathic Understanding Scale = CSO (12); Chandler Privileged Information Task = A/CSO (18); Davis Interpersonal Reactivity Index = A/CTO (15); Dymond Rating Test = CTO (9); Feffer Role-Taking Task = CSO (12); Feshbach Affective Empathy Scale = ASER (4); Hogan Empathy Scale = CTO (9); Kagan Affective Sensitivity Scale = ATO (3); Mehrabian and Epstein Emotional Empathy Scale = ATO (3); Truax Accurate Empathy Scale = CSO (12); Truax Relationship Questionnaire = A/CSER (16).

information. Each measure has been coded as to whose perspective is being used: Empathizer = ER, Empathizee = EE, Outsider = O. Each empathy type is categorized as either affective (Empathy A), cognitive (Empathy C), or affective-cognitive (Empathy A-C), as well as to whether it is a trait (Empathy T) or state (Empathy S). Hence, it is possible to code a measure as tapping one or more kinds of empathy. For example, the Carkhuff Empathic Understanding Scale would be coded Empathy CSO, standing for cognitive-state empathy as viewed by an outsider. By contrast, the OS Scale of the Barrett-Lennard Relationship Inventory would be coded Empathy A/CSEE, since it measures affective and cognitive-state empathy from the empathizee's perspective. It is interesting to note that these 13 commonly used measures tap 9 of 18 types of empathy. This helps to identify empathies that are typically not measured.

Table 11.2, therefore, gives an operational answer to the question, "What kinds of empathy exist?" Because the empirical evidence shows that these measures have little relationship to each other, and because theorists over the years have written about these different types, it can be estimated that there are at least 18 kinds of empathy (3 × 2 × 3 dimensions). In all likelihood, there are more, since empathy in childhood is probably different from empathy in adolescence and adulthood (see Chapter 1) and this difference is not accounted for in Table 11.2.

These 18 types of empathy are listed and defined in Table 11.3. This information can be used in a variety of ways. For example, it can help clarify Ham's (Chapter 2) research that demonstrated that different types of empathy exist. Table 11.3 can be used to identify the two types of empathy that she found, Empathy CTER and Empathy ATO.

Table 11.3 can also be used to determine which types of empathy have been frequently researched and which types neglected. For example, in the counseling/psychotherapy literature, a great many studies have used Carkhuff's EU Scale. This indicates that Empathy CSO is studied frequently.

The same analysis can be made of research reported in the literature. For example, Kurtz and Grummon's (1972) finding that their several empathy measures were unrelated is explained by the conclusion that these measures were tapping Empathy CTO, Empathy CSO, and Empathy A/CSEE, among others. A more recent study by Johnson, Cheek, and Smither (1983) showed that the Hogan Empathy Scale contained four generally different factors. Again, we can determine the types of empathy involved. In this instance, they are Empathy ATO and Empathy CTO.

Table 11.3 can also be used to discuss the reported research concerning empathy and sex differences. Some studies indicate that women are more empathic than men and that girls are more empathic than boys; others do

TABLE 11.3. Coded types of empathy and their definitions.

Coded type	Definition
1. Empathy ATER	Affective trait empathy from the empathizer's perspective; when the person perceives his or her own typical emotional responses to other people, things, or conditions
2. Empathy ATEE	Affective trait empathy from the empathizee's perspective; when a person perceives the typical emotional response of another to the former's emotional states
3. Empathy ATO	Affective trait empathy as perceived by an outsider; when a rater or observer judges the presence of emotional states that the empathizer typically displays in response to other people, things, or conditions
4. Empathy ASER	Affective state empathy from the empathizer's perspective; when the person perceives his or her own emotional response to a person, thing, or condition
5. Empathy ASEE	Affective state empathy from the empathee's perspective; when a person perceives an emotional response of another to the former's emotional state
6. Empathy ASO	Affective state empathy as perceived by an outsider; when a rater or observer judges the presence of an emotional state displayed by an empathizer in response to another person, thing, or condition
7. Empathy CTER	Cognitive trait empathy from the empathizer's perspective; when the person perceives his or her own typical role-taking responses to other people, things, or conditions
8. Empathy CTEE	Cognitive trait empathy from the empathizee's perspective; when a person perceives the typical role-taking response of another to the former's thinking and/or emotional states
9. Empathy CTO	Cognitive trait empathy as perceived by an outsider; when a rater or observer judges the presence of role taking that the empathizer typically displays in response to other people, things, or conditions
10. Empathy CSER	Cognitive state empathy from the empathizer's perspective; when the person perceives his or her own role-taking response to a person, thing, or condition
11. Empathy CSEE	Cognitive state empathy from the empathizee's perspective; when a person perceives a role-taking response of another to the former's thought or emotional state
12. Empathy CSO	Cognitive state empathy as perceived by an outsider; when a rater or observer judges the presence of role-taking displayed by an empathizer in response to another person, thing, or condition
13. Empathy A/CTER	Affective-cognitive trait empathy from the empathizer's perspective; when the person perceives his or her own typical emotional and role-taking response to other people, things, or conditions
14. Empathy A/CTEE	Affective-cognitive trait empathy from the empathizee's perspective; when a person perceives the typical emotional and role-taking responses of another to the former's thinking and/or emotional states
15. Empathy A/CTO	Affective-cognitive trait empathy as perceived by an outsider; when a rater or observer judges the presence of emotional states and role-taking that the empathizer typically displays in response to other people, things, or conditions

TABLE 11.3. (*Continued*)

Coded type	Definition
16. Empathy A/CSER	Affective-cognitive state empathy from the empathizer's perspective; when the person perceives his or her own emotional and role-taking response to a person, thing, or condition
17. Empathy A/CSEE	Affective-cognitive state empathy from the empathizee's perspective; when a person perceives an emotional and role-taking response of another to the former's thought or emotional state
18. Empathy A/CSO	Affective-cognitive state empathy as perceived by an outsider; when a rater or observer judges the presence of an emotional and role-taking response to another person, thing, or condition

not. Why is there inconsistency in the literature? By using Table 11.3, it can be determined that some of the studies of children's empathy were measuring Empathy ASEE (e.g., Feshback & Roe, 1968), while others were measuring Empathy A/CSO (e.g., Greenspan et al., 1976). Likewise, studies of adult empathy varied in what kinds of empathy were tested. Thus, the inconsistent sex findings appear to be a function of the types of empathy involved. (This does not eliminate other possible reasons as well. For example, as Feldstein noted in Chapter 7, using gender compared to sex role produces different findings.)

How Do These Different Kinds of Empathy Develop?

With the identification of these various empathies, we can now turn to this second question. Do each of these develop in the same manner? Are they the result of the same biological and/or environmental factors? Unfortunately, as noted earlier, there is very little clear-cut empirical evidence to use in answering these questions. What little exists suggests that mothers do have an impact on their daughters' cognitive and/or affective empathy. However, due to the limitations of these studies, it cannot be determined if this is Empathy CT or Empathy CS, Empathy CTEE or Empathy CTO.

Therefore, we must rely on the theorists' speculations that are summarized in Chapter 1. (For more detail, see Gladstein [1984].) Apparently Empathy CT and Empathy CS develop gradually as the infant is exposed to stimuli from the environment, particularly the mother (or mother-substitute). No theorist assumes that Empathy CT and Empathy CS are biologically inherited. From a self-centered, unconscious, concrete, nonabstract, infant evolves an adult who is capable of looking at himself or herself as different from others but capable of taking their roles. In essence, Empathy CT and Empathy CS are learned. Yet, as Piaget and other developmentalists have argued, natural maturational stages (meaning biological and environmental factors interacting) occur in all cultures. Thus, apparently this learning has some biological basis.

Regarding the development of Empathy AT and Empathy AS, the theorists are more vague. (There appears to be no empirical evidence regarding this development other than the fact that they increase as children get older.) Two lines of reasoning have been used: genetic and conditioning. For example, McDougall and Piaget wrote that the very young infant displays spontaneous emotional resonation or contagion (see Chapter 1). (A recent report by Condon [1984] indicated that within a few days the human neonate systematically responds to the mother.) By contrast, Allport argued that conditioning leads to these affective responses. Changes in Empathy AT and Empathy AS are cumulative, dependent on the particular conditioning history.

If the development of the *empathic process* is considered, however, the theoretical and empirical literature provides us with better answers. The empathic process itself can last for a few seconds or occur over several minutes. It can be conceived as having pre-, in-, and poststages. By using the information from Table 11.3, we can assume that all types of Empathy T exist in the *prestage*. In fact, the individual variations in Empathy T in this prestage are manifest when the various Empathy T tests are used. For example, norms for the Hogan CT, Mehrabian and Epstein AT, and Davis A/CT tests indicate considerable differences in scores.

During the *in-stage*, Empathy AS and Empathy CS differ in two respects. Empathy AS occurs unconsciously and rapidly. The empathizer is unaware that he or she is empathizing at that point in time. By contrast, the in-stage for Empathy CS occurs consciously and slowly—that is, longer than a few seconds. The empathizer chooses to be empathic. In the writings of the counseling/psychotherapy theorists (such as Stewart, Rogers, and Barrett-Lennard), there is considerable agreement concerning these points. All have identified the *initial* state as affective, which is then followed by role taking. A definite sequence occurs. Although the theorists agree on this, empirical evidence is missing here. It appears that no studies have been designed that clearly show this sequence. Research that has attempted to measure Empathy AS (e.g., Robinson et al., 1982) has usually used physiological indices, but no effort has been made to determine Empathy CS in a continuous sequence with Empathy AS.

In the *poststage*, Empathy AS occurs when the empathizer becomes aware of himself or herself again. At this point, the empathic process is over. The early aesthetic theorists were in agreement on this point (Gladstein, 1984). Therapists, such as Reik, wrote about moving in and out of Empathy AS as part of the therapeutic process. This movement occurs unconsciously. By contrast, the Empathy CS poststage occurs when the empathizer is no longer consciously attempting to act "as-if" he or she were the other. However, he or she can reactivate the process by taking on this attitude again.

In fact, this is what empathy training has focused on primarily. However, to get at Empathy CS, therapists have used Empathy CSO measures of the counselor's communicative skills. As discussed in Chapter 8 and documented in Chapters 9 and 10, most programs have tried to teach Empathy CS, even though the trainers have ideally sought to develop training in Empathy AS and Empathy A/CS. However, as noted earlier, the empirical evidence shows that even when the training has been limited to Empathy CS, only minimal levels of Empathy CS have been usually obtained.

What Are the Roles of the Different Kinds of Empathy in Counseling?

Even though this question is more awkward than the previously stated one (What is its role in counseling?), it should help us differentiate the possible roles that can be involved. Given the multiple types of empathy and their different developments and processes, we should expect different roles in counseling.

This position is briefly developed in the last section of Chapter 1 and is summarized in Table 1.1. It was argued that different counseling goals, stages, and client preferences would require differential use of Empathy A and Empathy C. Now, by using Tables 11.2 and 11.3, we can expand on those ideas. Table 11.4 incorporates the information included in Table 1.1 but recasts and adds to it. The first addition to be noted is the listing of separate columns for trait and state forms of empathy. Second, a column has been added for Empathy A/C for both the trait and state forms.

An analysis of Table 11.4 shows that out of the 78 possible situations where high empathy could have a definite positive role in counseling outcomes, only 34 (44%) are hypothesized. In addition, 18 (23%) situations are estimated to have a likely positive role.

As pointed out in the discussion of Table 1.1, these hypotheses are based upon existing empirical evidence, theoreticians' consensus of opinions, and this author's many years of counseling experience. There is nothing by way of new evidence presented in Chapters 2–10 that would argue for changing these determinations.

Several comments can be made from this expanded table. First, for certain counseling aspects, the effect of a high level of one type of empathy will be benefitted by high levels in the other types. For example, under "Stages" in Table 11.4, when Empathy AT and Empathy CT are high during "Initiation," Empathy A/C is effective also. By contrast, for "Exploration," when Empathy AT is listed as only "Maybe" and Empathy CT is listed as "Yes," their combination, Empathy A/CT, only is listed as "Maybe." Stating this another way, if a client is in the initiation, or beginning counseling stage, we can expect that all three types of high empathy will be helpful. However, during the exploration stage, if the counselor uses high levels of Empathy AT, high levels of Empathy CT, and high levels of Empathy A/CT, the effects on the counseling will be

TABLE 11.4. Expected relationships of various types of high empathy to positive counseling outcomes.

Counseling aspect	High trait			High state		
	Empathy A	Empathy C	Empathy A/C	Empathy A	Empathy C	Empathy A/C
Goals						
Self-exploration	Yes[a]	Yes	Yes	Yes	Yes	Yes
Problem-solving	No[b]	Maybe[c]	No	No	Maybe	No
Action-oriented	No	Maybe	No	No	Maybe	No
Stages						
Initiation	Yes	Yes	Yes	Yes	Yes	Yes
Rapport establishment	Yes	Yes	Yes	Yes	Yes	Yes
Problem identification	Maybe	Yes	Maybe	Maybe	Yes	Maybe
Exploration	Maybe	Yes	Maybe	Maybe	Yes	Maybe
Action	No	Maybe	No	No	Maybe	No
Termination	No	Maybe	No	No	Maybe	No
Client preferences						
Close emotional relationship	Yes	Yes	Yes	Yes	Yes	Yes
Neutral emotional relationship	No	Maybe	No	No	Maybe	No
Counselor to take client view	Yes	Yes	Yes	Yes	Yes	Yes
Counselor to present own self	No	No	No	No	No	No

[a]Yes = would help regarding positive outcome.
[b]No = would interfere regarding positive outcome.
[c]Maybe = may or may not help regarding positive outcome.

mixed. This example also illustrates a second point: high levels of all types of empathy will not, per se, lead to positive counseling outcomes. The results depend on the counseling goals, stages, and client preferences, as indicated in Table 11.4.

Another way of using Table 11.4 is to look at when high Empathy A and high Empathy C will most likely be helpful to counseling outcomes. Both would be useful for self-exploration goals, during the initiation and rapport establishment stages, when the client prefers a close emotional relationship with the counselor, and when the counselor takes the client's view. In addition, high Empathy C would be helpful during the problem identification and exploration stages.

Table 11.4 also indicates when high Empathy A/C would *not* be helpful: when the goals are problem solving and/or Action oriented, during the action and termination stages, when the client prefers a neutral emotional relationship, and when the client wants the counselor to present his or her own self.

All of the above adds up to a *practical principle: for maximum effectiveness, different types of high empathy must be used differentially, depending on the counseling goals, stages, and client preferences.*

Conclusions

In view of the above summary and discussion, the following conclusions are stated regarding our current state of knowledge and implications of this knowledge for research and practice.

State of Knowledge

1. *There is a considerable body of theoretical and research literature regarding the nature of empathy.* As indicated above, the empirical studies document its theorized multielements and multistages. This evidence is consistent across the social, developmental, and counseling/psychotherapy fields. Therefore, it is no longer legitimate to refer to the "nature of empathy." We must be concerned with various kinds of empathy.

2. *Although there is a considerable theoretical literature concerning empathy's development, the empirical research minimally supports the major propositions.* Even though the data show that children increase their Empathy A and Empathy C, there is no clear-cut evidence as to why this development occurs. Futhermore, research has not demonstrated Empathy A's and Empathy C's sequencing during the empathic process itself. Regarding counselor empathic training, despite numerous efforts to increase Empathy C, the evidence shows that only minimal increases occur. Very little research has attempted to increase counselor Empathy A.

3. *There is a large literature concerning empathy research approaches and measures.* Great strides have occurred during the last 30 years in the social, developmental, and counseling/psychotherapy fields. Many reasonably valid and reliable measures exist that tap each type of empathy from various perspectives. However, up to now, these fields have carried out their studies fairly independently of each other

4. *Although there is a sizeable literature concerning empathy's role in counseling, the empirical research evidence minimally supports the theoretical beliefs.* Since many research studies approach empathy as a unitary phenomenon, and since there are many design and measurement weaknesses, the available evidence is contradictory. The field appears to be at a point where major breakthroughs could occur.

From these conclusions, implications can be derived for research and practice.

Implications for Research

1. *Knowledge from the social, developmental, and counseling/psychotherapy fields must be used to plan and carry out basic and applied studies.* As noted above, without this integration, studies have been too narrow. Each field can benefit from the others' designs and measures.

2. *Research should approach empathy as a multielement and multistage construct.* Studies should identify the several types of empathy involved and measure them. Empathy should be looked at as in process, not as static. Because the empirical evidence clearly documents the existence of these various empathies, new research should focus on the processes.

3. *Appropriate empathy measures should be used for each type of empathy.* Table 11.2 categorizes and codes commonly used empathy measures. This information should be used when planning studies. In addition, new types of measures are needed regarding Empathy AS. This is the one area that is weak.

4. *Certain kinds of studies are expecially needed.* In the study of empathic development, longitudinal designs are needed for various types of empathy. So far, the typical approach has been cross-sectional. Also, a study should be made of the sequencing process. Theory indicates that Empathy A precedes Empathy C; however, solid evidence is lacking.

Regarding the roles that various types of empathy play in counseling, we need to follow-up some of the findings presented in Chapters 2-7. For example, would Empathy AS also show differences when counselor sex role versus counselor gender is used as an independent variable? In addition, studies should emphasize in vivo, not laboratory, designs. These are much harder and costlier to do, but they are needed to check out the analogue, laboratory results.

Implications for Practice

1. *Counselor empathy training should utilize a total comprehensive program.* Too many programs use only one modality or one training technique for only short time periods. The program described in Chapter 8 could be used as a model. These programs should emphasize Empathy AS, as well as including Empathy CS. Creative approaches need to be developed, since little attention has been given to this area. In addition, efforts should continue until the trainees can typically offer Empathy A/CS at a facilitative level. This is crucial, since the evidence indicates that this level is usually not achieved.

2. *Counselors should use various kinds of empathy differentially.* Table 11.4 can be used as a starting place to identify which empathy seems appropriate for which goals, for which stage, and for which client. The important thing here is to realize that flexibility is needed. This is also true regarding the use of empathy in conjunction with other aspects of counseling. The empathies are only one aspect of counseling. They must be integrated with others, such as diagnoses and information giving.

The above shows that, at this point, our knowledge about the empathies produces more implications for research than for practice. Perhaps after another 30 years of research the balance will be reversed. Let's hope so.

Appendix: Gladstein Nonverbal Empathy Scale

Rater Code ____
Segment # ____

General Instructions

As part of this research project you will be viewing a series of videotape segments of the nonverbal behavior of a counselor during an interview. Below you will find 5 definitions of different levels of nonverbal empathic understanding. Determine which level of the scale seems to be the most appropriate rating of the counselor's overall empathic understanding for that particular segment, and *CIRCLE* the number. Be sure to circle only 1 (ONE) number, and be sure that it is a whole number and not a space between two numbers.

LEVEL 1   The counselor's behavior during this segment suggests that s/he is NOT listening, not understanding, and gererally being insensitive.

LEVEL 2   The counselor's behavior indicates that s/he is responding but does so in a way that suggests a rather controlled or mechanical sensitivity.

LEVEL 3   The counselor's behavior indicates that s/he understands surface level feelings, but it does not demonstrate an understanding for deeper feelings.

LEVEL 4   The counselor's behavior during this segment indicates that s/he *generally* understands deeper level feelings that may be expressed.

LEVEL 5   The counselor's behavior indicates that s/he is responding with a full awareness of another's feelings, and also a comprehensive and accurate level of understanding.

LEVEL

1	2	3	4	5

References

Abramowitz, C.V., Abramowitz, S.I., & Weitz, L.J. (1976). Are men soft on empathy? Two studies in feminine understanding. *Journal of Clinical Psychology, 32,* 434-437.

Aderman, D., Brehm, S.S., & Katz, L.B. (1974). Empathic observation of an innocent victim: The just world revisited. *Journal of Personality and Social Psychology, 29,* 342-347.

Allport, F.H. (1924). *Social psychology.* Boston: Houghton Mifflin Co.

Altman, H.A. (1973). Effects of empathy, warmth, genuineness in the initial counseling interview. *Counselor Education and Supervision, 12,* 225-228.

Anderson, R.F., & Anderson, G.V. (1968). Interview rating scale—Form A. In L. Litwack, R. Getson, & G. Salzman (Eds.), *Research in counseling* (pp. 404-409). Itasca IL: F.E. Peacock, Inc.

Armstrong, G. (1982). The effects of a structured and unstructured group approach on the perceptual accuracy, empathy, and self-actualization of first-year human services students (Doctoral dissertation, Temple University, 1982). *Dissertation Abstracts International, 43,* 640-A.

Aronfreed, J. (1970). The socialization of altruistic and sympathetic behavior: Some theoretical and experimental analyses. In J. Macaulay & L. Berkowitz (Eds.), *Altruism and helping behavior.* New York: Academic Press.

Aylward, J.L. (1981). Effects of Alpha biofeedback training on empathy in counseling (Doctoral dissertation, Lehigh University, 1981). *Dissertation Abstracts International, 42,* 85-A.

Bandura, A. (1956). Psychotherapist's anxiety level, self-insight and psychotherapeutic competence. *Journal of Abnormal and Social Psychology, 52,* 333-337.

Bandura, A., Lipsher, D.H., & Miller, P.B. (1960). Psychotherapists' approach-avoidance reactions to patients' expressions of hostility. *Journal of Consulting Psychology, 24,* 1-8.

Banks, N.M. (1972). The differential effects of race and social class in helping. *Journal of Clinical Psychology, 28,* 90-92.

Barnett, M. A., Howard, J. A., King, L. J., & Dino, G. A. (1980). Empathy in young children: Relation to parent's empathy, affection, and emphasis on the feelings of others. *Developmental Psychology, 16,* 243-244.

Barrett-Lennard, G.T. (1962). Dimensions of therapist response as causal factors in therapeutic change. *Psychological Monographs, 76,* 1-33.

Barrett-Lennard, G.T. (1964). *The relationship inventory* (Form OS-M-64). Armidale, NSW, Australia: University of New England.

Barrett-Lennard, G.T. (1978). The relationship inventory: Later developments and adaptations. *Psychological Documents, 8,* 68. (Ms. No. 1732)

Barrett-Lennard, G.T. (1981). The empathy cycle: Refinement of a nuclear concept. *Journal of Counseling Psychology, 28,* 91-100.

Bath, K.E., & Calhoun, R.O. (1977). The effects of professional counselor training on empathy: Continued cause for concern. *Counselor Education and Supervision, 16,* 98-106.

Batson, C.D., Duncan, B.D., Ackerman, P., Buckley, T., & Birch, K. (1981). Is empathic emotion a source of altruistic motivation? *Journal of Personality and Social Psychology, 40,* 290-302.

Bender, I.E., & Hastorf, A.H. (1953). On measuring generalized empathic ability. *Journal of Abnormal and Social Psychology, 48,* 503-506.

Bem, S.L. (1974). The measurement of psychological androgyny. *Journal of Consulting and Clinical Psychology, 42,* 155-162.

Berenson, B.G., Carkhuff, R.R., & Myrus, P. (1966). The interpersonal functioning and training of college students. *Journal of Counseling Psychology, 13,* 441-446.

Berg, K.S., & Stone, G.L. (1980). Effects of conceptual level and supervision on counselor skill development. *Journal of Counseling Psychology, 27,* 500-509.

Bergin, A.E., & Jasper, L.G. (1969). Correlates of empathy in psychotherapy: A replication. *Journal of Abnormal Psychology, 74,* 447-481.

Bergin, A.E., & Suinn, R.M. (1975). Individual psychotherapy and behavior therapy. In M.R. Rosenzweig & L.W. Porter (Eds.), *Annual Review of Psychology* (p. 515). Palo Alto, CA: Annual Reviews.

Bergman, A., & Wilson, A. (1984). Thoughts about stages on the way to empathy and the capacity for concern. In J. Lichtenberg, M. Bornstein, & D. Silver (Eds.), *Empathy II* (pp. 59-80). Hillsdale, NJ: The Analytic Press.

Bieri, J. (1961). Complexity-simplicity as a personality variable in cognitive and preferential behavior. In D. Fiske & S. Maddi (Eds.), *Functions of varied experience* (pp. 355-379). Homewood, IL: Dorsey Press.

Birk, J.M. (1972). Effects of counseling supervision method and preference on empathic understanding. *Journal of Counseling Psychology, 19,* 542-546.

Blane, S.M. (1968). Immediate effect of supervisory experience on counselor candidates. *Counselor Education and Supervision, 8,* 29-47.

Bobker, L.R. (1979). *Elements of film* (3rd ed.). New York: Harcourt, Brace, Jovanovich.

Boomer, D.S., & Goodrich, D.W. (1961). Speech disturbances and judged anxiety. *Journal of Consulting Psychology, 25,* 160-164.

Bordin, E.S. (1979). The generalizability of the psychoanalytic concept of the working alliance. *Psychotherapy: Theory, Research and Practice, 16,* 252-260.

Borke, H. (1971). Interpersonal perception of young children: Egocentrism or empathy. *Developmental Psychology, 5,* 263-269.

Bowman, J., & Roberts, G. (1978). Counselor anxiety during a counseling interview. *Counselor Education and Supervision, 17,* 205-222.

Bowman, J., & Roberts, G. (1979a). Counselor trainee anxiety during counseling. *Journal of Counseling Psychology, 26,* 85-88.

Bowman, J., & Roberts, G. (1979b). Effects of tape-recording and supervisory evaluation on counselor trainee anxiety level. *Counselor Education and Supervision, 19,* 20-26.

Bowman, J., Roberts, G., & Giesen, J. (1978). Counselor trainee anxiety during the initial counseling interview. *Journal of Counseling Psychology, 25,* 137-143.

Bozarth, J.D., & Grace, D.P. (1970). Objective ratings and client perceptions of therapeutic conditions with university counseling center clients. *Journal of Clinical Psychology, 26,* 117-118.

Bradley, F.O. (1974). A modified interpersonal process recall technique as a training model. *Counselor Education and Supervision, 14,* 34-39.

Brams, J.M. (1961). Counselor characteristics and effective communication in counseling. *Journal of Counseling Psychology, 25,* 161-164.

Breisinger, G.D. (1976). Sex and empathy, reexamined. *Journal of Counseling Psychology, 23,* 289-290.

Brennan, J.N. (1979). *Counselor skill training: A critical review of the empirical literature.* Unpublished manuscript, University of Rochester. Completed as part of doctoral requirements.

Brewer, B.R. (1974). Relationships among personality empathic ability and counselor effectiveness. (Doctoral Dissertation, University of North Dakota, 1974). *Dissertation Abstracts International, 35,* 10-A, 6449. (University Microfilms No. DDJ75-09093)

Bronfenbrenner, U., Harding, J., & Gallway, M. (1968). The measurement of skill in social perception. In D. McClelland, A. Baldwin, U. Bronfenbrenner, & F. Grodbeck (Eds.), *Talent and society* (pp. 29-111). Princeton, NJ: Van Nostrand.

Brown, D., & Parks, J.C. (1972). Interpreting nonverbal behavior: A key to more effective counseling: A review of the literature. *Rehabilitation Counseling Bulletin, 15,* 176-184.

Bruning, J.L., & Kintz, B.L. (1977). *Computational Handbook of Statistics* (2nd ed.). Glenview, IL: Scott, Foresman and Co.

Bryan, J.H. (1972). Why children help: A review. *Journal of Social Issues, 28,* 87-104.

Budman, S.H. (1971). The effect of client lexical organization upon psychotherapist empathy level: A psychotherapy analogue study. (Doctoral dissertation, University of Pittsburgh, 1971). *Dissertation Abstracts International, 32* 6-B, 3629-3630. (University Microfilms No. 72-02047)

Burns, N., & Cavey, L. (1957). Age differences in empathic ability among children. *Canadian Journal of Psychology, 11,* 227-230.

Butler, E.R., & Hansen, J.E. (1973). Facilitative training: Acquisition, retention, and modes of assessment. *Journal of Counseling Psychology, 20,* 60-65.

Campbell, D., & Fiske, B. (1959). Convergent and discriminant validation by the multitrait multimethod matrix. *Psychological Bulletin, 56,* 81-105.

Campbell, D. & Stanley, J. (1966). *Experimental and quasi-experimental designs for research.* Chicago: Rand McNally.

Campbell, R.J., Kagan, N., & Krothwohl, D.R. (1971). The development and validation of a scale to measure affective sensitivity (empathy). *Journal of Counseling Psychology, 18,* 407-412.

Carkhuff, R.R. (1969a). *Helping and human relations: A primer for lay professional helpers: Vol. I. Selection and training.* New York: Holt, Rinehart & Winston.

Carkhuff, R.R. (1969b). *Helping and human relations: A primer for lay professional helpers: Vol. II. Practice and research.* New York: Holt, Rinehart & Winston.

Carkhuff, R.R. (1976). *HRD Audiotape Series, Forms I and II.* Amherst, MA: Human Resource Development Press.

Carkhuff, R.R. (1980). *The art of helping IV.* Amherst, MA: Human Resource Development Press.

Carkhuff, R.R., & Burstein, J. (1970). Objective therapist and client ratings of therapist offered facilitative conditions of moderate to low functioning therapists. *Journal of Clinical Psychology, 26,* 394-395.

Carkhuff, R.R., Pierce, R.M., Banks, G.P., Berenson, D.H., Cannon, J.R., & Zigon, F. J. (1980). *The art of helping IV—Trainers guide.* Amherst, MA: Human Resource Development Press.

Carkhuff, R.R., & Truax, C.B. (1965). Training in counseling and psychotherapy: An evaluation of an integrated didactic and experiential approach. *Journal of Counseling Psychology, 29,* 333-336.

Carlson, W. (1979). Increasing verbal empathy as a function of feedback and instruction. *Counselor Education and Supervision, 13,* 208-213.

Carter, C.A. (1971). Advantages of being a woman therapist. *Psychotherapy: Theory, Research and Practice, 8,* 297-300.

Carter, D.K., & Pappas, J.P. (1975). Systematic desensitization and awareness treatment for reducing counselor anxiety. *Journal of Counseling Psychology, 22,* 147-151.

Cartwright, R.D., & Lerner, B. (1963). Empathy, need to change, and improvement with psychotherapy. *Journal of Consulting Psychology, 27,* 138-144.

Cash, T., Kehr, J., & Salzbach, R. (1978). Help-seeking attitudes and perceptions of counselor behavior. *Journal of Consulting Psychology, 25,* 264-269.

Chandler, M.J. (1972). Egocentrism in normal and pathological childhood development. In F. Monks, W. Hartup, & J. DeWitt (Eds.), *Determinants of behavioral development.* New York: Academic Press.

Chandler, M.J. (1973). Egocentrism and anti-social behavior: The assessment and training of social perspective-taking skills. *Developmental Psychology, 9,* 326-332.

Chandler, M.J. (1976). Social cognition: A selective review of current research. In W.F. Overton & J.M. Gallagher (Eds.), *Knowledge and development: Advances in research and theory* (Vol. 1). New York: Plenum.

Chandler, M.J., Greenspan, S., & Barenboim, C. (1974). Assessment and training of role-taking and referential communication skills in institutionalized emotionally disturbed children. *Developmental Psychology, 10,* 546-553.

Charles, C.H.S. (1974). Correlates of adjudged empathy as early identifiers of counseling potential (Doctoral dissertation, The University of Alabama, 1973). *Dissertation Abstracts International, 34,* 6378. (University Microfilms, No. 74-9340)

Chesler, P. (1972). *Women and madness.* New York: Doubleday.

Chinsky, J.M. & Rappaport, J. (1970). Brief critique of the meaning and reliability of "accurate empathy" ratings. *Psychological Bulletin, 73,* 379-382.

Cochrane, C.T. (1974). Development of a measure of empathic communication. *Psychotherapy: Theory, Research, and Practice, 11,* 41-47.

Coke, J.S., Batson, D.D., & McDavis, K. (1978). Empathic mediation of helping: A two-stage model. *Journal of Personality and Social Psychology, 36,* 752-766.

Coleman, R., Gleenblatt, M., & Solomon, H.C. (1956). Physiological evidence of rapport during psychotherapeutic interviews. *Diseases of the Nervous System, 17,* 71-77.

Condon, W.S. (1984). Communication and empathy. In J. Lichtenberg, M. Bornstein, & D. Silver (Eds.), *Empathy II.* New York: The Analytic Press.

Corcoran, K.J. (1980). Experiential focusing and human resource development: A comparative study of pre-conceptual and conceptual approaches to the training of empathy (Doctoral dissertation, University of Pittsburgh, 1980). *Dissertation Abstracts International, 42,* 384-A.

Cottrell, L.S., Jr. (1942). The analysis of situational fields in social psychology. *American Sociology Review, 1,* 370-382.

Cowen, E.L. (1961). The experimental analogue: An approach to research in psychotherapy. *Psychological Reports, 8,* 9-10.

Cronbach, L.J. (1955). Processes affecting scores on "understanding of others" and "assumed similarity". *Psychological Bulletin, 22,* 177-193.

Daane, C.J., & Schmidt, L.G. (1957). Empathy and personality variables. *Journal of Educational Research, 51,* 129-135.

Dalton, R., Sunblad, L., & Hylbert, K. (1973). An application of principles of social learning to training in communication of empathy. *Journal of Counseling Psychology, 20,* 378-383.

Danish, S.J. (1971). Factors influencing changes in empathy following a group experience. *Journal of Counseling Psychology, 18,* 262-267.

Danish, S.J., & Kagan, N. (1971). Measurement of affective sensitivity: Toward a valid measure of interpersonal perception. *Journal of Counseling Psychology, 18,* 51-54.

Davis, M.H. (1980). A multidimensional approach to individual differences in empathy. *Psychological Documents, 10,* 85. (Ms. No. 2124)

Davis, M.H. (1983). Measuring individual differences in empathy: Evidence for a multidimensional approach. *Journal of Personality and Social Psychology, 44,* 113-126.

Davitz, J.R. (Ed.) (1964). *The communication of emotional meaning.* New York: McGraw-Hill.

Delaney, D.J. (1968). Sensitization to nonverbal communication. *Counselor Education and Supervision, 7,* 315-316.

Delaney, D.J. (1969). Simulation techniques in counselor education: Proposal of a unique approach. *Counselor Education and Supervision, 8,* 183-189.

Deutsch, F., & Madle, R.A. (1975). Empathy: Historic and current conceptualizations, measurement, and a cognitive theoretical perspective. *Human Development, 18,* 267-287.

DiMascio, A., Boyd, R.W., Greenblatt, M., & Solomon, H.C. (1955). The psychiatric interview. *Diseases of the Nervous System, 16,* 4-9.

Dispenzieri, A., & Balinsky, B. (1963). Relationship between the ability to acquire interviewing skills and authoritarianism and manifest anxiety. *Personnel and Guidance Journal, 42,* 40-42.

Dolan, V.L. (1983). The relationship of parent discipline and parent empathy to children's empathy and altruistic behavior. (Doctoral dissertation, University of Rochester, 1983). *Dissertation Abstracts International, 44,* 08A, 2358. (University Microfilms No. DEQ83-21710)

Dollard, J., & Miller, N. (1950). *Personality and psychotherapy.* New York: McGraw-Hill.

Dymond, R.R. (1949). A scale for the measurement of empathic ability. *Journal of Consulting Psychology, 13,* 127-133.

Edwards, H.P., Boulet, D.B., Mahrer, A.R., Chagnon, G.J., & Mook, B. (1982). Carl Rogers during initial interviews: A moderate and consistent therapist. *Journal of Counseling Psychology, 29,* 14-18.

Egan, G. (1975). *The skilled helper.* Monterey, CA: Brooks/Cole.

Eidsvik, C. (1978). *Cineliteracy: Film among the arts.* New York: Random House.

Eisenberg-Berg, N., & Mussen, P. (1978). Empathy and moral development in adolescence. *Developmental Psychology, 14,* 185-186.

Eisler, R.M., Hersen, M., Miller, P.M., & Blanchard, E.B. (1975). Situational determinants of assertive behavior. *Journal of Consulting and Clinical Psychology, 43,* 330-340.

Emmerling, F.C. (1961). A study of the relationships between personality characteristics of classroom teachers and pupil perceptions of these teachers. (Doctoral dissertation, Auburn University). *Dissertation Abstracts International, 22-*4, 1054. (University Microfilms No. 61-03002)

Endler, N.S., Hunt, J., & Rosenstein, A.J. (1962). An S-R inventory of anxiousness. *Psychological Monographs, 76,* 17 (whole No. 356).

Endler, N.S., & Okada, M. (1975). A multidimensional measure of trait anxiety: The S-R inventory of general trait anxiousness. *Journal of Consulting and Clinical Psychology, 43,* 319-329.

English, R.W., & Jelevensky, S. (1971). Counselor behavior as judged under audio, visual, and audiovisual communication conditions. *Journal of Counseling Psychology, 18,* 509-513.

Farnsworth, K.E. (1966). Application of scaling techniques to the evaluation of counseling outcomes. *Psychological Bulletin, 66,* 81-93.

Feffer, M.H. (1959). The cognitive implications of role-taking behavior. *Journal of Personality, 27,* 152-168.

Feffer, M.H., & Gourevitch, V. (1960). Cognitive aspects of role-taking in children. *Journal of Personality, 28,* 383-396.

Feldstein, J.C. (1979). Effects of counselor sex and sex role and client sex on clients' perceptions and self-disclosure in a counseling analogue study. *Journal of Counseling Psychology, 26,* 437-444.

Feldstein, J.C. (1982). Counselor and client sex pairing: The effects of counseling problem and counselor sex role orientation. *Journal of Counseling Psychology, 29,* 418-420.

Feldstein, J.C., & Gladstein, G.A. (1980). A comparison of construct validities of four measures of empathy. *Measurement and Evaluation in Guidance, 13,* 49-57.

Feshbach, N.D. (1978). Studies in empathic behavior in children. In B.A. Maher (Ed.), *Progress in experimental personality research* (Vol. 8) (pp. 1-47). New York: Academic Press.

Feshbach, N.D. & Feshbach, S. (1969). The relationship between empathy and aggression in two age groups. *Developmental Psychology, 1,* 102-107.

Feshbach, N.D., & Roe, K. (1968). Empathy in six- and seven-year-olds. *Child Development, 39,* 133-145.

Finn, J.D., & Mattson, I. (1978). *Multivariate analysis in educational research.* Chicago: National Educational Resources.

Flavell, J.H., Botkin, P.T., Fry, C.L., Jr., Wright, J.W., & Jarvis, P. (1968). *The development of role-taking and communication skills in children.* New York: Wiley.

Ford, J.D. (1979). Research on training counselors and clinicians. *Review of Educational Research, 49,* 87-130.

Ford, M.E. (1979). The construct validity of egocentrism. *Psychological Bulletin, 86,* 1169-1188.

Foushee, H.C., Davis, M.H., & Archer, R.L. (1979). Empathy, masculinity and femininity. *Psychological Documents, 9,* 85-86.

Freud, S. (1923). *Group psychology and the analysis of the ego.* New York: Boni and Liverright. (Original work published 1921)

Fridman, M.S., & Stone, S.C. (1978). Effect of training, stimulus presentation on empathy ratings. *Journal of Counseling Psychology, 25,* 131-136.

Gamsky, N.R., & Farwell, G.F. (1966). Counselor verbal behavior as a function of client hostility. *Journal of Counseling Psychology, 13,* 184-190.

Giannandrea, V., & Murphy, K.C. (1973). Similarity, self-disclosure and return for a second interview. *Journal of Counseling Psychology, 20,* 545-548.

Gladstein, G.A. (1970). Is empathy important in counseling? *Personnel and Guidance Journal, 48,* 823-827.

Gladstein, G.A. (1974). Nonverbal communication and counseling/psychotherapy. *The Counseling Psychologist, 4,* 34-57.

Gladstein, G.A. (1977). Empathy and counseling outcome: An empirical and conceptual review. *The Counseling Psychologist, 6,* 70-79.

Gladstein, G.A. (1983). Understanding empathy: Integrating counseling, developmental and social psychology perspectives. *Journal of Counseling Psychology, 30,* 467-482.

Gladstein, G.A. (1984). The historical roots of contemporary empathy research. *Journal of the History of the Behavioral Sciences, 20,* 38-59.

Gladstein, G.A., & Feldstein, J.C. (1983). Using film to increase counselor empathic experiences. *Counselor Education and Supervision, 23,* 125-131.

Glass, G.V., Willson, V.L., & Gottman, J.M. (1975). *Design and analysis of time-series experiments.* Boulder, CO: University of Colorado Press.

Goldstein, A.P., & Michaels, G.Y. (1985). *Empathy: Development, training, and consequences.* Hillsdale, NJ: Lawrence Erlbaum Associates.

Gormally, J., & Hill, C.E. (1974). Guidelines for research on Carkhuff's training model. *Journal of Counseling Psychology, 21,* 539-547.

Gough, H.G. (1964). *Manual for the California psychological inventory* (rev. ed.). Palo Alto, CA: Consulting Psychologists Press.

Graves, J.R., & Robinson, J.D. (1976). Proxemic behavior as a function of inconsistent verbal and nonverbal messages. *Journal of Counseling Psychology, 23,* 333-338.

Greene, E. (1970). *Counselor verbal behavior as a function of client demeanor.* Unpublished doctoral dissertation, Teachers College, Columbia University. (ERIC Document Reproduction Services No. ED 046 047)

Greenberg, R.P., & Zeldon, P.B. (1980). Sex differences in preferences for an ideal counselor. *Journal of Personality Assessment, 44,* 474-477.

Greenson, R.R. (1967). *The technique and practice of psychoanalysis* (Vol. 1). New York: International Universities Press.

Greenson, R.R. (1978). *Explorations in psychoanalysis.* New York: International Universities Press.

Greenspan, S., Barenboim, C., & Chandler, M.J. (1976). Empathy and pseudo-empathy: The affective judgments of first- and third-graders. *Journal of Genetic Psychology, 129,* 77-78.

Greif, E.B., & Hogan, R. (1973). The theory and measurement of empathy. *Journal of Counseling Psychology, 20,* 280-284.

Gross, H.S., Herbert, M.M., Knotterud, G.L., & Donner, L. (1969). The effect of sex and race on the variation of diagnoses and disposition in a psychiatric emergency room. *Journal of Nervous and Mental Disease, 148,* 638-646.

Guilford, J.P., & Fruchter, B. (1978). *Fundamental statistics in psychology and education* (6th ed.). New York: McGraw-Hill.

Gurman, A.S. (1977). The patient's perception of the therapeutic relationship. In A.S. Gurman & A.M. Razin (Eds.) *Effective psychotherapy: A handbook of research.* New York: Pergamon Press.

Haase, R.F., & Tepper, D.T. (1972). Nonverbal components of empathic communication. *Journal of Counseling Psychology, 19,* 417-424.

Hackney, H. (1974). Facial gestures and subject expression of feelings. *Journal of Counseling Psychology, 21,* 173-178.

Hackney, H. (1978). The evolution of empathy. *Personnel and Guidance Journal, 57,* 35-38.

Ham, M.D. (1981). The effects of the relationship between client behavior and counselors' predicted empathic ability upon counselors' in-session empathic performance: An analogue study (Doctoral dissertation, University of Rochester, 1980). *Dissertation Abstracts International, 41,* 2939A. (University Microfilms No. 8025044)

Hathaway, S.R., & McKinley, J.C. (1943). *Manual for the Minnesota multiphasic personality inventory.* New York: Psychological Corp.

Hansen, J.C., Stevic, R.R., & Warner, R.W., Jr. (1982). *Counseling: Theory and practice* (3rd ed.) Boston: Allyn and Bacon.

Harrison, R.P., & Knapp, M.L. (1972). Toward an understanding of nonverbal communication systems. *Journal of Communication, 22,* 339-352.

Heck, E.J., & Davis, C.S. (1973). Differential expression of empathy in a counseling analogue. *Journal of Counseling Psychology, 20,* 101-104.

Heller, K., Myers, R.A., & Kline, L.V. (1963). Interview behavior as a function of standardized client roles. *Journal of Consulting Psychology, 27*(2), 117-122.

Hill, C.E. (1974). *An investigation of the effects of therapist and client variables on the psychotherapy process.* Unpublished doctoral dissertation, Southern Illinois University.

Hill, C.E. (1975). Sex of client and sex and experience level of counselor. *Journal of Counseling Psychology, 22,* 6-11.

Hill, C.E., & King, J. (1976). Perceptions of empathy as a function of the measuring instrument. *Journal of Counseling Psychology, 23,* 155-157.

Hill, C.E., Tanney, M.F., Leonard, M.M., & Reiss, J.A. (1977). Counselor reactions to female clients: Type of problem, age of client and sex of counselor. *Journal of Counseling Psychology, 24,* 60-65.

Hoffman, M.L. (1977a). Empathy, its development and pro-social implications. In H. E. Howe, Jr., & C.B. Keasey (Eds.), *Nebraska Symposium on Motivation* (Vol. 25) (pp. 169-217). Lincoln: University of Nebraska Press.

Hoffman, M.L. (1977b). Sex differences in empathy and related behavior. *Psychological Bulletin, 84,* 712-722.

Hoffman, M.L., & Levine, L.E. (1976). Early sex differences in empathy. *Developmental Psychology, 12,* 557-558.

Hogan, R. (1969). Development of an empathy scale. *Journal of Consulting and Clinical Psychology, 33,* 307-316.

Hogan, R. (1975). Empathy: A conceptual and psychometric analysis. *The Counseling Psychologist, 5,* 14-17.

Hogan, R., & Dickstein, E. (1972). A measure of moral values. *Journal of Consulting and Clinical Psychology, 39,* 210-214.

Hogan, R., & Henley, N. (1970). A test of the empathy-effective communication hypothesis. Unpublished paper, Johns Hopkins University. Center for the Study of Social Organization of Schools Report, No. 84.

Hogan, R., & Mankin, D. (1970). Determinants of interpersonal attraction: A clarification. *Psychological Reports, 26,* 235-238.

Hogan, R., Mankin, D., Conway, J., & Fox, S. (1970). Personality correlates of undergraduate marijuana use. *Journal of Consulting and Clinical Psychology, 35,* 58-63.

Horney, K. (1937). *The neurotic personality of our time.* New York: W.W. Norton.

Hountras, P.T., & Anderson, D.L. (1969). Counselor conditions for self-exploration of college students. *The Personnel and Guidance Journal, 48,* 45-48.

Irwin, R.L. (1974). The relationship of counselor empathy and genuineness to client self-experiencing with two types of clients at a university counseling center (Doctoral dissertation, Washington State University, 1973). *Dissertation Abstracts International, 34,* 4045B. (University Microfilms No. 74-4107)

Ivey, A.E., & Authier, J. (1978). *Microcounseling* (2nd ed.) Springfield, IL: Charles C Thomas.

Janofsky, A.I. (1971). Affective self-disclosure in telephone versus face-to-face interviews. *Journal of Humanistic Psychology, 11,* 93-103.

Jansen, D.G., Bonk, E.C., & Garvey, F.J. (1973). MMPI characteristics of clergymen in counseling training and their relationship to supervisors' and peers' ratings of counseling effectiveness. *Psychological Reports, 33,* 695-698.

Jensen, L., Perry, C., Adams, G., & Gaynard, L. (1981). Maternal behavior and the development of empathy in preschool children. *Psychological Reports, 48,* 879-884.

Johnson, D.H. (1978). Student sex preferences and sex role expectancies for counselors. *Journal of Counseling Psychology, 25,* 557-562.

Johnson, J.A., Cheek, J.M., & Smither, R. (1983). The structure of empathy. *Journal of Personality and Social Psychology, 45,* 1299-1312.

Johnson, M.D. (1983). The relationship between the empathy cycle and psychological type in marital interaction. (Doctoral dissertation, University of Rochester, 1983). *Dissertation Abstracts International, 45,* 03A, 791. (University Microfilms No. DEQ84-13061)

Kagan, N. (1975). *Interpersonal process recall: A method of influencing human interaction* (rev. ed.). East Lansing, MI: Mason Media.

Kagan, N. (1978). *Influencing human interaction: Fifteen years with IPR.* Unpublished paper.

Kagan, N., Kratchovil, D., & Miller, R. (1963). Simulated recall in therapy using videotape: A case study. *Journal of Counseling Psychology, 10,* 237-241.

Kagan, N., Krathwohl, D.R., & Associates. (1967). *Studies in human interaction.* East Lansing: Educational Publication Services, College of Education, Michigan State University.

Karr, J.T., & Geist, G.O. (1977). Facilitation in supervision as related to facilitation in therapy. *Counselor Education and Supervision, 16,* 264-268.

Kasl, S., & Mahl, G.F. (1965). The relationship of disturbances and hesitations in spontaneous speech to anxiety. *Journal of Personality and Social Psychology, 1,* 425-433.

Katz, D., & Resnikoff, A. (1977). Televised self-confrontation and recalled affect: A new look at videotape recall. *Journal of Counseling Psychology, 24,* 150-152.

Katz, R. (1963). *Empathy: Its nature and uses.* New York: Free Press.

Kazdin, A.E. (1978). Evaluating the generality of findings in analogue therapy research. *Journal of Consulting and Clinical Psychology, 46,* 673-685.

Kell, B.L., & Mueller, W.J. (1966). *Impact and change.* New York: Appleton-Century-Crofts.

Kelly, G.A. (1955). *The psychology of personal constructs: Vol. I. A theory of personality.* New York: W.W. Norton.

Kendall, P.C., & Wilcox, L.E. (1980). Cognitive-behavioral treatment for impulsivity: Concrete versus conceptual training in non-self-controlled problem children. *Journal of Consulting and Clinical Psychology, 48,* 80-91.

Kerlinger, F.N. (1973). *Foundations of Behavioral Research* (2nd ed.). New York: Holt, Rinehart & Winston.

Kerr, W.A., & Speroff, B.J. (1954). Validation and evaluation of the empathy test. *Journal of General Psychology, 50,* 269-276.

Kimberlin, C.L., & Friesen, D.D. (1980). Sex and conceptual level empathic responses to ambivalent affect. *Counselor Education and Supervision, 19,* 252-257.

Kingdon, M.A. (1975). A cost/benefit analysis of the interpersonal process recall technique. *Journal of Counseling Psychology, 22,* 353-357.

Kirk, R.E. (1968). *Experimental design: Procedure for the behavioral sciences.* Belmont, CA: Brooks/Cole.

Kohut, H. (1977). *The restoration of the self.* New York: International Universities Press.

Kohut, H. (1978). *The search for the self* (Vols. 1 & 2). New York: International Universities Press.

Kratchovil, D., Aspy, D., & Carkhuff, R.R. (1967). The differential effects of absolute level and direction of growth in counselor functioning upon client level of functioning. *Journal of Clinical Psychology, 23,* 216-218.

Kratchowil, T.R. (Ed.). (1978). *Single subject research: Strategies for evaluating change.* New York: Academic Press.

Krebs, D. (1975). Empathy and altruism. *Journal of Personality and Social Psychology, 32,* 1134-1146.

Kreiser, J. (1978). *Counselor trainee anxiety level and concurrent counselor behavior.* Paper presented at the annual meeting of the American Educational Research Association, Toronto. (ERIC Document Reproduction Service No. ED 156 997)

Krug, S.E., Scheier, I.H., & Cattell, R.B. (1976). *Handbook for the IPAT Anxiety Scale.* Champaign, IL: Institute for Personality and Ability Testing.

Kuder, F. (1976). *Occupational interest survey—General manual.* Chicago: Science Research Associates, Inc.

Kurtines, W., & Hogan, R. (1972). Sources of conformity in unsocialized college students. *Journal of Abnormal Psychology, 80,* 49-51.

Kurtz, R.R., & Grummon, D.L. (1972). Different approaches to the measurement of therapist empathy and their relationship to therapy outcome. *Journal of Consulting and Clinical Psychology, 39,* 106-115.

Lake, D.G., Miles, M.B., & Earle, R.B. (1973). *Measuring human behavior: Tools for the assessment of social functioning.* New York: Teachers College Press, Columbia University.

Lamb, R., & Mahl, G.F. (1956). Manifest reactions of patients and interviewers to the use of sound recording in the psychiatric interview. *American Journal of Psychiatry, 112,* 731-737.

Lambert, M.J., DeJulio, S.S., & Stein, D.M. (1978). Therapist interpersonal skills: Process, outcome, methodological considerations and recommendations for future research. *Psychological Bulletin, 85,* 467-489.

Lanning, W.C., & Lemons, S.L. (1974). Another look at the factor structure of the Barrett-Lennard Relationship Inventory. *Measurement and Evaluation in Guidance, 6,* 228-231.

Larrabee, M.J., and Froehle, T.C. (1979). Estimating role fidelity and consistency in coached client performance. *Counselor Education and Supervision, 19,* 165-170.

Latane, B., & Darley, J. (1970). Bystander intervention in emergencies. In J. Macaulay & L. Berkowitz (Eds), *Altruism and helping behavior.* New York: Academic Press.

Lesh, T.V. (1971). Zen meditation and the development of empathy in counselors. In T. Barber (Ed.), *Biofeedback and self-control.* Chicago: Atherton.

Lichtenberg, J., Bornstein, M., & Silver, D. (Eds.). (1984). *Empathy* (Vols. I & II). Hillsdale, NJ: The Analytic Press.

Linden, J.D., Stone, S.C., & Shertzer, B. (1968). Development and evaluation of an inventory for rating counseling. In L. Litwack, R. Getson, & G. Salzman (Eds.), *Research in counseling.* Itasca, IL: F.E. Peacock, Inc.

Loesch, L.C. (1975). Nonverbalized feelings and perceptions of the counseling relationship. *Counselor Education and Supervision, 15,* 105-113.

Lord, F.M. (1967). A paradox in the interpretation of group comparisons. *Psychology Bulletin, 681,* 304-305.

Luborsky, L. (1952). The personality of the psychotherapist. *Menninger Quarterly, 5,* 1-6.

Luborsky, L., Averbach, A.H., Chandler, M., Cohen, J., & Bachrach, H.M. (1971). Factors influencing the outcome of psychotherapy: A review of quantitative research. *Psychological Bulletin, 75*(3), 145-161.

MacKrell, S.M. (1983). The effects of counseling supervision method, trainee level of sophistication and sex of trainee on empathic understanding. (Doctoral Dissertation, University of Rochester, 1983). *Dissertation Abstracts International, 44,* 03A, 675. (University Microfilms No. DA 8313591)

Mahl, G.F. (1956). Disturbances and silences in the patient's speech in psychotherapy. *Journal of Abnormal and Social Psychology, 53,* 1-15.

Mahl, G.F. (1961). Measures of two expressive aspects of a patient's speech in two psychotherapeutic interviews. In Louis A. Gottschalk (Ed.), *Comparative psycholinguistic analysis of two psychotherapeutic interviews* (pp. 91-114). New York: International Universities Press.

Mahon, B.R., & Altman, H.A. (1977). Skill training: Cautions and recommendations. *Counselor Education and Supervision, 17,* 42-50.

Mann, B., & Murphy, K.C. (1975). Timing of self-disclosure, reciprocity of self-disclosure, and reactions to an initial interview. *Journal of Counseling Psychology, 22,* 304-308.

Maslow, A.H. (1962). *Toward a psychology of being.* New York: Van Nostrand.

McDougall, W. (1908). *An introduction to social psychology.* Boston: Luce & Co.

Mead, G.H. (1934). *Mind, self, and society.* Chicago: University of Chicago Press.

Mehrabian, A.E. (1968). Communication without words. *Psychology Today, 2,* 52-56.

Mehrabian, A.E. (1971). Verbal and nonverbal interaction of strangers in a waiting situation. *Journal of Experimental Research in Personality, 5,* 127-138.

Mehrabian, A. & Epstein, N. (1972). A measure of emotional empathy. *Journal of Personality, 40,* 525-543.

Melnick, R.R. (1974). Counseling response as a function of type of client problem and method of problem presentation. (Doctoral dissertation, Syracuse University, 1973). *Dissertation Abstracts International, 34,* (11-A) 6981-6982. (University Microfilms No. 74-10, 160)

Merbaum, M. (1963). The conditioning of affective self-references by three classes of generalized reinforcers. *Journal of Personality, 31,* 179-191.

Meyers, J.L. (1969). *Fundamentals of experimental design.* Boston: Allyn and Bacon.

Mitchell, K.M., Bozarth, J.D., & Krauft, C.C. (1978). A reappraisal of the therapeutic effectiveness of accurate empathy, nonpossessive warmth, and genuineness. In A.S. Gurman and A.M. Razin (Eds.), *The therapists contribution to effective psychotherapy: An empirical analysis* (pp. 482-502). New York: Pergamon Press.

Morocco, D.R. (1979a). *The nonverbal facilitative components of a helping process: A methodological review.* Unpublished paper, University of Rochester.

Morocco, D.R. (1979b). *Client self-exploration as a psychological function of counselor nonverbal empathy.* Unpublished paper, University of Rochester.

Morocco, D.R. (1981). The psychological impact of varying counselor level of empathic understanding and communication modality on selected in-counseling outcomes. (Doctoral dissertation, University of Rochester, 1981). *Dissertation Abstracts International, 42,* 01A, 88. (University Microfilms No. DDJ81-13620)

Munley, P.H. (1974). A review of counseling analogue research methods. *Journal of Counseling Psychology, 21,* 320-333.

Munsterberg, H. (1970). *The film: A psychological study.* New York: Dover Publications.

Murphy, W.A., & Lamb, D.H. (1973). The effects of training in psychotherapy on therapists' responses to client hostility. *Journal of Community Psychology, 1,* 327-330.

Myers, J.L. (1972). *Fundamentals of experimental design* (2nd ed.). Boston: Allyn and Bacon.

Orlinsky, D.E., & Howard, K.I. (1975). *Varieties of psychotherapeutic experience, multivariate analysis of patients' and therapists' reports.* New York: Teachers College Press.

Paar, H.J., & Seeman, J. (1973). Experimental psychotherapy: Effectiveness of therapist response under two conditions of threat. *Journal of Clinical Psychology, 20,* 100-103.

Panek, C.M., & Martin, B. (1959). The relationship between GSR and speech disturbances in psychotherapy. *Journal of Abnormal and Social Psychology, 58,* 402-405.

Parker, G.V. (1967). Some concomitants of therapist dominance in the psychotherapy interview. *Journal of Consulting Psychology, 31,* 313-318.

Parloff, M., Waskow, I., & Wolfe, B. (1978). Research on therapist variables in relation to process and outcome. In S.L. Garfield & A.E. Bergin (Eds.), *Handbook of psychotherapy and behavior change: An empirical analysis* (2nd ed.). New York: Wiley.

Payne, P.A., Weiss, S.D., & Kapp, T.A. (1972). Didactic, experiential, and modeling factors in the learning of empathy. *Journal of Counseling Psychology, 19,* 425-429.

Peabody, S.A., & Gelso, C.J. (1982). Countertransference and empathy: The complex relationship between two divergent concepts in counseling. *Journal of Counseling Psychology, 29,* 240-245.

Pennscott, W.W., & Brown, D.F. (1972). Anxiety and empathy in a counseling and guidance institute. *Counselor Education and Supervision, 7,* 257-261.

Perry, M.A. (1975). Modeling and instructions in training for counselor empathy. *Journal of Counseling Psychology, 22,* 173-179.

Petro, C.S., & Hansen, J.C. (1977). Counselor sex and empathic judgment. *Journal of Counseling Psychology, 24,* 373-376.

Piaget, J. (1959). *Judgment and reasoning in the child.* Paterson, NJ: Littlefield, Adams. (Original work published 1928)

Piaget, J. (1965). *The moral judgment of the child.* New York: Free Press. (Original work published 1932)

Piaget, J. (1975). *The child's conception of the world.* Totowa, NJ: Littlefield, Adams. (Original work published 1929).

Pierce, R., Carkhuff, R.R., & Berenson, B.G. (1965). The differential affects of high and low functioning counselors upon counselors-in-training. *Journal of Clincial Psychology, 29,* 333-336.

Pierce, R. M., & Schauble, P. G. (1970). Graduate training of facilitative counselors: The effects of individual supervision. *Journal of Counseling Psychology, 17,* 210–215.

Pierce, R.M, & Schauble, P.G. (1971a). Follow-up study on the effects of individual supervision in graduate training. *Journal of Counseling Psychology, 18,* 186-187.

Pierce, R.M., & Schauble, P.G. (1971b). Toward the development of facilitative counselors: The effects of practicum instruction and individual supervision. *Counselor Education and Supervision, 11,* 83-89.

Pope, B., & Siegman, A.W. (1972). Relationship and verbal behavior in the initial interview. In A.W. Siegman and B. Pope (Eds.), *Studies in dyadic communication.* (pp. 69-89). New York: Pergamon Press.

Pope, B., Siegman, A.W., & Blass, T. (1970). Anxiety and speech in the initial interview. *Journal of Consulting and Clinical Psychology, 35,* 233-238.

Rappaport, J., Gross, T., & Lepper, C. (1973). Modeling, sensitivity training, and instruction: Implications for the training of college student volunteers and for outcome research. *Journal of Consultation and Clinical Psychology, 40,* 99-107.

Rappoport, D.N. (1975). *Client behaviors effecting [sic] the therapist offerings of nonpossessive warmth, accurate empathy and genuineness.* Unpublished doctoral dissertation, California School of Professional Psychology.

Reddy, W.B., & Lippert, K.M. (1981). A bibliography of small group training, 1976-1979. In J. Jones & Pfeiffer (Eds.), *The 1981 annual handbook for group facilitators* (pp. 284-292). San Diego: University Associates.

Reik, T. (1964). *Listening with the third ear.* New York: Pyramid.

Rice, D.G. (1969). Patient sex differences and selection for individual psychotherapy. *The Journal of Mental and Nervous Disease, 148,* 124-133.

Robinson, J.W., Herman, A., & Kaplan, B.J. (1982). Automatic responses correlate with counselor-client empathy. *Journal of Counseling Psychology, 29,* 195-198.

Robinson, S.E., Froehle, T.C., & Kurpius, D.J. (1979). Effects of sex of model and media of model presentation on skill development of counselor trainees. *Journal of Counseling Psychology, 26,* 74-80.

Roe, K.V. (1980). Toward a contigency hypothesis of empathy development. *Journal of Personality and Social Psychology, 39,* 991-994.

Rogers, C.R. (1957). The necessary and sufficient conditions of therapeutic personality change. *Journal of Consulting Psychology, 21,* 95-103.

Rogers, C.R. (1975). Empathic: An unappreciated way of being. *The Counseling Psychologist, 5,* 2-10.

Rogers, C.R., & Truax, C.B. (1967). The therapeutic conditions antecedent to change: A theoretical view. In C.R. Rogers (Ed.), *The therapeutic relationship and its impact: A study of psychotherapy with schizophrenics.* (pp. 97-108). Madison: University of Wisconsin Press.

Roulx, K.R. (1969). Some physiological effects of tape recording on supervised counselors. *Counselor Education and Supervision, 8,* 201-205.

Rosenblum, R. & Karen, R. (1980). *When the shooting stops . . . the cutting begins: A film editor's story.* New York: Penguin.

Ruesch, J. (1965). Nonverbal language and therapy. *Psychology, 18,* 323-330.

Ruesch, J., & Bateson, G. (1951). *Communication: The social matrix of psychiatry.* New York: W.W. Norton.

Rushton, J.P. (1980). *Altruism, socialization, and society.* Englewood Cliffs, NJ: Prentice-Hall.

Rye, D.R. (1970). A comparative study of three small group treatments and their effects on accurate communication between counselor trainees and their clients (Doctoral Dissertation, Indiana University, 1969). *Dissertation Abstracts International, 30,* 554-A.

Saltmarsh, R.E. (1973). Development of empathic interviewing skills through programmed instruction. *Journal of Counseling Psychology, 20,* 375-377.

Salzinger, K., & Pisoni, S. (1958). Reinforcement of affect responses of schizophrenics during the clinical interview. *Journal of Abnormal and Social Psychology, 57,* 84-90.

Salzinger, K., & Pisoni, S. (1960). Reinforcement of verbal affect responses of normal subjects during the interview. *Journal of Abnormal and Social Psychology, 60,* 127-130.

Sarbin, T.R., & Allen, V.L. (1969). Role theory. In G. Lindzey (Ed.), *The handbook of social psychology* (Vol. I). (pp. 223-258). Cambridge, MA: Addison-Wesley.

Seay, T.A., & Altekruse, M.K. (1979). Verbal and nonverbal behavior in judgments of facilitative conditions. *Journal of Counseling Psychology, 26,* 108-119.

Selfridge, F., Abramowitz, S.I., Abramowitz C., Weitz, L., Calabria, F., & Steger, J.

(1975). Sensitivity-oriented versus didactically oriented in-service counselor training. *Journal of Counseling Psychology, 22,* 156-159.

Seligman, L. (1978). The relationship of facilitative functioning to effective peer supervision. *Counselor Education and Supervision, 17,* 2454-260.

Selman, R.L. (1980). *The growth of interpersonal understanding.* New York: Academic Press.

Shapiro, J.G., Foster, C.P., & Powell, T. (1968). Facial and bodily cues of counselor warmth and empathy. *Journal of Counseling Psychology, 24,* 87-91.

Shostrom, E. (Producer). (1977). *Carl Rogers counsels an individual on hurt and anger* [film]. Alexandria, VA: American Association for Counseling and Development.

Siegman, A.W., & Pope, B. (1972). The effects of ambiguity and anxiety on interviewee verbal behavior. In A.W. Siegman and B. Pope (Eds.), *Studies in dyadic communication* (pp. 29-68). New York: Pergamon Press.

Silverman, M. S., & Quinn, P. F. (1974). Co-counseling supervision in practicum. *Counselor Education and Supervision, 13,* 256-260.

Sladen, B. J. (1982). Effects of race and socioeconomic status on the perception of process variables in counseling. *Journal of Counseling Psychology, 29*(6), 560-566.

Smith-Hanen, S. S. (1977). Effects of nonverbal behaviors on judged levels of counselor warmth and empathy. *Journal of Counseling Psychology, 24,* 91-97.

Smither, S. (1977). A reconsideration of the developmental study of empathy. *Human Development, 20,* 253-276.

Snelbecker, G. E. (1961). Factors influencing college students' person-perceptions of psychotherapists in a laboratory analog (Doctoral   dissertation, Cornell University, 1961). *Dissertation Abstracts International, 22-11,* 3928. (University Microfilms No. 62-00966)

Steiberg, J. K. (1967). *Counselor anxiety and interview behavior* Unpublished doctoral thesis, Columbia University, New York.

Stengel, J. B. (1976). Counselor response as a function of client's sex, counselor's sex and client's presenting affect (Doctoral dissertation, Boston University, 1976). *Dissertation Abstracts International, 36,* 11-B, 5819. (University Microfilms No. DDJ76-11831)

Stewart, D. (1956). *Preface to empathy.* New York: Philosophical Library.

Stone, G. L., & Vance, A (1976). Instruction, modeling, and rehearsal: Implications for training. *Journal of Counseling Psychology, 23,* 272-279.

Stotland, E. (1969). Exploratory investigations of empathy. In L. Berkowitz (Ed.), *Advances in experimental social psychology*(Vol. 4). New York: Academic Press.

Stotland, E., & Dunn, R. (1963). Empathy, self-esteem and birth order. *Journal of Abnormal and Social Psychology, 66,* 610-614.

Stotland, E., Mathews, K. E., Jr., Sherman, S. E., Hansson, R. O., & Richardson, B. Z. (1978). *Empathy, fantasy and helping.* Beverly Hills: Sage Publications.

Strupp, H. H., & Luborsky, L. (Eds.). (1962). *Research in psychotherapy* (Vol. II). Washington, DC: American Psychological Association.

Sullivan, H. S. (1954). *The psychiatric interview.* New York: W. W. Norton.

Sullivan, H. S. (1956). *Clinical studies in psychiatry.* New York: W. W. Norton.

Taylor, C. (1972). *Counselor's level of empathic understanding as a function of counselor sex and client sex.* Unpublished doctoral dissertation, University of South Carolina.

Tepper, D. T., & Haase, R. F. (1978). Verbal and nonverbal communication of facilitative conditions. *Journal of Counseling Psychology, 25,* 35–44.

Therrien, M., & Fischer, J. (1978). Written indicator of empathy in human-relations training: A validation study. *Counselor Education and Supervision, 17,* 272–277.

Thoresen, C. E., & Anton, J. L. (1974). Intensive experimental research in counseling. *Journal of Counseling Psychology, 21,* 553–559.

Travers, R. M. N. (1959). Critical review of techniques for evaluating guidance. *Educational and Psychological Measurement, 9,* 211–225.

Truax, C. B. (1966). Therapist empathy, warmth, and genuineness and patient personality in group psychotherapy: A comparison between interaction unit measures, time sample measures, and patient perception measures. *Journal of Clinical Psychology, 22,* 225–229.

Truax, C. B., Altmann, H., & Millis, W. A. (1974). Therapeutic relationships provided by various professionals. *Journal of Community Psychology, 2,* 33–36.

Truax, C. B., & Carkhuff, R. R. (1964). Significant developments in psychotherapy research. In L. Abt and J. Reiss (Eds.), *Progress in clinical psychology* (Vol VI) (pp. 124–155). New York: Grune & Stratton.

Truax, C. B., & Carkhuff, R. R. (1967). *Toward effective counseling and psychotherapy: Training and practice.* Chicago: Aldine.

Tubesing, D. A., & Tubesing, N. C. (1973) *Tune-in: Empathy training workshop.* Milwaukee: Listening Group.

Vargas, A. M., & Borkowski, J. G. (1982). Physical attractiveness and counseling skills. *Journal of Counseling Psychology, 29*(3), 246–255.

Vesprani, G. J. (1969). Personality correlates of accurate empathy in a college companion program. *Journal of Consulting and Clinical Psychology, 33,* 722–727.

Vitalo, R. L. (1971). Teaching improved interpersonal functioning as preferred mode of treatment. *Journal of Clinical Psychology, 27,* 166–171.

Walker, R. B., & Latham, N. L. (1977). Relationship of a group counseling course, hours in counselor education, and sex to empathic understanding of counselor trainees. *Counselor Education and Supervision, 16,* 269–274.

Wedeking, D. G., & Scott, T. B. (1976). A study of the relationship between supervisor and trainees behaviors in counseling practicum. *Counselor Education and Supervision, 15,* 259–266.

Whitley, J. (Producer). (1974). *Carl Rogers on empathy* [film]. Alexandria, VA: American Association for Counseling and Development.

Wicas, E., and Mahan, T. W., Jr. (1966). Characteristics of counselors rated effective by supervisors and peers. *Counselor Education and Supervision, 6,* 150–155.

Wiggers, T. T. (1978). *The effects of client sex, counselor sex and counselor role on selected client nonverbal behaviors in a counseling analogue.* Unpublished doctoral dissertation, University of Rochester, Rochester, NY.

Williams, J. H. (1977). *Psychology of women: Behavior in a biosocial context.* New York: W. W. Morton & Co.

Winer, B. J. (1971). *Statistical principles in experimental design* (2nd ed.). New York: McGraw-Hill.

Wogan, M. (1970). Effects of therapist-patient personality variables on therapeutic outcome. *Journal of Consulting and Clinical Psychology, 35,* 356–361.

Wolpe, J. (1958). *Psychotherapy by reciprocal inhibition.* Stanford, CA: Stanford University Press.

Wrenn, C. G., & Parker, C. A. (1960). Counseling theory. *Encyclopedia of educational research* (3rd. ed.), pp. 341–348. New York: Macmillan.

Wundt, W. (1892/1897). *Ethics: Vol. 1. The facts of the moral life* (2nd ed.). New York: Macmillan. (Original work published 1892)

Young, D. (1979). *The meanings of counselor nonverbal gestures.* Unpublished paper, University of Rochester.

Young, D. (1980). Meanings of counselor nonverbal gestures: Fixed or interpretive? *Journal of Counseling Psychology, 27,* 447–452.

Author Index

Subject Index